PRAISE FOR BEYOND THE PIPELINE

"This book is a game-changer for women in STEMM and the allies championing progress. It dismantles outdated career pipeline narratives, revealing the resilience and innovation of those forging new paths. A must-read for anyone committed to building a more equitable and sustainable future for women in STEMM."

– Kerrie L. Greenfelder, *PE, FY26 President-Elect, Society of Women Engineers*

"Reading *Beyond the Pipeline* felt like someone finally put words to what so many of us have lived. As a Black woman in engineering and the founder of an organization dedicated to creating space for girls who look like me, I've seen firsthand how powerful it is when we're not just invited in—but truly seen and valued. This book doesn't just name the problems—it offers hope, clarity, and actionable solutions. It's a must-read for anyone serious about building a better, more inclusive future in STEMM."

– Kara Branch, *Chemical Engineer, Founder and CEO, Black Girls Do Engineer*

"If we are to achieve lasting and effective change, we need to draw together many voices with lived experience. *Beyond the Pipeline* explores a range of barriers and provides considered advice from those who have walked the path."

– Dr Shane Huntington OAM, *CEO of the Australian Society for Medical Research*

"*Beyond the Pipeline* delivers both solidarity and strategy for surviving STEMM's most broken systems. As a queer, femme, neurodivergent scientist, this book made me feel seen AND armed."

– Ashley Ruba, PhD, *Founder of After Academia*

"The field guide I needed 20 years ago—part compass, part reality check. Forget the leaky pipeline. Women in STEMM aren't dripping away. We're dodging potholes, facing detours, and rerouting toward workplaces that align with our values. Share this book with every brilliant STEMM woman you know, and remind her: *You deserve to be seen, supported, and respected. Don't settle for less.* A must-read for charting a course in STEMM without losing yourself along the way."

– Emily Nichols, *P.Eng., Keynote Speaker and Emcee, Connect Better Inc.*

Beyond the Pipeline

Beyond the Pipeline

Redefining Value, Success, and the Future of Women in STEMM—Together

Karli M. Auble   Emily L. Bishop

Jessica G. Borger   Rachael Browning

Jennifer G. Christensen   Jaymi T. Cormier

Jane Desrochers   Belinda A. Di Bartolo

Trevor C. George   Manpreet Kaur

Tais S. Kraljević   Cassie Leonard

Monika McDole-Russell   Laura Marie Rivera

Kelly A. Seiler Vocke   Mindy Ursino

Megan Wendell   Ashley C. Wynne

Edited by Cassie Leonard

ELMMPRESS

Credits: Cover design and illustrations by Anna Korlath, www.korlath.at.
Diagrams by Cassie Leonard.

ISBN 979-8-9887205-3-9 (paperback)
ISBN 979-8-9887205-4-6 (ebook)

Library of Congress Control Number: 2025904355

A heartfelt thank you to everyone who contributed to this project. We are grateful for your expertise, courage, and dedication.

We'd like to acknowledge the following key collaborators whose support went above and beyond in making *Beyond the Pipeline* what it is.

Michelle C. Andersen

Sanchari Banerjee

Alex Egeler

Eleonora Grandi

Okereke Jasper

Christina Look

Monika McDole-Russell

Bridgette D. Semple

Katie Wilson

Contents

Section 2

Introduction

WHERE OUR STORIES TAKE SHAPE

by Cassie Leonard, engineer, leader, mom, and mentor dedicated to elevating diverse voices, shifting systems, and sparking change.

I was 12 years old when I first watched the movie Apollo 13.

It was mesmerizing. When catastrophic failures sabotaged NASA's third mission intended to land on the Moon, rocket scientists back on Earth were called into action to solve what seemed like an unsolvable problem: toxic carbon dioxide gas in the Lunar Module was literally poisoning the astronauts with every breath, and the available functioning equipment was the wrong shape.

It was time to invent a way to put a square peg in a round hole.[1] At that moment, watching the scene unfold, I knew I was going to be a rocket scientist. I wanted to solve the hardest problems, work with the smartest people, and create a lasting impact.

It wasn't until many years later, when I watched my favorite movie again, that I noticed an important detail: there wasn't a single woman in the scene working to solve the toxic air problem.

---

[1] The scrubbers on the Apollo 13 Command Module used cubic cartridges, while the scrubbers on the Lunar Module used cylindrical cartridges.

As a senior aerospace engineer who's done the homework, I now know just how wrong that omission was. Women were there.[2] We've always been there. But our stories are rarely told.

It's time to change the narrative.

– Cassie

Today women are in the room, at the table, and leading from the front. We are thought leaders, managers, and core contributors solving the hardest problems.

When the real Apollo 13 mission launched, women were often relegated to separate rooms to perform their calculations. Thankfully, due to the hard work of countless women, allies, and advocates, opportunities for women to wholeheartedly pursue Science, Technology, Engineering, Mathematics, and Medicine (STEMM) have expanded dramatically.

Companies, institutions, and governments have launched programs specifically aimed at inspiring girls to pursue lucrative STEMM careers.

IDWGS (International Day of Women and Girls in Science) was established in 2015 and is celebrated annually on February 11.

Ada Lovelace, the world's first computer programmer, is celebrated each year on the second Tuesday of October.

Impactful organizations like **Black Girls Do Engineer**, **Techbridge Girls**, **oSTEM**, and **Mothers in Science** are addressing the intersecting barriers that many girls and women face around the world.

Within academia, curricula have been updated to include images and examples of women in STEMM. Word problems in math books now feature girls as the protagonists.

In industry, new levels of support are being offered to early-career professionals through training programs tailored for

---

[2] Check out *Rise of the Rocket Girls* by Nathalia Holt (2016) and *Hidden Figures* by Margot Lee Shetterly (2016) to explore more.

women, broad mentoring initiatives, and the formation of employee resource groups (ERG).

We've seen so many focused efforts. Surely, we must be getting close to parity, right? Well... no.

While the number of women entering STEMM fields has more than tripled over the past 50 years, the vast majority of that progress occurred during the 1970s and 1980s. Since then, progress has been slow, and in some disciplines, virtually nonexistent.

- Since the mid-1990s, biology has continued to grow, with employed women surpassing 50% of the total around 2010.
- In contrast, the percentage of women working in chemistry and materials science has remained largely unchanged.
- Engineering and architecture have seen a frustratingly slow climb, increasing from 14.1% to just 16.7% over the past 20 years.
- Meanwhile, the percentage of women earning computer science bachelor's degrees has dropped sharply, from its peak of 37% in the late 1980s to less than half of that today.[3]

Why is this happening? And why does this matter?

Let's think about it.

A CORRODING PIPELINE ANALOGY

The answer we've been told is simple. Too simple.

The prevailing narrative is that STEMM careers resemble a pipeline from which women just seem to "leak out." For decades, this pipeline has been used to describe the progression (or lack thereof) of women and people of color through academic STEMM careers, from undergraduate students to postdoctoral researchers. The "leaks" represent the points where under-represented and marginalized groups exit the pipeline.

---

[3] HP Developers have done a wonderful job consolidating NCES's data for percentage of bachelor's degrees conferred to females in the U.S. from 1970 to 2010, peaking at 37%. NCES's latest data shows Engineering Technologies is now at 14% women.

Over time, this analogy has been extended to corporate STEMM careers, but the premise remains the same.

While the metaphor once served a purpose, providing language to spark important conversations, it is time to move beyond the **leaky pipeline**. That image is rusting. It values only who is "in" and who is "out," and it fails to capture the complexity of real lives and real decisions.

> Women are making choices.
> We are active in this process.
> *The conversation needs to evolve.*

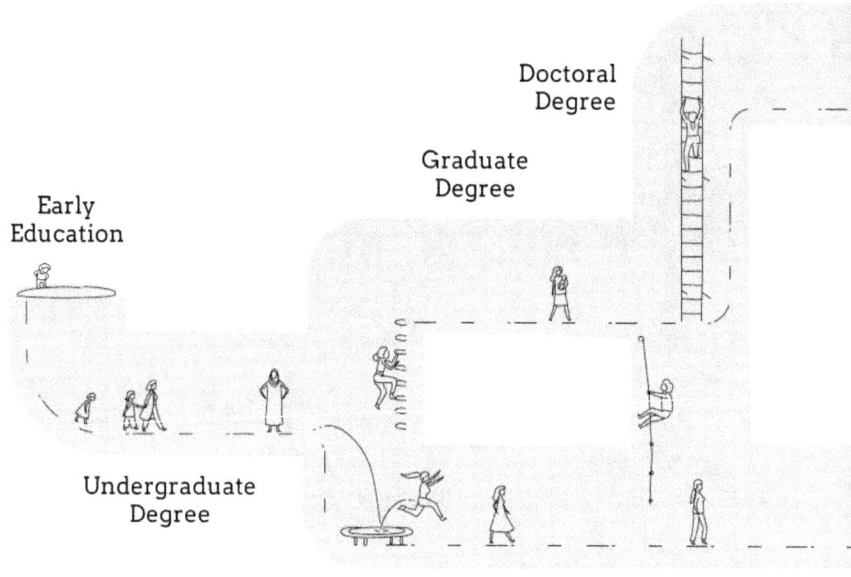

A simplified and idealized view of the classic academic and corporate pipelines, implying (not so subtly) a narrow definition of "success" in STEMM careers.

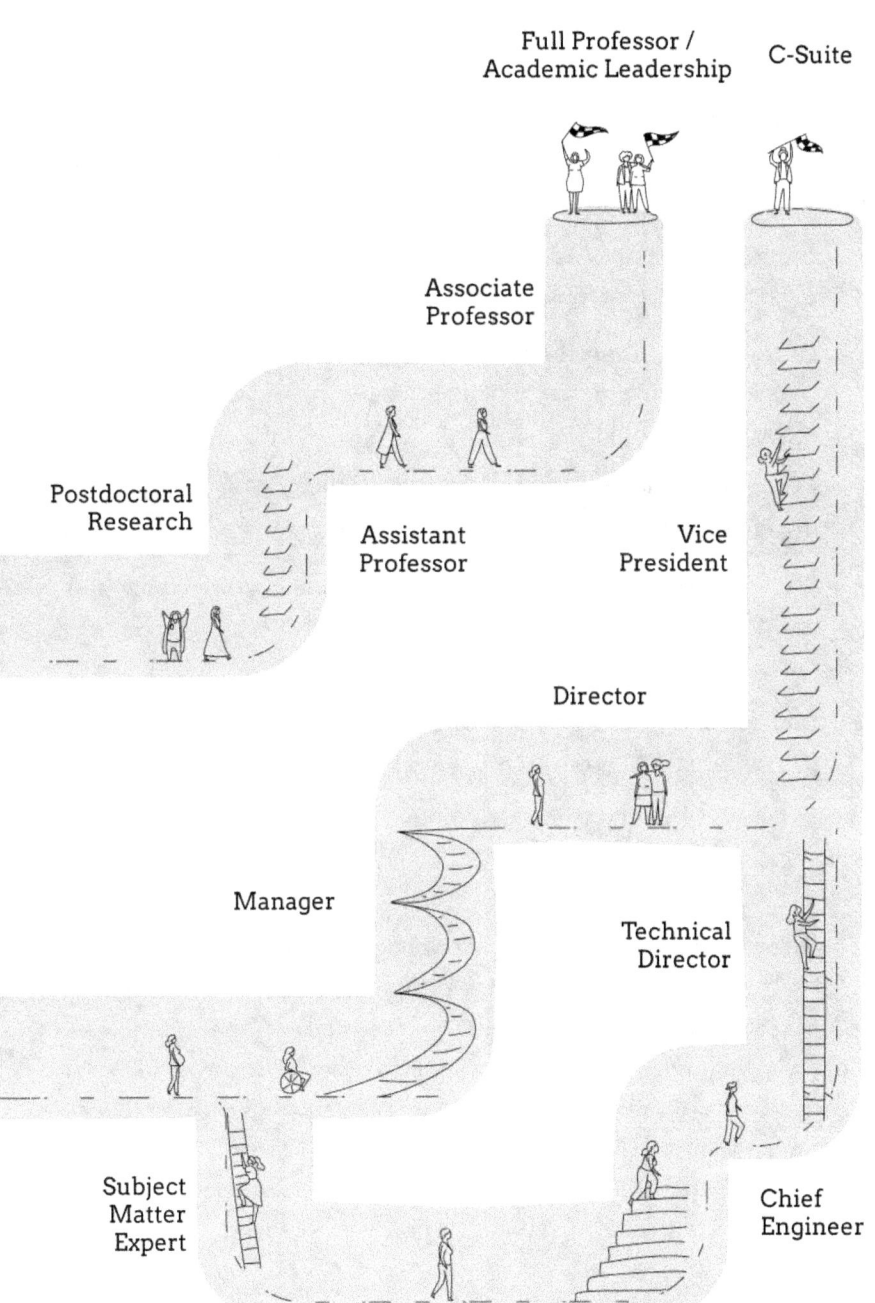

BEYOND ELASTIC LIMITS

When I chose to leave my corporate STEMM career, I was unaware of how systemic factors had influenced my decision. I could feel the tension but did not yet have the space to recognize that I had internalized societal narratives. I was over-constrained, overstretched, and burned out.

> I wanted to be the **ideal leader**, ready at a moment's notice to answer any call or solve any problem, always doing the very best work.

> I wanted to be the **ideal parent**, fully invested in supporting my boys' emotional, physical, and intellectual growth in every way a "good" mom should.

> I was constantly walking a **tightrope** between assertiveness and friendliness, masculine and feminine.

> My office loved me when I was **the glue** holding everything together, but I noticed too late how these non-technical roles moved me farther from my engineering.

> And in hindsight, I now realize I was up against a recurring **prove-it-again bias** my peers never seemed to face.

And when the global shutdown in 2020 meant childcare vanished? That was when I reached my irreversible state of change.[4]

This system, with its rigid schedules, spoken and unspoken gender norms, intersecting biases, and infrastructure never designed for the details of my life, pushed me from elasticity to plasticity.

But despite all this, I know that leaving my corporate aerospace job was my choice. Blame it on the seven years I spent as a structural engineer, but I choose to reframe my pipeline metaphor as a stress-strain curve. On my curve, at the point where stress and strain reach their peak, where irreversible change must occur (plasticity), something beautiful happens: we adapt.

---

[4] When a material (or person) is strained beyond its modulus of elasticity, it enters plasticity—a state of irreversible change (or maybe we should call it growth?).

The idea that women are leaking out suggests we have no agency in the situations we find ourselves in, that we are merely along for the ride.

We do not accept this.

OPPOSING FORCES

In this book, you will meet dozens of women and allies who are bravely sharing their own stories. As you read through each experience, I hope you will agree that there are no passive bystanders here.

We do, however, recognize that every decision is nuanced. There are both internal and external forces at play.

We are drawn to STEMM careers for the immense responsibility and opportunity they offer. Every day, we have the chance to innovate, tackle the world's most pressing problems at scale, and shape the future. As STEMM professionals, whether in academia, the corporate world, or non-profits, we are tasked with mitigating the effects of climate change, developing life-saving medicines and medical devices, transforming the digital landscape, or exploring and connecting the world. Whatever field we choose, our work has the power to create lasting value.

These careers also offer opportunities for professional advancement, collaboration within inspiring teams, flexibility, prestige, and the promise of a comfortably compensated lifestyle.

That is the pull. *But there is also a push.*

We are being pushed away from STEMM by unpalatable systemic issues. Leadership training encourages us to be authentic, while the same organizations pass us up for promotions because we do not represent their ingrained ideals of executive presence.

> Have you ever been told to talk in a deeper voice so the men in the room will listen to you? I have.

> Have you been told you didn't get the promotion because you were too brash "for a woman?" Monika has.

> Have you ever been told not to lean in a doorway because women apparently lean in a way that is "suggestive?" Jessica has.

But for every action, there is an equal and opposite reaction.

> We have been told to smile more because it will "help our careers."

> We have been told not to worry. "Just do what you do, and the company will take care of you."

> We have been told to just act like one of the guys.

How in the world could a single analogy, let alone a two-dimensional, zero-curiosity pipeline, capture all the complexities of retaining and losing women in STEMM today?

BEYOND THE PIPELINE

Welcome to our collaborative project, Beyond the Pipeline. This book aspires to capture the truths we live, the choices we make, the contradictions, the sticky realities, and the actions you can take to define your own version of success.

This work has been crafted by a diverse cross-section of women and allies from around the world, all willing to share their stories so you can see a broader range of what STEMM might be for you.

Our contributors represent a wide spectrum of lived experiences. Some authors have PhDs, while others entered industry right after undergrad. Some have kids, and some do not. Some are executives in technically demanding industries, and others are engineers, neuroscientists, and technologists. And some thought they had left, only to find themselves thriving in nontraditional STEMM pursuits.

> We are senior consultants, directors, principals, postdoctoral researchers, entrepreneurs, stay-at-home parents, and radar specialists. We have mentored peers, championed women and underrepresented minorities of the next generation, and celebrated countless personal and professional triumphs along the way.

> Our collective experience spans six continents: Africa, Asia, Australia, Europe, North America, and South America.[5]

---

[5] Shout out to Antarctica—*I'm saving space for you in the second edition!*

Together, we speak Arabic, Bengali, English, French, Hindi, Igbo, Italian, Punjabi, Spanish, and Tamil, and for 22% of us, English was not our first language.

We have published industry-leading papers, delivered cutting-edge products, presented at conferences, and volunteered in schools.

We have simultaneously cared for children, partners, and aging parents. Together, we are single, married, divorced, and separated. We have navigated depression and postpartum depression, perimenopause and menopause, miscarriages, chronic conditions, and life-altering diagnoses.

"Women in STEMM" is not a homogeneous entity. The personal stories we offer are never intended to imply they represent the only experience.

With over 9 million people of all genders graduating in STEM globally each year, every story we share is merely a starting point.[6] Perhaps our stories will add dimensions to your understanding of a given topic and spark your curiosity to seek out more perspectives.[7]

As authors and storytellers, we recognize that each of us carries a unique tapestry of both privileged and marginalized identities. We also acknowledge the inherent discomfort this may bring to the conversation.

In thinking about how to reflect the range of lived experiences represented in this book, we looked for ways to acknowledge both our shared perspectives and our differences.

The following pie charts offer a snapshot of our authors' and collaborators' identities and backgrounds, helping set the stage for the nuanced and occasionally conflicting conversations ahead. Each is offered to reflect the diversity that shapes this project, not to categorize or define.

---

[6] For clarity and consistency, the acronym STEM is used when referring to studies or datasets that do not consider medicine, even though the broader context of *Beyond the Pipeline* encompasses STEMM (Science, Technology, Engineering, Mathematics, and Medicine).

[7] The numbers are hard to find, but the Center for Security and Emerging Technology states China and India awarded 3.57M and 2.55M tertiary STEM degrees in 2020. Add this to the Organisation for Economic Co-operation and Development (OECD) recorded 3.59M tertiary STEM degrees for 39 additional countries in 2021, and we're at about 9M. Tertiary includes international equivalents for associates, bachelors, masters, and doctoral degrees.

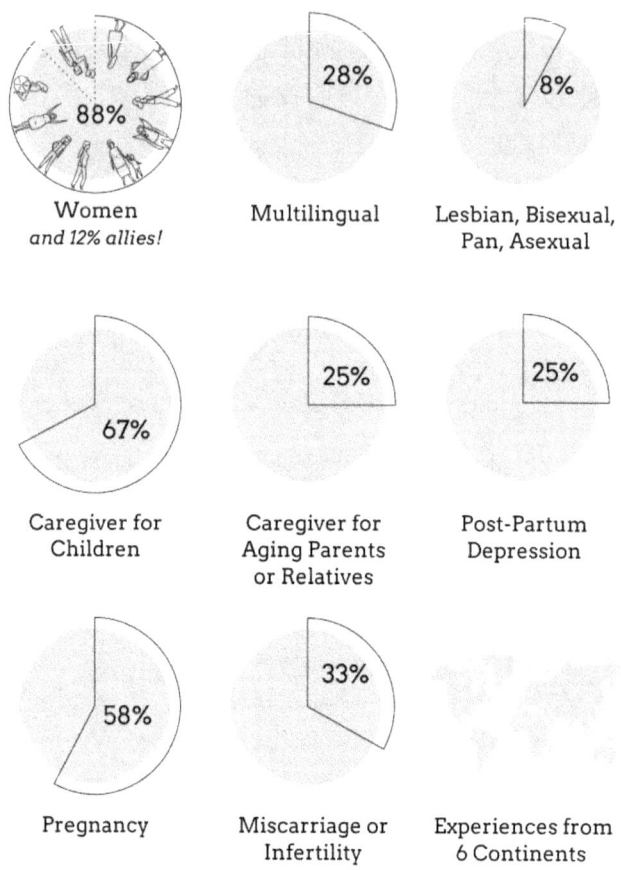

88% Women *and 12% allies!*	**28%** Multilingual	**8%** Lesbian, Bisexual, Pan, Asexual
67% Caregiver for Children	**25%** Caregiver for Aging Parents or Relatives	**25%** Post-Partum Depression
58% Pregnancy	**33%** Miscarriage or Infertility	Experiences from 6 Continents

WELCOME TO THE CONVERSATION

You are welcome with all the identities you carry.

Women are welcome. Allies of all genders are welcome.

HR leaders, policymakers, and managers are welcome.

LGBTQ+ students dreaming of seeing themselves in this profession, welcome.

You, exactly as you are, are welcome.

This book is not a collection of stand-alone thoughts. Instead, you will find many narratives woven together within each chapter. Its development included brainstorming sessions, shared digital whiteboards, and active Slack channels. With contributors spread across 17 time zones, it was both a joy and a challenge to put all the virtual team-building skills we developed in 2020 to good use.

While most personal stories have been simplified for clarity, and occasionally anonymized for discretion, they are all based on true experiences. None have been exaggerated for dramatic effect.[8] Each reveals the forces women encounter every day in STEMM, so often normalized that we hardly notice them in our own lives. I encourage you to stay curious and open-minded as you move through this book. Notice where your story aligns with others and where it does not. You may find perspectives or solutions that seem to conflict with one another, that is expected, because this is sticky.

Some stories, when taken alone, may not demand sweeping systemic change. Others will.

When we start collecting all the unintended slights, the "that's just the way it has always been" pain points, the assumptions that change will happen on its own, and the egregious misconduct, we illuminate the urgent need for action.

DISMANTLING MYTHS, BUILDING SOLUTIONS

Within these pages, we seek to expand the conversation. So, let's dive in.

We have organized *Beyond the Pipeline* into three sections to support your exploration and honor your valuable time. You are welcome to read this book in any order that suits you, whether you choose to jump to topics that resonate or explore chapters that might broaden your perspective.

Section 1 lays the foundation, considering how we've arrived where we are today and opening the conversation for systemic change. We examine current systems and how conventional wisdom still focuses on recruitment, often overlooking the benefits of retention. We also explore the contradictions

---

[8] With one exception: the three idealized women we meet in Chapter 4, *Ideal Worker vs. Ideal Parent*, are fictional composites drawn from many real experiences within our community.

we carry day in and day out and consider the fundamentals of values, choice, and what it means to thrive.

Section 2 highlights the unseen but deeply felt realities of working in STEMM. We present a range of lived experiences grounded in personal stories and data. Our global survey revealed patterns that echo across diverse workplaces: every woman who responded had encountered at least one of the topics covered in this section, and more than two thirds had left a job because of it.

Section 3 shifts fully toward action. We will investigate how everyone can drive change, both in their own lives and at systemic levels. We will take a hard look at what is and what isn't working in the current effort to grow women's representation in STEMM. And we will present a business case for why change is critical at every level.

My original motivation for this project was to shed light on those times when something felt just a bit off but I couldn't quite put my finger on it. I am so thankful to the authors and collaborators who have joined me in giving voice to these experiences.

Our goal is to create a lasting, positive impact on diversity, inclusion, equity, acceptance, and belonging in STEMM. By sharing our stories, we hope women will feel seen, and be seen. By connecting our experiences with data, positive examples, and action, we aspire to support women, allies, and advocates in creating meaningful change for themselves and within their organizations.

> *It's no longer 'I want to leave the profession better than I found it,' but 'I want to live it better than I found it.'*
>
> – Dr. Ami Sawran
> *FRCVS, Clinical Director and Veterinarian*

If, like the Apollo 13 astronauts, your "lunar module" feels inhospitable, let our personal stories, research, and insights inspire you to redesign the system. Whether you choose to reshape the square peg or the round hole, or perhaps redesign the entire lunar mission, the choice is yours.

You are worthy of working in an environment where you are seen, supported, and respected.

Don't accept anything less.

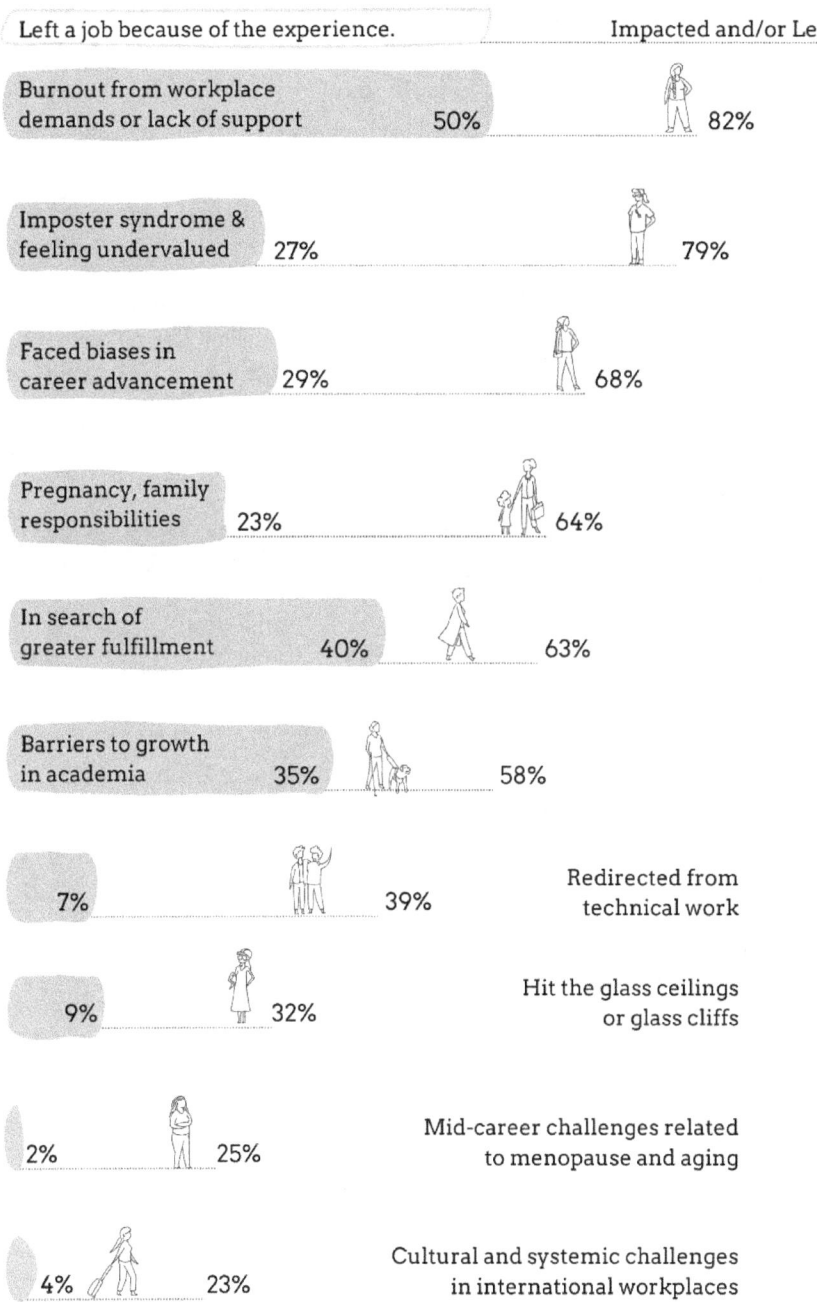

Left a job because of the experience.

Impacted and/or Left

Burnout from workplace demands or lack of support — 50% — 82%

Imposter syndrome & feeling undervalued — 27% — 79%

Faced biases in career advancement — 29% — 68%

Pregnancy, family responsibilities — 23% — 64%

In search of greater fulfillment — 40% — 63%

Barriers to growth in academia — 35% — 58%

7% — 39% — Redirected from technical work

9% — 32% — Hit the glass ceilings or glass cliffs

2% — 25% — Mid-career challenges related to menopause and aging

4% — 23% — Cultural and systemic challenges in international workplaces

Global survey results: Have you ever left a STEMM job or seriously considered leaving due to any of the following reasons? (n = 55)

Mental Wellness Moment | An Introduction

I was 16 when I was handed my first official mental health diagnosis, and it would hardly end up being my last. Add to that my thirst for knowledge and a pathological need to achieve, and you have a recipe for mental disaster. I've spent years trying to understand my brain well enough to rise to what I thought was my peak, my potential, only to be frustrated by new symptoms or manifestations of my brain chemistry that I saw as failures.

While I am under no illusions that my mental health journey is magically resolved, I am finally reaching a point where I no longer wish for it to "end" or go away. Yes, there are hard days and moments when I hate feeling the way I do. But some of the qualities I love most about myself stem from my neurodivergence and mental vulnerabilities.

My name is Megan, and although I must emphasize that I am not a mental health professional, I am excited to share what I've learned along my personal mental health journey and as a STEMM leader who cares deeply about helping individuals thrive in systems that aren't always conducive to those who are neurodivergent or not mentally "robust."

I will pop in throughout this book, along with other contributors from time to time, to offer context on how mental wellness challenges can add complexity to your STEMM journey. I'll also share stories and tips that have helped me and others like me navigate technical workplaces. I hope some of them can help you or someone you love thrive in the face of tough moments, and maybe even reframe your neurodivergence or symptomatology as the superpower they truly can be.

– Megan Wendell

Section 1

One

Shattering the Pipeline

Imagining a More Meaningful Metaphor

by Jane Desrochers, hard-headed, soft-hearted Canadian engineer, recovering academic and certified overthinker.

The pipeline was a mess.

Rusty, cracked, and groaning under pressure, fluid bubbled out of cracks, spurted from misaligned joints, and seeped from places no one had even noticed. A big group of really smart people gathered around, wide-eyed and panicked. They frantically raced to stem the leaks. Someone slapped on a piece of duct tape. Someone else jammed a crack with a wad of goo. Another pressed both palms over a geyser.

But the leaks kept coming.

Each "fix" sprung two more.

"I think it needs a redesign!"
an observer called out from the sidelines.

The foremen didn't even look up. As the water around them steadily rose, they barked back,

"No time! Too expensive!"

This is the so-called leaky pipeline: a simple, visual shorthand used to illustrate an outdated system of channels that carry people from one time and place in their career to another. Its simple, linear logic effectively highlights the alarming rates at which women exit STEMM, especially as they progress in their careers.

And exit we do.

Global data modeling suggests that one woman leaves her STEMM career every three minutes. This means that in the span of a solid workday, the equivalent of a 20-story office tower full of women in STEMM clears out.

This chapter acknowledges the value of the leaky pipeline metaphor in calling attention to this grim reality but argues that it is time for an evolution. The factors that influence who enters, who stays, who leaves, and who returns to STEMM are diverse, intersecting, and nonlinear. Our understanding and our visual language need to reflect that complexity.

ORIGIN STORY

While most scholars attribute the origin of the "leaky pipe" metaphor to papers from the 1990s, the first published reference seems to have emerged much earlier. An excerpt in a 1910 issue of *Nature*, entitled *Education During Adolescence*, references a paper read by Professor M.E. Sadler called *The Relation of Elementary Schools to Technical Schools, Day and Evening*. In this work, Sadler describes a phenomenon of educational attrition among adolescent students (and notably for the time, includes both boys and girls). He likens the shortsightedness and dysfunction of developing academic systems, rife with "educational leakage," to investing in "a costly system of water supply, [only to] have left a badly leaking pipe just behind the tap."

Fast forward to the 1980s, when there was a surge in research exploring women's underrepresentation in science and engineering, and efforts to figure out how to encourage and retain women and other underrepresented minorities in the field. When researchers began investigating the trajectories of education and academic career paths for women in STEM, they uncovered a disturbing trend: women were less likely to advance to senior academic positions despite entering doctoral programs. This issue was thoroughly examined by the National Academy of Sciences in a 1979 report titled

Climbing the Academic Ladder: Doctoral Women Scientists in Academe. Key findings from that report indicate that, despite women in science demonstrating better grades and completing their PhDs more quickly, their representation at the faculty level declined with seniority. Women were disproportionately concentrated in lower academic ranks, but were significantly outnumbered at higher ranks, with fewer holding tenure. They also continued to face salary disparities, particularly in fields like chemistry.

Sue Berryman (1983) introduced the "pipeline" as a conceptual metaphor to illustrate the representation of minorities and women across academic levels in advanced science and mathematics programs. Her model was a significant innovation in advancing the empirical analysis of minorities and women in post-secondary degree pathways.

In the early 1990s, a flood of papers began using the term "leaky pipe" to describe the loss of women at various stages of educational and career pathways in STEM fields. Sheila Tobias (1990) described upstream attrition in the academic pathway, and she doesn't mince words. The pipeline is not merely leaking; it's "hemorrhaging ... during the college years," she writes. Early in the evolution of the metaphor, Tobias recognized that attrition was not only due to suitable students being pushed out, but also due to suitable students being pulled elsewhere. She refers to this group as a "second tier" of untapped

The factors that influence who enters, who stays, who leaves, and who returns to STEMM are diverse, intersecting, and nonlinear.

scientific ability and suggests that this subset of perfectly competent individuals might be persuaded to (re)enter science if the system adopted more flexible curricula and teaching approaches, in which a broader range of ways of thinking and problem-solving were recognized, accommodated, and valued.

Barinaga (1992) analysed career paths of women in neuroscience, and notes with dismay that even though nearly half the students in neuroscience graduate programs within the ANDP were women, "the pipeline ... is leaking - like a sieve."

While women represent nearly half of graduate school entrants, PhD graduate representation drops to 38%; postdoctoral representation drops to about one-third; and women hold twice as many non-tenure-track (36%); compared to tenure-track positions (18%). These data are consistent with U.S. national studies reported by Pell (1996): women represent 40% of science and engineering undergraduate degree holders, but only 22% of university faculty and a mere 8% of full professors in these fields.

In Alper (1993), *The Pipeline Is Leaking Women All the Way Along*, published in *Science*, Sue V. Rosser, director of Women's Studies at the University of South Carolina, reflects on the fact that "the pipeline is leaking women ... and unless this country does something to plug those leaks, women will continue to be denied opportunities in rewarding, high-paying careers, and this country is going to be worse for it."

By 1993, use of the term had expanded to include the attrition of other minority identities, as in Hill (1993), which emphasizes how systemic barriers in special education intersect to limit the advancement of culturally and linguistically diverse professionals in the field.[1]

In *Talking About Leaving: Why Undergraduates Leave the Sciences*, Seymour and Hewitt (1997) explore the experiential and extrinsic factors that influence program switching out of science, mathematics, and engineering (SME) majors among undergraduate students. Their work revealed several key intersecting influences that shaped program trajectories. In particular, the rigid structure of the educational experience and the culture of the discipline drove more students out of SME programs than it brought in.

By the 2010s, the leaky pipe metaphor had been adopted beyond academia to describe attrition in corporate leadership and other industries outside STEM. Discussions in living rooms, boardrooms, and classrooms focused on the factors driving career attrition among women and other minorities, including work-life balance pressures, lack of mentorship, and exclusionary organizational cultures.

The model had gained traction and broad utility, but its growing popularity also began to expose its limitations.

---

[1] The authors don't define special education, but the paper is an analysis of the intersectionality of diverse learning needs and physical disabilities, as well as cultural and linguistic diversity (CLD). The article emphasizes the importance of recruiting and retaining CLD teachers in special education to better serve the growing diversity of students in public schools in the U.S., particularly those with disabilities.

An Incomplete Story

> *As always in life, people want a simple answer...*
> *and it's always wrong.*

> – Baroness Susan Greenfield
> *Neuroscientist*[2]

While effective in its simplicity, the metaphor of the leaky pipeline risks narrowing our collective imagination about both the challenges and the opportunities of careers in STEMM.

Visual language plays a critical role in shaping understanding.[3] Compelling images, like that of a leaking pipe, can crystallize complex ideas, make patterns and connections more accessible, and transcend linguistic or disciplinary boundaries. Yet even when we lack the words to describe what we perceive, images have the power to shape our internal beliefs, sometimes with unintended consequences: subtly reinforcing assumptions, flattening critical complexities, and constraining how problems are defined and how solutions are imagined.

The Passive and Negative Framing Implies that Women are Quitters

In its most extreme oversimplification, the leaky pipeline depicts STEMM career paths as a single, linear channel, and the people navigating these paths as fluid molecules uniformly flowing through it. This pipeline is *perfect* (ignoring, of course, a few spontaneous cracks or holes at specified junctions), and the fluid is homogeneous.

In this oversimplified framing, harmful implications that might otherwise be subtle enough to miss become glaringly obvious.

It suggests that those who "leaked out" or were "lost" passively washed out through discrete flaws in an otherwise functional design, drawing attention to isolated defects or weak spots rather than to the design of the system or the nature of the flow.

---

[2] Often attributed to Baroness Susan Greenfield, though no original source has been verified.

[3] A picture is worth a thousand words, after all.

If the fluid is uniform, then all else is presumed equal too. And so, by extension, those who "leak out" must be inherently weak, deficient, or otherwise unsuitable.

Either that or we're quitters. But none of these is accurate.

We are not passive.

We are intentional.

We are active agents in our own lives, making reasoned choices based on a multitude of factors.

We are not weak.

We are powerful. We are strong, smart, generous, and disciplined.

We take calculated risks to drive sustainable progress, balancing strategic priorities with insight and agility. We deliver results by investing in collective success and by holding ourselves and our teams accountable.

We do not quit.

We persevere. We adapt. We pivot.

We are resilient and committed, ambitious and resourceful. We are strategic, decisive, and self-aware.

We overcome challenges and adversity with ingenuity, persistence, and resolve. We adjust and recalibrate as we learn and grow, individually, in teams, and across organizations. We make goal-oriented, future-forward decisions, shifting course when necessary to pursue opportunities that align with our strengths, our values, and our potential, and charting new paths where existing ones fail to lead where we need to go.

We are brave.

At its most oversimplified extreme, the subtle but real and potentially harmful implications of the leaky pipeline model become clear. It flattens critical complexities and nuanced decisions into a single, shallow narrative of passive loss. In truth, our departures are deliberate, discerning acts of survival, ambition, and hope.

A Little Too Little About Prevention

Framing departures from STEMM as passive losses also shifts the focus "a little too much on how we fix it, and a little too little on how we prevent it."

Such a myopic and simplistic "plug-and-fix" approach promotes superficial solutions aimed at merely preventing leaks, rather than addressing the underlying individual, cultural, institutional, and systemic factors that intersect to influence career satisfaction and progression. As the upstream parable reminds us, instead of scrambling to catch those who are struggling downstream, we would be much better off addressing the upstream causes that push women out of STEMM in the first place.[4]

Misdirected Focus of "Waste"

Wasted knowledge. Wasted talent. Wasted productivity. Wasted money.

In the leaky pipeline framework, the dominant narrative for departures from STEMM frames "exits" as "losses" and "losses" as "waste." From the perspective of the establishment, it makes perfect sense. Within a closed system like an engineering company or a university, a STEMM graduate who becomes a physics teacher is seen as a "drip" from the pipeline. A chemistry lab director who shifts to science communication or politics is regarded as "wasted potential." An engineering professional who transitions to law, music, or public policy is logged as a "loss."

But real life is an open system, and the full arc of a real-life career can include any variety of dynamic transitions, such as promotions, pivots, part-time roles, multiple roles, pauses, re-entries, and lateral moves. Some women feel pushed out of STEMM by barriers and threats; others feel pulled toward opportunities that better align with our ambitions. Many of us feel the torsion of both.

---

[4] The *upstream parable*, often attributed to Saul Alinsky, is commonly used in public health to emphasize the importance of addressing root causes rather than only reacting to symptoms. The parable asks: If people keep falling into a river, should we continue rescuing them or investigate what's causing them to fall in?

There is waste in the system, indeed. There is waste when we are pushed out. There is waste when we are pulled elsewhere. And there is certainly waste when we stay.

But *who* wastes *what* matters.

This central point is not captured at all in the leaky pipe model. When strong, capable women are pushed out the waste is extensive and layered.

> **Women themselves stand to lose** momentum toward positions of power, along with the professional, financial, social, and emotional security that come with career advancement.[5] We can lose our ability to earn a living doing what we love and do best. We can lose confidence, credibility, relationships, influence, and the reputation we've worked hard to build.

> **Organizations can lose** time, money, and productivity. They can also lose trust, institutional knowledge, role models, and future talent.

> **Society loses too**, bearing the massive opportunity cost of all that unrealized possibility. When women are pushed away from positions of influence, the entire system forfeits the diverse perspectives and problem-solving approaches that drive meaningful, inclusive change. The whole world pays the price.

When strong, capable women are pulled to other opportunities the gains and losses are complex.

We may trade power, prestige, and financial returns for other valid pursuits like activism, autonomy, balance, challenge, creative expression, fulfillment, growth, impact, innovation, mental health, passion, independence, legacy, and purpose. We may reclaim our time, our health, and our sense of self.

We may discover new ways to lead, build, and innovate.

But we leave other things behind. We may lose stability, status, or the cumulative benefits of staying on a conventional path. And we might have to

---

[5] Sometimes a lateral move is the best strategic step. Shout out to all those women who launched themselves forward by stepping back for a beat.

walk away from communities we helped build, from people and projects we care deeply about, and from systems and ideals we once believed in.

When our transitions are seen through a lens of "loss," changing course can be confused with failure: if change = loss, and loss = failure, then change = failure. Women internalize this messaging, and we beat ourselves up. *Twice.*

Once for "failing" the establishment.

And then again (even worse) for "failing" other women and girls.

The gains and losses to organizations and communities that arise from our career transitions are unevenly distributed, but they do not simply diffuse away. Organizations and sectors that fail to retain us lose out, while others stand to benefit from the STEMM knowledge, skills, mindsets, and perspectives we carry forward to enable innovation in every job, every field, and every sphere of influence.

Paid or not.

When strong, capable women choose to stay in STEMM the waste can be invisible, but burdensome, nonetheless.

Women in many STEMM workplaces spend an extraordinary amount of precious emotional energy biting our tongues, code-switching, compensating for others, enduring hostility, humiliation, and harassment, fighting for recognition, justifying ourselves, and proving again and again.

What a waste.

That same energy, if redirected, could deepen discussions, accelerate innovation, strengthen teams, solve more technical challenges, make organizations more productive and more fair, engage with more communities, or mentor more students. That same energy, if redirected, could also go toward caring for our own wellness and connecting more with the people and causes that matter most to each of us.

Collective progress slows when we mistake survival for success. When women's time and brilliance are consumed by navigating bias and broken systems, rather than driving innovation and progress, organizations risk exhausting their most committed talent. Society, in turn, loses out on the competitive advantages that inclusive leadership brings.

A BETTER STORY

THERE IS NO PATH; THERE ARE INFINITE PATHS

Our lives and our careers are shaped by intrinsic, interpersonal, institutional, and systemic influences, as well as by the opportunities available or unavailable at a given time. Some of us enter STEMM in grade school and continue in the same field throughout our entire careers; others move on to pursue opportunities in completely different fields and never look back; still others shift into peripheral fields and later return, bringing renewed energy and fresh perspectives.

If we want the next generation "leaky pipe" metaphor to be meaningful and effective, it must evolve to reflect the full complexity of this real-world experience. It needs to be less about passive leaking; and more about active pivoting; less about failing; and more about consciously pursuing meaningful, inspiring, engaging, satisfying, high-impact careers and other life goals.

Imagine a labyrinth, a game of pinball, or an obstacle course, like the one imagined in our Rubik's Cube illustration. Each has multiple pathways, optional workarounds, and also dead ends. There are aid and rest stations here and there, but sometimes they're hidden or blocked off. Sometimes you can clearly see a route ahead, but sometimes you're blindfolded. Sometimes it's a team challenge; sometimes you're on your own.

Or picture a biological cell, with intricate machinery that miraculously maintains equilibrium but can swell to bursting or dry out to dust.

It could be a garden ecosystem with fertile soil, sun, fresh water, and mutualists, but also pests, predators, and seasonal cycles. Or perhaps it's a satellite, held in orbit by a strong gravitational pull, equipped with sophisticated sensing for precise course corrections, but vulnerable to drift and signal interference, and reliant on exorbitant amounts of fuel.

For some, it's an iceberg, with the visible surface veneer masking a much deeper reality: tidy narratives for messy truths, band-aid fixes for systemic issues, shallow recognition for deep contributions, and narrow ideals blocking infinite potential. And yet, somehow, it stays afloat.

Or maybe it's the big bang, a constellation of attractive and repulsive forces so intense they can generate an explosion if not handled with care, one that could give birth to a whole new universe or tear another apart.

It's got all sorts of interacting components, like…

Wheels, ramps, springs, levers, cranks, gears, bearings, chains, magnets, hinges and locks, valves, dampers, pistons, turbines, regulators, pumps, and vacuums.

Also pillars, bridges, staircases and secret passageways, front doors, back doors, elevators, building codes, blueprints, scaffolding, hard hats, power drills, levels, jackhammers, chisels, forges, nuts and bolts, insulation, glass, concrete, and rebar.

With non-Newtonian fluids, solvents and solutes, acids, bases, buffers, isomers, polymerizers, catalysts, heat sinks, and covalent networks.

And quantum states, paradoxes and proofs, non-linear equations, limits and asymptotes, integrals, transformations, multidimensional matrices, and fractals.

And feedback loops, network protocols, encryption languages, idle states, variable bandwidth and system compatibility, archives, updates, routers, sensors, switches, batteries, capacitors, resistors, amplifiers, diodes, transformers, circuit breakers, and operating system interfaces.

And semi-permeable membranes, and skin, muscles, brains, lungs, guts, enzymes, and antibodies.

And uteruses, cocoons, shells, caves, nests, hives, greenhouses, seeds and soil, roots and shoots, fossils and diamonds, mountains, valleys, waterfalls, geysers, hurricanes, droughts, sun showers and rainbows.

With prisms, paint, pencils and erasers, stencils, rulers, mirrors, lenses, light and shadow.

And magic.

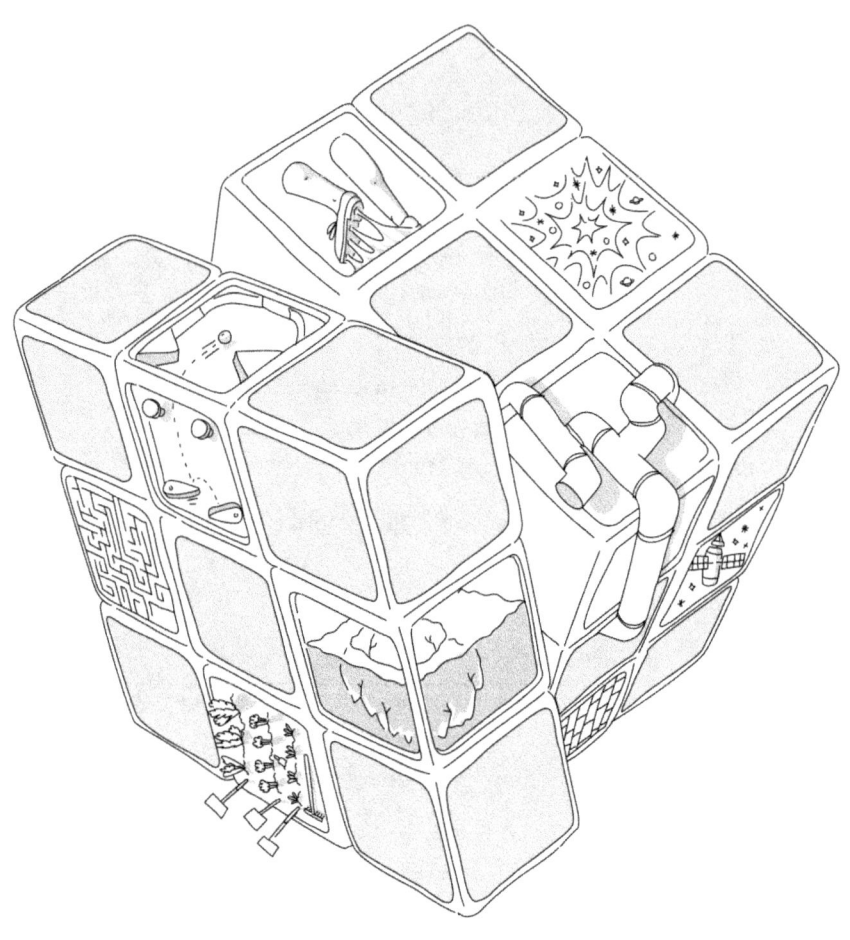

A dynamic reimagining of the leaky pipeline metaphor.

A HUMAN STORY

I've learned that making a living is not the same thing as making a life.

– Dr. Maya Angelou
Poet and Civil Rights Activist

Behind all the models and metaphors are the human stories. Here's one from me.

I sent out an SOS following a deeply troubling series of events at work one day, and my best friend in the world said something to me that I will never forget:

"Jane, we all know you can handle this.
You can handle your shit better than anyone else I know.
But you don't have to.
It's ok to say you don't want to.
It's not the same as you can't."

It's ok to say I don't want to. It's not the same as I can't.

Those words struck a chord that day that will resonate forever. They catalyzed my own permission to think about what I actually wanted in my career, rather than chasing the outer limits of my ability to endure.

It took another year or so to move on from that job, but I did. Not because I couldn't handle it, but because I didn't want to.

Creating my next fit took a lot of reflection, time and effort. I'm reinventing myself (again) and I can't really say for sure if I'm still "in" STEMM.[6]

- I still design and run experiments, but I no longer use microscopes or scalpels.
- I still build things, but rarely in CAD models anymore.
- I still analyse and document results, but I don't publish them in peer-reviewed journals like I used to.
- I still teach and learn, but almost never in a classroom.

---

[6] Positioning STEMM as something you're either "in" or "out" of is absurd, anyways. We can't even agree on the letters in the acronym (is it STEM or STEMM?). How could we possibly define the arbitrary boundaries of an entire constellation of fields?

- I still write code, but not to control robots.
- I still give the occasional talk, but not at research conferences.
- And I still build new tech, but more often with my heart and mind than my hands.

I didn't "leak out." And I didn't quit.

I persevered. I adapted. I pivoted.

I persevered under extreme workloads: designing, building, programming, writing, presenting, teaching, traveling, negotiating, project managing, experimenting, and meeting impossible deadlines.

I persevered through the subtle (but constant) fear of working in basement labs in the middle of the night.

I persevered through the impossible balancing act of raising babies while building a career: breastfeeding my infant son in one arm while cranking out MATLAB code with my other, and writing winning proposals with my tiny daughter bouncing around on my lap.

I persevered under the burden of my own perfectionism, but outworking it sure made me tired.

I persevered through blatant sexism, like when I was told to "show up in a little black dress, so we'd get better funding."

I persevered when I discovered I was being paid less than my colleagues because I cared so deeply about my projects and clients.

I persevered when so-called "leaders" stole my hard work and passed it off as their own.

I persevered when so-called "leaders" stopped short of patting me on the head, but told me to my face that I should "leave this to the big boys."

I adapted my boundaries.

I chaired EDI committees.

I chose my academic supervisors and managers extremely carefully, and I got to work with some great ones.

I sought out teams I respected and opportunities I valued.

I built informal support systems where formal support was missing.

I strategically leveraged my voice: speaking loudly when I had the advantage, biting my tongue when it wasn't worth the work.

I pivoted from engineering to research because I could get paid to be curious.

I pivoted from research to innovation because I was more excited about turning ideas into solutions and getting them to market than I was about lab work, and it seemed more amenable to the work-life balance I envisioned for myself at the time.

I pivoted from innovation to writing, consulting, and investing because I was so burned out and cynical I could hardly recognize myself.

My career "path" is nothing like cruising down a clear channel. It's more like surfing in Tofino. There is bright sun and frigid water. It's calm and serene in certain seasons, wild and unpredictable in others. Sometimes the beach is empty, and sometimes it's crowded. Most surfers are friendly and helpful; a few guard their turf. I can catch the odd wave, but mostly I have to fight like hell just to stay up.

I stall and wipe out. I change course. I carve my own.

Good thing I'm a strong swimmer.

END OF THIS STORY

Women transition away from STEMM at alarming rates, and the leaky pipeline metaphor has been effective at calling attention to this fact. But its very simplicity limits its utility in representing the truth. Women's career and life choices are complex and multidimensional, and cannot be reduced to a single, straight channel.

Representing attrition as "leaks" implies that it's a passive process, which couldn't be further from the truth. No one passively leaks out of STEMM.

We persevere. We adapt. We pivot.

Framing departures from STEMM as passive losses shifts time and energy toward plugging discrete holes rather than interrogating the flawed design of the system itself.

The narrative of "loss" equates intentional career transitions with waste. There is waste, indeed, but the model flattens crucial realities. It focuses "losses" on institutional metrics while overlooking both the costs and rewards women themselves may experience when they transition, and it erases the very real waste that might occur when we stay.

As conversations about equity and inclusion in STEMM continue to evolve, so too must the visual language we use to represent them. It's time to retire a simple leaky pipeline in favor of a more dynamic framework, one that reflects the complex, intersecting factors that influence why we enter, stay, leave, and return to STEMM.

TL;DR

1. The leaky pipeline metaphor evolved to draw attention to the fact that women are exiting STEMM careers at alarming numbers.

2. The concept of a one-dimensional pipe with a single inlet and outlet that passively leaks talent is simple and convenient, but it fails to capture the diverse and intersecting forces that push and pull women toward and away from STEMM careers.

3. No single framework will ever fully encompass the range of influences that shape our decisions to enter, stay in, or leave STEMM careers. But if we use our imaginations, and lean into the symbolic power of STEMM-y tools and concepts, we can invent a metaphor all our own.

Two

Values and Choice

PURSUING FULFILLMENT ON OUR OWN TERMS

by Cassie Leonard, amateur beach volleyball player and baker, semi-pro boy mom, and executive-level spreadsheet enthusiast.

I used to define my success in the way I had inadvertently been taught. I've always been an ambitious, self-driven individual, striving to excel in whatever I am doing. These traits are readily fostered and encouraged in academic STEMM environments, and I fell right into the trap of always pushing towards the next grant, the next publication, the next graduation, and the next external accolade.

The awareness that this lifestyle was increasingly incompatible with my personal and professional values came gradually, but it crystallised when I was awarded a significant research grant. Instead of feeling elated, grateful, and excited, I was filled with a sense of dread and simmering anxiety. The thrill of this external validation of 'success' was undermined by the realisation that I should already be focused on achieving the next grant to keep the success ship afloat.

I realised that my sense of self-worth and identity had become so intimately tied to how we typically define academic success that it was just not sustainable.

This realisation prompted me to transition from academia to management consulting. One year into my new role, I still feel excited and open to the wide range of opportunities where my skills and values could take me, rather than being confined to a predetermined career trajectory.

Now, success to me means working as an efficient, effective team to generate a result that will have an impact, whatever that may be and however big or small. Success to me means being fully present with my kids at moments that count and not feeling guilty about it. Success to me means defining myself as more than just 'a neuroscientist' and more than what is listed on my CV.

– Bridgette Semple
Neuroscientist and Management Consultant

How many times have you been asked this seemingly benign question; "So... what do you do?"

I have encountered variations of this query countless times, from fellow soccer parents making small talk on the sidelines, at conferences and holiday parties, during book clubs, and even with (overly) inquisitive strangers at the grocery store.

And I've done it, too. Reducing a new acquaintance's full identity to just their occupation is quick and easy. Welcome to Social Skills 101!

At one point, my answer was quick and easy too: "I'm an engineer."

I'll admit, I enjoyed how this broad job category often garnered impressed and surprised eyebrow raises. I let people jump to their own favorable conclusions about my intelligence, diligence, ambition, and affluence based on my three-word reply.

And then I went and changed everything.

Like so many, the 2020 pandemic and global shutdown became a catalyst for deep reflection, driving me to reconsider my entire value system. After months away from the office, I started questioning why I had allowed daily commutes, daycare drop-offs, school pickups, subpar cafeteria lunches, fluorescent lighting, and windowless office buildings to dominate my waking hours for the previous 16 years.

Self-reflection also revealed that my enthusiasm for aerospace products was waning. I found myself far more excited about investing my time in coaching, writing, and playing beach volleyball in the sunshine. In 2022, I chose to leave my corporate aerospace career.

First emotion: Elation.

Second emotion: *Terror!*

For the entire first year, I struggled. How could I decouple my sense of worth, *who I am*, from my professional identity? "I'm an engineer" had been my magic tool to efficiently (and with the societally required dash of modesty) articulate my value.
But how do I answer this damn question now?

Bridgette's perpetual grant application story, always chasing the next success, highlights how societal pressures in Australia inhibited her efforts to separate what she does, and how well she does it, from who she is. Like many of us, Bridgette had fallen into the enmeshment trap, discovering that her professional identity was consuming her entire sense of self.

But she also shows us that there is hope. Through self-awareness, active choice, and determination, Bridgette has successfully reclaimed her identity.

DEFINING VALUE & VALUES

The journey of defining your values and understanding how they correlate with the decisions you make is deeply personal. For the sake of discussion, we'll separate the definition of this complex word into two distinct concepts.

> **Value** (in its singular form) is our sense of self-worth. It's how we measure ourselves. Our identity, achievements, recognition, self-compassion, and growth all play into value.

> **Values** (plural), on the other hand, are our principles, beliefs, and standards that guide every decision we make. Examples include communication, commitment, and creativity.

Value and values are involved in every decision we make. Take something as simple as choosing what to have for lunch. If your measure of self-worth tells you today's presentation was amazing and you deserve sushi, that's your value in action. However, if your values include frugality, you might still opt for your packed lunch instead.

As decisions become larger, value and values become even more influential. This is why the choices we make, both personally and professionally, are completely unique to each individual.

Ultimately, it's only what you, the smart reader you are, choose that matters. For example:

- A market-leading salary may be very important because you have large student loans to pay off.
- Stability might be a consideration because you didn't enjoy moving from school to school as a kid.
- Or variety might be what you're seeking because, thanks to your neurodivergence, novelty helps you focus.

There is no such thing as the "right" answer for any decision you're faced with, even if external pressures suggest otherwise. The belief that one singular choice is 'best' can hinder our ability to move forward with confidence.

No chapter in any book can define who you are or how you choose to invest your energy. What we can do, however, is explore value frameworks as a way of establishing a common language to reflect on our self-worth and allow those reflections to guide our next steps.

We'll examine the internal and external factors influencing our active (and passive) choices, offering a glimpse into the abundance of contradictions women in STEMM face. Additionally, I'll share a simple tool, consisting of just two questions, to help us reclaim the power to make decisions independent of current social norms and external expectations.

MODELS, MODELS, EVERYWHERE

All models are wrong, but some are useful.

– George E. P. Box
British Statistician

Before we explore, let's align on one ever-present truth: these models are wrong.[1]

Of course they are. Like the pursuit of modeling turbulent flow using unsolvable partial differential equations, the topics we are tackling are unquantifiable. However, like good scientists, we are going to try anyway.

Models offer value through the discussions they inspire. Remember, the leaky pipeline model has driven conversation about attrition in STEMM for half a century. Well done, leaky pipeline. But as we learned from Jane's chapter, it's time to shatter that model and start a new conversation.[2]

For our conversation on values and value, I selected the following two models because:

- Their overlapping themes are presented in very different ways.
- I was able to translate both into equations, and equations make me happy.

MODEL 1: EXPECTANCY-VALUE THEORY

We'll explore Expectancy-Value Theory (EVT) first. This model came to my attention when a fellow collaborator directed me to Jacquelynne Eccles's paper, where she applied EVT to substantiate her 1983 research on why girls opt out of mathematics. In her work, Eccles considers the intrinsic and extrinsic factors that motivate the choices girls make, compared to boys their age.

Developed by John William Atkinson in the 1950s and 1960s, EVT seeks to acknowledge the interplay of three unique types of self-value: attainment value, intrinsic value, and utility value. It also accounts for the cost associated with each choice we make. Even though its intent is to simplify, this is far from basic algebra; it's more like calculus.

Social and personal expectations, our sense of self, and a diverse array of competing forces all shape our personalized measurement of value and, ultimately, our expected returns on investment (ROI). Eccles captured the multi-dimensional influences of value in her work, stating, "it is not reality itself (i.e., past successes or failures) that most directly determines children's expectancies, values, and behaviors, but rather the interpretation of that reality."

---

[1] Or at least incomplete.
[2] See Chapter 1, *Shattering the Pipeline*.

$$ROI = \frac{f(Attainment\ Value, Intrinsic\ Value, Utility\ Value)}{f(Effort, Loss\ of\ Alternative, Cost\ of\ Failure)}$$

We all run inputs through our own ROI formula countless times each day. While every individual's valuation will be unique, the fundamental variables are similar.

> **Attainment Value** is how we qualify the importance of success as we consider each decision. It's tied to a sense of accomplishment, validation of self-worth or identity, and external recognition. This could be a new title, a pay increase, or a handwritten thank-you note from a peer.

> **Intrinsic Value** correlates to our "why." It's the satisfaction we gain when we focus our energy on tasks that align with our personal values and reinforce our understanding of who we are.

> **Utility Value** represents our external needs such as job security, income, data, and lab space. It might mean putting in work now for gratification later: a hard day's work for a handshake at the end of the day, a paycheck at the end of the month, or a pension at the end of our career. While it might not feel fulfilling in the moment, we understand the ROI is coming.

But for every return, there must be an investment.

> **Effort** is the energy we exert, or sometimes over-exert, to achieve the value we seek. Burnout becomes a significant risk when we fail to account for this cost.

> **Loss of Valued Alternatives** refers to the opportunities we miss because we chose a different path. If you decide to buy this house, you won't have the resources to buy that one too. If you decide to champion one rising star, you may not have the political capital left to support another.

> **Psychological Cost of Failure** recognizes the inherent risks and their connection to our sense of self-worth and confidence.

I find Expectancy-Value Theory to be a useful model because it illustrates mathematically what I've learned in parallel through life experience and my time training to be a professional coach: never give advice! With all the ways we can interpret value, all the costs and trade-offs, how in the world can you possibly know exactly what someone else should do?

Kelly learned this firsthand when people started giving her unsolicited career advice. She made the choice to move from a stable, prestigious job to an unknown subsea sensor company in a cyclical industry. To her peers, this seemed like a crazy decision, and they told her just that. When compared with their own values, she was taking on too much risk for too little reward.

So, when Kelly was laid off two years later, along with the rest of the production support team, were the nay-sayers proven right?

Not according to Kelly. She still knows it was the best decision.

That was the career move that reignited her passion for engineering. She loved working in a smaller business that afforded opportunities to engage with all aspects of a project, from proposal to design, build, test, and sell-off. Most importantly, she found a team culture that valued her ideas.

If her previous peers had known she was leaving to get away from a toxic workplace, would their advice have been different? Perhaps. But even she hadn't realized how toxic her previous job had been until she attended her first meeting at her new company, armed with a laundry list of reasons to validate her idea. Instead of being put on the spot to justify herself, her new team loved the idea immediately, and the meeting moved on. She was left discombobulated.

While everyone had warned her "the grass isn't always greener on the other side," Kelly followed her own intuition. She let her values and her sense of self-worth be her guide. By doing so, she discovered, in her own words, "the grass wasn't just greener. *It was fucking technicolor.*"

MODEL 2: TYPES OF FUN

Our second model, Type I and II Fun, entered my lexicon when I moved to Seattle and started playing beach volleyball on near-freezing winter days. Some people told me I was crazy (there's that word again), but I was having Type II fun!

I realize this expression isn't globally popular yet, so I'll explain.

Coined in the mid-1980s by professor and outdoor enthusiast Dr. Rainer Newberry of the University of Alaska, Fairbanks, this model sorts "fun" into distinct categories, differentiated by whether you enjoyed the experience in the moment or in retrospect.[3]

> **Type I Fun** refers to experiences you enjoy both in the moment and when you look back on them. Type I fun for me is floating on a paddle board at sunset or playing a board game with my boys.

$$Type\ I\ Fun = Pleasure(During) + Pleasure(Retrospect),$$

$$if\ Experience \geq 0\ during\ the\ activity.$$

> **Type II Fun** is an experience you find challenging in the moment, but in retrospect, you are grateful it happened. It's the strenuous hike to a summit that leaves you sore but with a sense of accomplishment.

$$Type\ II\ Fun = Struggle(During) + Pleasure(Retrospect),$$

$$if\ Experience > 0\ only\ in\ retrospect.$$

When applied to chilly January beach volleyball adventures, some days are Type I and some are Type II. When the sand is so cold it's a struggle, I remind myself about the benefits extra practice before the season offers (Utility Value).

You might be wondering what fun has to do with value and values in a professional conversation. Compared to EVT, I agree that the Types of Fun is a more playful model, but does that make it any less relevant? Let's look at examples in a STEMM workplace.

---

[3] A lesser-known third category, Type III Fun, is when something is not fun in the moment or in hindsight, and you'd never choose to do it again. The only 'fun' part is getting to recount your harrowing story over a pint. It applies to being chased by a bear but is (hopefully) less relevant in a workplace discussion.

Type I work is tasks throughout the day that are enjoyable right away. It's a mentoring where everything just clicked or, like me, having the time to dive deep into a beautiful spreadsheet.

Type II work is when it's not sunshine and rainbows, but you recognize that the energy you're investing will yield lasting value, including but not limited to attainment, intrinsic, and utility. It might be your first lead project with a demanding customer or the weeks of analysis to validate the structural integrity of a fuselage cutout. Both are grueling, but in the end, you feel proud of what you achieved.

Quantifying what we do as *fun* furthers the conversation by distilling the complexities of the EVT model into two simple questions:

Am I enjoying this right now?

Will I be happy that I did it afterward?

Notice that neither of these questions references extrinsic value. By bringing fun into the conversation, we shift the focus inward. Only you can decide if you're having fun. Others might feel irrationally comfortable advising you on your value and values, but you get to decide what's fun.

We all have different motivations, different end games, and different definitions of enjoyment. Perhaps, if we spent less time handing out unsolicited advice, we would all feel a bit less external pressure as we navigate our professional and personal lives.

EXTERNAL FORCES AT PLAY

Of course, clarity on our self-worth and values is only part of a larger equation. We live in an interconnected world. With that come external forces such as societal norms (gendered and not gendered), economic pressures, and expectations from bosses, peers, mentees, parents, partners, and friends; the list goes on.

You have to never get old, never be rude, never show off, never be selfish, never fall down, never fail, never show fear, never get out of line. It's too hard! It's too contradictory...

– Gloria, played by America Ferrera,
Barbie

With its two-minute-long third-act monologue, the movie Barbie brought the tightrope of external pressures women navigate into the spotlight. Thanks to Greta Gerwig and America Ferrera, we now have a globally recognized resource to describe the daily tensions women face.

My favorite part of the monologue is the rapid-fire series of contradictions, each one starting with "You have to" or "You're supposed to," only to be instantly undercut by a "but." The following table captures key double standards that resonated with me as a woman in STEMM.[4]

You have to / You're supposed to	But (also)
Always be extraordinary.	Somehow, we're always doing it wrong.
Have money.	You can't ask for money because that's crass.
Be a boss.	You can't be mean.
Lead.	You can't squash other people's ideas.
Be a career woman.	Always be looking out for other people.
Always be grateful.	Always stand out.
Find a way to acknowledge that the system is rigged.	Always be grateful.

To explore more, with a much less pink color scheme, check out Cynthia Nixon's viral video montage of impossible standards, *Be a Lady They Said.*[5] "Don't talk too loud, don't talk too much, don't be intimidating... Why are you so miserable?"

---

[4] Watch the full monologue at roughly the 1:15:00 timestamp of Barbie (2023).
[5] "Be a Lady They Said," a poem by Camille Rainville, performed by actor and activist Cynthia Nixon.

External forces will always play a role. By acknowledging them, we can approach our choices more strategically. After all, we can't solve for variables if we don't know they're part of the equation.

Barbie and *Be a Lady They Said* are helping us with awareness—check.

SHOULDS

Next, it's time to look for our "shoulds." *Shoulds* are things we do primarily to satisfy others, not ourselves. When left unchecked, my *shoulds* kept me climbing the corporate ladder away from the job I actually loved. Bridgette's *shoulds* encouraged her to continuously apply for the next grants, chasing external validation as her measure of success.

Recognizing these patterns was a turning point for both Bridgette and me, allowing us to pause, reassess, and proactively make choices to realign with our own values.

When we stop focusing on what we think we *should* do and instead offer ourselves the freedom to make choices based on what we truly value, whether it's a new career path, side gig, volunteer opportunity, vacation, promotion, or even intentional demotion, we begin moving in a more authentic direction.

AUTHENTIC CHOICES

When I chose to open a small coaching business, pivoting away from my hard-earned path toward chief engineer, I was once again reminded that I might be crazy.

But that's ok. I had done the math.

My new path offered more of what I valued:

> **Attainment value**. Shifting my definition of worth from salary to fulfilling "ah-ha" moments with coaching clients.

> **Intrinsic value**. Creating opportunities to align each day with my passions. Making space to be a volleyball player and quality time with my kids.

> **Utility value**. Recognizing how my needs have shifted. After 16 years of pretty aggressive saving, I had reduced my reliance on external income—thanks in part to FIRE movement principles!

I also looked at the cost. Over time, I realized the loss of valued alternatives would be greater if I stayed in my corporate job than if I forged my own path, with effort required either way. And the psychological cost of failure? It seemed worth the risk.

I was ready.

I chose to have some Type I fun at work!

> *The awareness that this lifestyle was increasingly incompatible with my personal and professional values came gradually...*
>
> – Bridgette

When Bridgette left her prestigious academic career, she still had external forces to navigate. Her good friend, and author of our *Academia* chapter, Jessica, recalls how others tried to pull Bridgette back in with more attainment and utility offerings.

> *Bridgette called me telling me she had left academia but then was awarded a very prestigious grant. Suddenly her perceived value had increased in the eyes of her workplace, who tried to persuade her to reconsider her decision to leave. She maneuvered the decision so expertly. I couldn't be prouder of how she navigated this and all she has achieved since. Bridgette is an absolute role model for anyone considering leaving academia.*
>
> – Jessica

Jessica's reflections also highlight that not all external forces are unwelcome. Bridgette made a professional choice that offered true intrinsic value. This example of glowing support from a friend during pivotal decisions reinforces the immeasurable value of being truly understood and trusted to chart your own course.

Imagine if we could decouple the conflict around what we want to be and who we think we should be. What if we were able to crystallize all the frameworks, models, and unsolicited advice to focus just on you?

I encourage you to get curious about every decision you make, big or small, by asking yourself these two (deceptively) simple questions:

What value does this offer me?

Do I personally value that value?

Derived from our Types of Fun questions, these Intrinsic Value questions are your new tool. They are designed to help you explore what you want, free from external input. Adjust the phrasing of these two questions as needed until they resonate with you and reflect your true values.

When faced with a decision, whether it's going for that promotion, negotiating your salary, working late, leaving early, speaking up in the meeting, taking a career break, pivoting, moving internationally, prioritizing time with loved ones, advocating for change, embracing the unknown, or anything else pressing on your mind, these questions can help cut through the noise.

They're focused squarely on you, not the system, not what's best for humankind, or even womankind. The insights they offer will support any decision you make, even when you ultimately choose to prioritize external factors over your intrinsic motivations. After all, we are navigating an imperfect, complex system; this is calculus.

What will you do?

You get to choose.

I chose to write books, coach, and play beach volleyball regardless of the season. When people inevitably ask me the dreaded, "What do you do?" question, I have a new answer for them— "I'm having so much fun!"

Three

Inlet Forces

ON PUSHING AND PULLING WOMEN & GIRLS INTO STEMM

by Jane Desrochers, engineer's brain, researcher's toolkit, explorer's compass; relentless excavator of deep questions.

A thin steel rod is great in tension and useless in compression.
Pull it and it holds strong and steady.
Push it and it will probably wobble, buckle, and then fail.
So is the argument for pulling women and girls into STEMM.
As is the argument against pushing them.

PULLING

Pulling women and girls into STEMM means creating STEMM education and workplace environments that are safe, attractive, productive, and accessible. It's about building equitable systems that accelerate inclusive innovation and progress. It's about shaping workplace cultures where being human is an asset, not a liability. It's about ensuring that transparency, fairness, decency, and respect are the standard, not the exception.

But it's also about recognizing what naturally draws women in: the promise of financial stability, the joy of problem-solving, the chance to build a meaningful and impactful career, and the opportunity to use our skills in ways that challenge us intellectually and serve others in practical and meaningful ways. STEMM can be a place to do what we love, strengthen our innate talents, and open doors to leadership across industries.

When women and girls see a workplace that reflects both our values and our potential, we will naturally be *pulled* toward it.

PUSHING

Pushing women and girls into STEMM is often forceful and careless. It reduces women and girls to statistics and quotas, ignoring whether the path is desirable, fair, or even safe for those expected to traverse it, all in an impulsive effort to satisfy arbitrary targets, impress funders, improve rankings, and gloss up annual reports.

But pushing isn't always loud or obvious.

Sometimes it comes wrapped in praise and encouragement, in subtle actions that reward ambition and excellence only when they align with narrow ideals. It shows up in well-meaning teachers and caregivers who celebrate girls for outperforming boys in math but dismiss us when we show interest and talent in art or caregiving. It hides in the quiet pressure not to "waste" potential, not to let anyone down, not to "squander your talents on hobbies that will never pay the bills."

Pushing funnels women and girls into rigid, outdated classrooms, labs, and offices that haven't adapted, turning a blind eye to systemic dysfunction and assuming that meeting quotas somehow equates to progress.

When learning institutions and workplaces fail to evolve, *pushing* harder doesn't fix the path. It breaks it.

REAL STORIES

It wasn't until I was almost 40 that it occurred to me that maybe this STEMM career I had wasn't actually the best choice for me. Perhaps it was the leading edge of a midlife crisis. Perhaps it was the fact that, as my career expanded, I was increasingly surrounded by incredibly diverse, talented, capable, and inspiring people of all genders. Perhaps it was that my daughter was coming out of her squishy childhood and growing into her adolescence.

Whatever the reasons that encouraged it, the realization feels like a distinct before and after. The thing is, I was good at STEMM. I had the privilege of a great support network: incredible parents, great teachers, and lots of other champions. But I had also worked damn hard to get where I was. My identity as an engineer was an important part of myself, and for a long time I couldn't afford to wonder whether I could have been better at something else.

Maybe I just didn't want to.

But one evening, a bright young colleague was contemplating going back to school to pursue a PhD, and she asked me an explosive question that caught me off guard.

"Would you do it again?"

And I had to confront her question and all the layers behind it.

What would my life look like if I'd made a different choice?

Who would I be without my iron ring and my PhD?[1]

What did it cost me and what did I gain?

Why did I pick engineering, anyways?

And was it really a choice I made on my own accord?

My response that night was a torrent of emotionally fueled word vomit, punctuated by long pauses while my brain caught up to my feelings and fumbled desperately to put them into words. Certain influences were clear and obvious then. Others have taken a lot more reflection.

I was pulled into the field because I inherited the benevolent helper gene and saw engineering as a way to do good for the world.

My dad was a doctor, and I wanted to help people be healthy too, but without all the blood and guts and talking to sick strangers. Engineering gave me a way to do real, tangible good for people from behind the scenes, where I could think and build all day in the comfort of my small team.

---

[1] The iron ring is a symbolic band worn by Canadian engineers on the pinkie finger of our dominant hand. It has a unique meaning to each engineer, but generally symbolizes unity, humility, and our ethical obligation to serve the public through the practice of engineering.

I was pulled in because I saw engineering as a straightforward path to a stable and well-paying job.

I was pulled in because I liked doing really hard things.

I was pulled in because I saw engineering as a way to contribute to meaningful impact that fit how I was naturally wired: quietly, rigorously, with tangible outcomes.[2]

But I was pushed as well, even if I didn't know it or feel it back then. I see now that my logic was shaped by a cultural undercurrent that was easy to miss at the time.

I was pushed in by an internalized idea that being a good feminist meant going where the smart boys were and outperforming them.

I was pushed in by an understanding that women's representation in STEMM was too low, and I felt a strong sense of duty to help change that.

I was pushed away from the identity threat of disappointing anyone. I couldn't stomach the thought of letting down my family, my teachers, my coaches, or my peers. Out loud, they all told me that I could do anything, but I could see their faces drop if I ever suggested creative or relational work. Their voices were silent, but their body language was loud and clear: smart girls did STEMM.

There were both pushing and pulling influences that shaped my own path into STEMM, and I am still working on uncoupling what I feel like I am supposed to want from what I think I want, from what I really want in my career. Those reflections have revealed a deeper truth.

How we frame STEMM for women and girls matters.

There is a case for pulling, and a case against pushing, women and girls into STEMM. A deeper understanding of these opposing drivers will help readers reflect on the forces that influence decisions to come and go from STEMM.

---

[2] Or, as straightforward as it got, at least.

THE CASE FOR PULLING

Hell yes, we should be pulling women and girls into STEMM!

THE BENEFITS STEMM OFFERS TO WOMEN AND GIRLS

The best argument for pulling women and girls into STEMM is that STEMM education and careers can offer extraordinary opportunities and benefits to us. STEMM is an incredible intellectual playground.

> **For women and girls who love pulling things apart** to understand how they work, or imagining systems that don't yet exist, STEMM provides an expansive canvas for exploration, creativity, and building.

> **For women and girls who love patterns and logic**, who can get lost in the rhythm of code or the beauty of an elegant equation, STEMM offers the opportunity to use those skills to shape the future through data science and technology development.

> **For women and girls who are fascinated by the natural world** of water, soil, plants, animals, and stars, STEMM provides the tools to explore, understand, and protect the environment.

> **For women and girls who are committed to improving** public health, reducing inequities, or developing groundbreaking medical innovations, STEMM is a vehicle to serve humanity through technical skill.

At their heart, STEMM education and careers provide a means to do what we love. But they also fortify our toolkit of cognitive and professional skills, all of which are valuable for both technical and non-technical roles across a wide range of industries and career paths.

STEMM disciplines train individuals to think critically, evaluate evidence, and approach complex problems with creativity and structured reasoning. Success requires breaking down open-ended (often ambiguous) challenges into manageable parts and addressing them with logic, precision, and ingenuity. These cognitive habits, which are transferable skills, are consistently cited by employers as essential across fields. Research also shows that participation in STEM-based learning environments increases cognitive **versatility**, **metacognition**, systems thinking, and the capacity for lifelong learning.

In a world that demands interdisciplinary thinking and agile leadership to respond to rapidly changing workplaces and global challenges, this kind of mental flexibility is a powerful asset.

But skills alone aren't the only return on a STEMM investment for women and girls. A STEMM education and career can also offer strong economic value, unlocking financial stability, upward mobility, and long-term opportunity.

Many STEMM careers rank among the highest-paying and most stable occupations worldwide. In the U.S., women in STEM occupations earn, on average, 67% more than women in other fields. Across OECD countries, graduates in engineering, information and communication technology (ICT), and health sciences tend to report significantly higher earnings than their peers in the humanities, arts, or social sciences. STEMM roles often offer faster entry into livable-wage careers, which can accelerate progress toward paying off student loans, saving for a home, or building financial independence. For example, engineering and computer science graduates in Canada report some of the shortest payback periods for education-related debt. Globally, STEMM jobs also tend to have lower unemployment rates and higher projected demand, especially in areas such as AI, health, and clean energy. This makes a STEMM career not just lucrative, but resilient.

STEMM education and careers can open doors to economic opportunity, but this does not excuse or minimize the infuriating reality that gender pay gaps persist across nearly all STEMM disciplines, and that these disparities tend to widen with career progression.[3] Still, for many women, especially when compared to other fields, the economic benefits are substantial. A STEMM background not only increases earnings and job security, it also catalyzes opportunity for leadership, influence, and advancement.

The case for pulling women and girls into STEMM for our own sake is strong: the benefits are tangible, the investment is as future-proof as it gets, and

---

[3] This whole book is about that truth.

the gains are long-term. So yes, pull women and girls in. STEMM can offer a lot to us, and we can offer a lot in return.

THE BENEFITS WOMEN AND GIRLS OFFER TO STEMM

Women and girls bring immense value to STEMM.

Women in STEMM contribute essential perspectives that deepen the understanding of complex problems and drive creative solutions. A landmark study by Anita Woolley and colleagues reported that collective group intelligence was not associated with IQ, but was correlated with the proportion of females in the group. Articles from *Harvard Business Review* support these findings and show that diverse teams, which have varied life experiences and ways of thinking, are better at solving complex problems because they bring more ideas to the table, increasing the range of potential solutions. These teams don't just generate better outcomes in the moment; they also enrich problem-solving processes themselves, which accelerates future innovation.

Collective group intelligence correlates with the proportion of women in the group, not with IQ.

Diverse teams also show clear advantages when it comes to decision-making. Research has shown that diverse teams make faster, more informed, and more resilient decisions because they are more likely to challenge assumptions, consider alternative viewpoints, and examine issues from multiple angles. Better decision-making leads to solutions that are both more robust and more adaptive, essential qualities in critical sectors such as climate tech, healthcare, and AI. Better decision-making also results in faster project completion, fewer costly errors, and greater adaptability to change.

Expanded market intelligence to identify new product opportunities is a clear competitive advantage, one that extends to the bottom line.[4] So, it's no surprise that companies with gender-diverse leadership are consistently shown to perform better financially. McKinsey & Company (2020) reports that such companies are 25% more likely to exceed profitability averages, while a Boston

---

[4] Especially for folks historically overlooked by mainstream design and development.

Consulting Group (2018) study found that diversity in management is associated with 19% higher innovation-related revenue.

In addition to our contributions to economic and technical outcomes, women in STEMM also contribute to building organizations that are safer, more ethical, and better equipped for both short- and long-term challenges. Diverse teams have been shown to make more accurate assessments and respond more effectively to risk. These qualities are essential for agile decision-making in the near term, especially in rapidly changing fields such as artificial intelligence, biotechnology, and climate science.

In parallel, gender-diverse teams are also more likely to prioritize sustainability, social responsibility, and ethical governance, which are critical for long-term resilience and reputational integrity. Alongside our technical brilliance, women in STEMM bring a broad awareness of how decisions affect people, systems, and ecosystems, both now and in the future. This future-oriented mindset is especially valuable in domains that demand a balance between innovation and stewardship, such as health, energy, infrastructure, and environmental design. Research also suggests that women in leadership tend to engage in collaborative, inclusive negotiation strategies, leading to durable and socially beneficial outcomes. In this way, women help build STEMM teams and cultures where a striking combination of empathy, systems thinking, and technical excellence helps ensure that innovation remains human-centered and future-ready.

> *There is no such thing as a single-issue struggle because we do not live single-issue lives.*
>
> – Audre Lorde
> *Writer, Poet, and Civil Rights Activist*

Women and girls can derive huge benefits from STEMM education and careers. Likewise, STEMM fields can derive huge benefits from including us. But if we focus only on getting more women and girls into STEMM without addressing the structural inequities, toxic cultures, and systemic barriers that we may encounter within it, we risk doing more harm than good. Inclusion without reform isn't progress. It's a setup.

THE CASE AGAINST PUSHING

There are so many ripple effects that emanate from increasing diversity in STEMM. Discussions about innovation, equity, justice, and the future of STEMM itself are happening in living rooms, classrooms, and boardrooms alike. However, while the emotional, psychological, and human costs of women's participation in STEMM are finally receiving some attention, there is still not much in the literature that speaks directly to these effects.

Given the limited published research on this vital topic, the arguments that follow are presented as a (woefully) incomplete series of opinion vignettes, each offering a different angle on the potential harm done to women and girls when we are carelessly pushed into a system that has not evolved to work with us.[5] I call attention to these harms not to argue against inclusion, but to advocate for a more thoughtful, more judicious approach to how we pursue it.

RECRUITMENT IS EASY, RETENTION IS HARD

> **Recruiting** more women and girls into STEMM is a win. No question. It's a win that generations of women fought hard for. But it's also the easy part. Recruitment is a short-term, outward-facing project with a well-defined timeline, relatively low costs, concrete scope, and clear, quantifiable metrics.

> **Retention**, by contrast, demands everything that recruitment neatly avoids. It requires an introspective approach from the highest levels of leadership and the courage to confront uncomfortable truths about organizational culture, power dynamics, and systemic bias. Leaders must examine not just policies, but people, including themselves. That kind of reckoning is existentially threatening. It is also more operationally complex: timelines are long and unpredictable, costs are high, and the scope is slippery, with complex, intersecting variables that

---

[5] I use the term *harm* in the broadest possible sense, much like in the classic saying "do more good than harm." Harm can be life-altering, or it can go unnoticed in the moment, but little harms always add up.

defy simple ROI calculations. As a result, retention work is often postponed or neglected completely.

Of course, the cost of that neglect is paid for by women ourselves.[6]

There are a growing number of phenomenal STEMM workplaces led by trailblazers of all genders who have done the hard work. This is real progress, to be sure. But these are outliers. Most workplaces have still not yet adapted to the point where a diverse workforce can thrive and where organizations can realize the full value of our contributions.

Still today, in many STEMM workplaces, women are under-supported at best. At worst, we are actively harmed. Chronic stress, burnout, demoralization, mental and physical dysregulation, pay inequity, stalled advancement, underemployment, and attrition are all predictable outcomes, not unfortunate anomalies.

Women don't suffer these effects because we are too fragile to "make it" in STEMM. We suffer these effects because institutions still refuse to do the hard, unglamorous work of becoming worthy of the people they claim to want.

JUST BECAUSE YOU CAN DOESN'T MEAN YOU HAVE TO

"You're smart. We need women and girls like you in STEMM."

Intended as a compliment, this seemingly innocuous statement is meant to be encouraging. But there is an implicit message that walks a fine line between invitation and expectation. It is a message that can be internalized not as aptitude, but as obligation. It also blurs the lines between *can*, *should*, *want*, and *need*.

Intentional or not, positioning STEMM careers as the best (or only) option for smart girls risks undercutting the equity movements that fought for women's right to work, to lead, and to be taken seriously in fields once walled off to us. It doesn't expand choice; it constrains it, undermining the very agency these movements fought to protect.

Framing STEMM as the only acceptable option also reinforces an unspoken hierarchy that places STEMM above all other domains. This is

---

[6] Organizational cultural neglect harms everyone, regardless of gender, but the burden of that neglect falls disproportionately on women and other marginalized groups. Candid conversations about how the "patriarchy" also harms men are becoming more common in public discourse, but they are, unfortunately, out of scope for this book.

especially problematic when STEMM is positioned in opposition to fields historically filled mostly by women, because it explicitly devalues the care, education, community, and creative work done almost exclusively by women in the past. These relational domains are absolutely vital to a strong society and equally deserving of a talented, ambitious workforce.

Strong societies run on a collective total of individual strengths. We all have a duty to contribute in the best way we can. But a just society, one that is truly free, means we all have the ability to decide how. Enabling women to choose how, what, and with whom we add value to our communities and workplaces may very well be the most radical form of equity we can offer.

OUR RELATIONSHIP TO WORK IS CHANGING

Women suffer these effects because institutions still refuse to do the hard, unglamorous work of becoming worthy of the people they claim to want.

Pushing women down a career path (no matter how prestigious or high paying the prize at the end may seem) will never work better than building workplaces that *pull* us in.

Women today know this better than ever before. We are making intentional, balanced career choices. Choices that prioritize mental health, flexibility, personal growth, and social impact.

We're not just asking, "What job can I do?"

We are asking, "What kind of world do I want to live in? What kind of life do I want? And how can I build a career that supports it?"

For many, this means stepping off traditional career paths and away from outdated and myopic definitions of success in favor of something more adaptive, humane, and aligned with our core values.

This shift is both inspiring and unsettling, hopeful, and disorienting. It is liberating for individuals, but disruptive for institutions. It upends decades of presumptions about career loyalty, narrow definitions of ambition, and the assumed virtues of grind culture. But for organizations willing to evolve, it opens up access to a new wave of brilliant, values-driven, and deeply committed talent. Women today are every bit as ambitious as our mothers and grandmothers. We are just very selective about how we orient that ambition.

If the work is worthy, if it aligns with our values, complements our other life goals, supports our well-being, and makes a meaningful impact, then smart, resourceful, creative, driven women will gravitate toward it.

And we will show up.

With enthusiasm. Commitment. Strength. Energy. Passion. Purpose. Drive. Focus. Resilience.

And each other.

But we have to be *pulled* in.

FINAL THOUGHTS

I think back to the conversation with my young colleague that cracked this all open. Her question was simple and direct: if I had the choice, would I take the academic STEMM path again?

I never really answered her. It is years later, and I am still untangling my thoughts and feelings about it all.

I don't regret a minute of my education. My engineering degree comes with me wherever I go, and I lean on the skills and knowledge I gained from my STEMM training and experience in all aspects of my life. Certain workplace experiences cost me dearly, but I also recognize the incredible opportunities my career has afforded me. I will quietly admit that I do feel a certain pride in my iron ring and my PhD. But I would still be enough without them.

So, would I do it again?

Honestly, I think I would.

I just wish I could say I did it because I really wanted to.

Not because I felt like I should.

TL;DR

1. The benefits to women and girls who pursue STEMM education and careers can be extraordinary

2. The benefits to companies and communities and innovation and progress at large from attracting more women and girls to pursue STEMM education and careers can be extraordinary

3. There are plenty of arguments for why we need to make STEMM careers more attractive, productive, and equitable for women and girls whose talents and values and career goals align well, so there is a natural *pull* in that direction.

4. But carelessly *pushing* women and girls down these career paths without first making organizations more supportive for us sets the whole system up for failure.

Four

Ideal Worker vs. Ideal Parent

THE HIGH COST OF COMPETING IDENTITIES

by Emily L. Bishop, mother and engineer turned entrepreneur challenging the status quo.

I grew up in a lower-middle-class family on the east coast of Canada. My dad was an engineer and my mom was a nurse before staying home with us. Growing up, I was told I could do anything. If I worked hard, I'd be successful. So, I followed the path laid out for me: good grades, a strong university education, and a secure career.

I chose to pursue engineering, and everyone around me cheered me on. It was smart, stable, and well-paying.

But when I graduated with my Mechanical Engineering degree, I felt no excitement about the jobs in front of me. Then I discovered Biomedical Engineering and thought, "Now that's something I can get behind." I went to grad school, and a master's degree turned into a PhD. Nine years of higher education later, I was finally ready to join the workforce.

At 31, I landed a research job with a knee brace company. I was thrilled! I had everything I thought I wanted: a good job, a beautiful home, a supportive husband, and three weeks' vacation.

It was a great fit... for a time.

As a young, married professional, trading 40 hours a week for a good paycheck felt like a fair exchange. I had my evenings, my weekends, a couple of vacations a year. Life was good.

Then, at 33, I had my first son. I took a year off to raise and nurture this new human and returned to work. Honestly, I never questioned going back. I had worked too hard to get where I was. Walking away wasn't even a consideration. But when I went back to work, everything changed.

Suddenly, the systems I had trusted all my life no longer worked for me. I felt like I was failing, both at work and at home. I questioned everything. Was I doing something wrong? Was I just not cut out for this?

I also knew that having a career and purpose outside of motherhood would only enhance my role as a mother.

Eventually, I saw the truth. The problem wasn't me. It wasn't a lack of effort or grit. It was that the system was never built for someone like me. A woman in STEMM, and especially not a mother.

– Emily

As a young biomedical engineer, I never questioned the systems of today's workplace. But when my title changed to *Mama*, everything shifted. Motherhood opened my eyes to the deep misalignment between workplace structures and the realities of parenting today. Through entrepreneurship and by coaching other ambitious mothers, I've embraced the opportunity to reimagine work and family life in a way that honours both my ambition and my motherhood.

THREE 'IDEAL' DAYS

Let's explore a typical day in the lives of three women:

Taylor wakes at 5:30 a.m. and heads to the office before anyone else. Her inbox is cleared by 8:00, and she's fully prepped for the day. In meetings, Taylor offers insightful suggestions and takes on extra tasks without hesitation. By lunchtime, she has completed two major projects. She stays late to ensure everything is perfect, always going the extra mile.

Taylor represents the **ideal worker.** Work always comes first. Personal life never interferes. Productivity is constant. Well done, Taylor.

Morgan also wakes at 5:30 a.m., but her morning starts with prepping a nutritious breakfast for her kids and catching Dr. Becky's latest podcast on raising confident, resilient kids. After school drop-off, she double-checks the family calendar, making sure appointments, extracurricular activities, and other family commitments are up to date. Next, she fires off a few emails from her school treasurer account, pops back to the school to volunteer at reading time, zooms home to update the hockey fundraising tally on the team website, and then cooks dinner from scratch.

After school, while shuttling the kids to their activities, Morgan listens attentively as they share the highs and lows of their day. She offers thoughtful advice, encouragement, and a steady presence while modeling clear, compassionate boundaries. After bedtime, she tidies up, tackles laundry stains, inventories the pantry, and thoughtfully updates the family memory book, ensuring every special moment is preserved.

Morgan represents the **ideal parent.** Her kids always come first. She gives endlessly and rests rarely. Her family is so lucky to have her.

Jordan wakes at 4:30 a.m. She drags herself out of bed for a quick workout while mentally planning the day. By 5:15, she's prepping lunches while double-checking the quarterly report slides she's presenting that morning. At 6:00, she wrangles kids through breakfast and tantrums on four hours of sleep, replying to "urgent" emails between bites.

By 7:30, Jordan is out the door, coffee in one hand and school permission slips in the other, signing them at stoplights. She slips into work five minutes late, still managing to nail her presentation, earning a "great work" nod from the senior manager. On the way out, she calls the pediatrician and schedules a follow-up for her youngest, all while mentally drafting the proposal she needs to send by the afternoon.

At 5:00 p.m., she races to soccer practice, laptop bag slung over one shoulder and snacks for the team in the other. She cheers loudly while finalizing a budget spreadsheet on her phone, catching judgmental glances from the nearby "ideal parents." By 7:30, she's home, reheating dinner, helping with homework, prepping for tomorrow. At 10:00, after the kids are asleep and the house is tidied up, Jordan opens her laptop again, because deadlines don't wait. By midnight, she finally collapses into bed, still wondering: Have I done enough?

Jordan is attempting to be both the *ideal worker* and the *ideal parent*. She's doing it all and losing herself in the process. It's not sustainable, and it's definitely not enjoyable.

THE PARADOX

This chapter explores the structural and cultural challenges inherent in today's STEMM workplaces, highlighting the tension between outdated expectations and modern parenting realities. It lays the foundation for reimagining a more inclusive, balanced, and human approach to work and life, especially for women and mothers in STEMM.

Before moving on, take a moment to reflect.

Reflections | The Paradox

How do you feel about the way you're working and living today? What are the best three parts? What are three things you'd like to change?

Consider the systems and structures at your workplace. Which ones support you? Which ones work against you?

A career in STEMM can be deeply fulfilling, offering pride, purpose, and financial stability. But to sustain that, we have to untangle our identity and self-worth from our work. We're not here just to hustle for the promise of freedom in retirement. Perhaps we can learn from the lessons of those who reflect on their lives in their final moments.

I wish I hadn't worked so hard.

– Bronnie Ware
The Top Five Regrets of the Dying

Life is meant to be lived now, not just after decades of sacrifice. We're here to thrive in all aspects of life, including our careers. And for that to happen, our work has to serve us, not the other way around.

THE HISTORY OF THE 9-5

To understand the nine-to-five work model that still dominates STEMM today, we need to go back to the early 1900s. In 1926, Henry Ford made a groundbreaking move when he introduced the 40-hour workweek for his employees. This marked a dramatic shift from the grueling 10 to 16-hour workdays, six days a week, that were standard for factory workers at the time.

Why did he do it?

Ford understood that well-rested employees were more productive, and also that more leisure time meant more people buying and enjoying his cars.

Well played, Mr. Ford.

By 1940, the 40-hour workweek was U.S. law. Canada followed suit in the 1960s.

At the time, the norm was a single-income household: one person (typically a man) worked outside the home, while the other (typically a woman) managed everything inside it. The system was built around male physiology, following a 24-hour hormonal cycle, which made a predictable, repetitive schedule more manageable.

But this model did not reflect women's reality then, and it still does not today. Women operate on a roughly 28-day hormonal cycle, with physical and emotional shifts across the month, not to mention the life stages of pregnancy, perimenopause, and beyond. A rigid nine-to-five structure rarely accounts for these natural ebbs in energy, focus, and physical needs.

While traditional practices in Indigenous cultures, Chinese medicine, and Ayurveda have long supported slowing down during menstruation, many women today push through with painkillers and back-to-back meetings, trying to keep up in a system that was never built for them.

Add to that the demands of caregiving and domestic responsibilities in dual-income households, and the nine-to-five model becomes even more outdated.

So why, despite massive technological advances, are so many of us still clocking in and out like factory workers from a century ago?

Since 1950, women's workforce participation has skyrocketed. In Canada, the number of dual-income families nearly doubled between 1976 and 2015. Yet most companies still cling to the 40-hour workweek model. Even after the pandemic proved that remote work is effective, many organizations, and even entire countries, are now forcing a full return to the office. A step backward, if you ask me.

STEMM fields, historically male-dominated, weren't built with women in mind, and it shows. Ill-fitting safety gear, cold offices calibrated to male physiology, and insecure change rooms are just a few examples. Beyond physical design, social and cultural gaps persist. Women remain underrepresented in many STEMM sectors today, and these systemic oversights continue.

And yet, women want to work. In the U.S., 77.9% of prime-age women (24 to 54 years) were active in the workforce by the end of 2024. We play a critical role in driving economic growth, and research shows that companies with greater gender diversity, especially in leadership, perform better financially.

Still, we're navigating a system built for someone else.

It's time to reimagine the workplace beyond the 9-5.

What if we built systems that honoured the needs of all workers, including women, parents, and multidimensional professionals, rather than forcing them to conform?

The future of work demands innovation, inclusivity, and equity. Let's rise to the challenge and create workplaces that truly work for everyone.

THE IDEAL WORKER

There's no question that our society is built around professional identity. Our careers often define who we are and how we're perceived.[1] This is especially true in STEMM, where titles like "Engineer," "Research Scientist," or "R&D Specialist" carry significant weight. And while our careers matter, it's worth examining how much of our worth we attach to them, particularly in North American culture.

Consider a familiar scene:

> Jessica and Emma reconnect at their mutual friend Ariel's birthday.
>
> "Hey! It's been too long. How are you?"
>
> Without thinking, Jessica responds, "Oh, I'm good—busy, you know!"

We've normalized being busy as a way of life and a marker of success. Not being busy? That can feel like failure. In STEMM, where pressure is high and expectations are relentless, the urge to stay "on" is constant. From a young age, we're rewarded for our output: the grades, the ribbons, the quick responses. So it's no surprise we carry that conditioning into adulthood, pushing ourselves beyond our limits, often at the expense of our health and well-being.

Today's work culture expects us to prioritize career over everything: health, family, even ourselves. The traditional trajectory assumes we start working in our 20s and continue for the next 40 or more years. But with rising living costs and delayed retirement, that number is growing. In fact, workers aged 75 and older are now the fastest-growing demographic in the workforce.

Technology promised flexibility but delivered constant connection. Work can follow us anywhere, and it does. The boundaries between work and life blur as we answer emails during dinner or finish slide decks after bedtime. This "always-on" culture is taking a toll on our well-being and our relationships too.

The results are stark. The World Health Organization has called stress the health epidemic of the 21st century. Long hours, high expectations, and non-stop demands lead to burnout, reduced productivity, and serious health issues

---

[1] See Chapter 2, *Values and Choice*.

such as high blood pressure, stroke, obesity, and diabetes. For women in STEMM, the load is heavier, as they juggle career demands with caregiving and social expectations. Unsurprisingly, women consistently report higher stress levels than men, have a higher prevalence of anxiety disorders, and are significantly more likely to experience job burnout.

How long can we sustain this pace?

Or has the cost of the "ideal worker" identity already outweighed its benefits?

It's time to stop measuring ourselves against a broken ideal and start defining success on our own terms.

What would it look like if we stopped chasing work-life balance and started building work-life integration, where career and life flow together instead of constantly competing?

THE PAINFUL TENSION BETWEEN MOTHERHOOD AND CAREER AMBITION

So... today's work systems are outdated, designed in an era when women's roles in the workplace were marginal at best. Our society's obsession with productivity and with work as a central part of our identity creates challenges for everyone, and those challenges are magnified for women, particularly those in demanding STEMM careers. Add motherhood into the mix, and it becomes a recipe for disaster.

The result?

Many of us are left feeling overwhelmed, ineffective, and burnt out.

While women have made significant strides in STEMM, the simultaneous rise in work and parenting expectations pulls mothers in STEMM in opposite directions. STEMM careers often demand long hours, rigid schedules, and continuous professional development. At the same time, societal norms expect perfection, both at work and at home. And while we continue to define ourselves by our professional achievements, research shows that women still carry the majority of household and childcare responsibilities, even in dual-income households.

So, while one hand grips late-night coding sessions, research deadlines, and boardroom presentations, the other holds bedtime stories, school pickups, and science fair projects. STEMM mothers find themselves in the middle of a relentless tug-of-war between being the "ideal parent" and the high-achieving professional. And it is stretching us very thin.

To make matters worse, our culture has embraced intensive parenting. This model demands hands-on, emotionally involved, and child-centered care. Instead of decompressing on our commute, we're tuning in to Dr. Shefali, trying to master conscious parenting. For college-educated mothers, including many in STEMM, the time devoted to childcare has doubled since 1990.

The pressure to provide constant enrichment, such as zoo visits, sensory bins, and kids' yoga, is real. While these activities can be wonderful, they add to an already crushing mental load.

STEMM careers require a high level of cognitive engagement, and when mothers also serve as the default parent at home, the invisible labor piles up quickly. Social media only amplifies this pressure, making it all too easy to compare our parenting to polished, curated images from *momfluencers* and Pinterest-perfect lives.

It's no wonder that in 2023, 65% of working moms reported struggling with the mental load of balancing work and family responsibilities.

Cultural narratives reinforce these pressures. Take Procter & Gamble's 2010 *Thank You, Mom* campaign. It was emotionally powerful (it made me cry every time), but it subtly reinforced the idea that a mother should be the central figure in her child's success, with little acknowledgment of fathers or shared caregiving.

This idea is rooted in the concept of intensive mothering, which suggests a mother's time, energy, and emotional resources should be fully devoted to her children. That's a heavy expectation, especially for women in STEMM who have worked hard to build careers that bring them joy, purpose, and pride.

Too often, the cost of trying to do both is our own well-being. The yoga class, the massage, the night out with friends? Usually, these are the first things to go.

When we're burnt out, it affects everything: our work, our families and our sense of self. It leaves everyone in a state of imbalance.

We need a new narrative, one that centers well-being instead of self-sacrifice. When STEMM mothers put their needs first, prioritizing rest, mental clarity and personal fulfillment, they show up more grounded, more present, and more powerful in all areas of life.

This shift isn't just good for women, it's essential for creating sustainable, thriving STEMM environments where diversity, balance, and brilliance can coexist.[2]

WORK, REIMAGINED

Here's the good news: change is happening.

Research on the four-day workweek continues to show promising results for both employees and employers. Benefits include improved mental and physical well-being, better work-life balance, and greater overall happiness. Companies see boosts in productivity, employee retention, and revenue. Influential companies like Microsoft Japan have adopted this model in favor of more efficient meetings, happier employees and increased output.

Globally, we're also seeing movement toward healthier boundaries. In 2017, France passed a labour law, the "right to disconnect," giving employees the legal right to ignore work-related communication outside of working hours. Since then, countries including Spain, Italy, Portugal, Belgium, and Germany have adopted similar measures. And while the surge of return-to-work policies is making headlines in 2025, over two-thirds of employers in the U.S. continue to offer work location flexibility.

We're also seeing the early stages of workplace recognition around women's unique health needs. Conversations around menstrual leave are gaining traction, with a few countries and progressive companies implementing policies that provide time off for painful periods. While more research is needed to fully understand the benefits and potential drawbacks of offering menstrual leave, the conversation is growing, and that matters.[3]

These are just a few examples of how the landscape of work is evolving. From rethinking hours and availability to recognizing diverse physical and emotional needs, the shift toward more inclusive, flexible, and sustainable work cultures is gaining momentum, and I'm here for it.

---

[2] If you'd like to explore more about navigating motherhood alongside a STEMM career, head over to Chapter 9, *Navigating Motherhood Alongside Career*, next.

[3] See Chapter 16, *Menopause & Perimenopause*, for more on how companies are starting to support employees through menopause.

The future of work is being redefined.

And these early changes? They're just the beginning.

Now that we've explored the history of the workplace, today's work culture, and the added complexity of motherhood in a system that is still catching up, take a moment to revisit the reflection questions from the beginning of the chapter.

Reflections | Checking In

Have your answers shifted?

Do you see your work and life differently?

What new insights or possibilities have emerged?

CELEBRATING YOU

Before we close, I want to celebrate you: for your perseverance, your passion, and your leadership in STEMM. For continuing to show up and push forward in a system that was never built with you in mind.

As women in a historically male-dominated field, we have the opportunity and the responsibility to reimagine what it means to work and lead today. Not just as professionals, but as whole humans with lives outside of work: families, friends, passions, periods, babies.

We are human beings, not human doings.

– Rick Warren
The Purpose Driven Life

For women navigating parenthood and STEMM, consider these suggestions for practical steps forward on your personal quest to navigate the ideal worker versus ideal parent paradox.

This week, notice where the "ideal worker" and "ideal parent" narratives show up: in your workplace, your routines, even your inner dialogue.

This month, get clear on your own ideals: What actually matters to you? What does success look like for you, not just at work but in life? Where are you acting from external expectations rather than your own truth?

This quarter, begin making small, meaningful shifts to align your daily actions with your personal definition of success. Let your values guide the way you live and work.

For everyone looking to create change in this space, consider if you could:

Start prioritizing life outside of work: your hobbies, relationships, and rest, and encourage others to do the same. Life is meant to be lived, not just worked through.

Stop glorifying busyness, overwork, and productivity at the expense of your well-being. These are not badges of honour; *they're warning signs.*

Continue supporting women in STEMM. Celebrate their brilliance, resilience, and leadership. Acknowledge the challenges they face in systems never built for them.

You are a part of shaping the future of work in STEMM, not only for our generation but for generations to come.

And the future?

It's full of possibility.

Mental Wellness Moment | The Weight of Over-Responsibility

Over-responsibility is a common experience, especially for women. We often feel responsible not just for ourselves, but for what others think or feel about us, how our kids are doing, and even how our coworkers are performing.

High expectations, often rooted in perfectionism, can lead us to hold too much ownership, which in turn can lead to stress and burnout. And no, you don't have to do anything perfectly to be a perfectionist. Just believing that perfection is possible is enough to trigger self-criticism.

A drive to be everything for everyone can make it hard to delegate. You may believe no one can do it as well as you, or feel frustrated when they don't meet your (possibly unrealistic) expectations.

Imposter syndrome can compound the problem. If you question whether your accomplishments were earned on merit, you might feel like you can't afford to slow down or take a break.

One helpful concept for reframing this mindset is the 80/20 rule: 80% of your results often come from just 20% of your effort. How hard are you pushing to achieve the last 20% of results? Sometimes, the extra push only adds marginal value but comes at the highest personal cost.

If you see yourself in these patterns, remember that you are not responsible for everything. Practice letting go of unrealistic expectations, both of yourself and of others. Start noticing when "good enough" truly is good enough.

Take care of yourself,

– Kelly A. Seiler Vocke

Five

From Surviving to Thriving

THOUGHTS, HABITS, RELATIONSHIPS, INSTINCTS, VALUES, AND ENVIRONMENTS

by Karli M. Auble, engineer, coach, and mom of three thriving through chaos and baskets of unfolded laundry.

On January 1st, the night typically dedicated to fresh beginnings, I found myself sobbing into my pillow, desperate to muffle the sound so my husband wouldn't hear. This wasn't just the ultimate Sunday scaries; it was the culmination of months of relentless stress and uncertainty.[1]

For the record, this is wildly uncommon for this "rub some dirt on it and make a to-do list" kind of girl. But this time, even I had my limits. In just four months, I had been thrust into a challenging role with no pay increase, asked to help "fix" a toxic work environment, become pregnant with my third child, and faced the looming threat of layoffs.

That night, as I lay sobbing into my pillow, a thought struck me: If I can use the THRIVE framework to thrive through childbirth, the most physically and mentally challenging thing I've ever done, surely, I can use it to thrive at work.

---

[1] The "Sunday scaries," a term popularized by Urban Dictionary in 2009, are feelings of anxiety or dread that occur on Sundays, especially when the workweek begins again. If you've never heard of them or felt them, congrats to you!

I developed the *THRIVE framework* during my master's in Positive Psychology, and it was the foundation of my capstone project: The Positive Childbirth Course. This course is designed to help birthing mothers and their partners optimize their **Thoughts, Habits, Relationships, Instincts, Values,** and **Environments** to thrive through the beautiful and challenging experience of childbirth.[2]

Could these same principles help me move from survival mode to a place of strength? Spoiler alert: They did.

Over the past decade, I've navigated the STEMM world as a leader and a mother, and the THRIVE framework helped me navigate both life and labors toughest challenges. I share it now in hopes it can help you do the same.

– Karli

THOUGHTS

Let's revisit my meltdown. In my head, a constant loop looked like this:

I hate my job.

Everything at work is terrible.

I never want to go back to the office.

Cognitive Behavioral Theory (CBT) tells us that our thoughts create our feelings, our feelings create our behaviors, and our behaviors reinforce our thoughts.[3] That night, those negative thoughts created feelings of resentment and self-pity, which led to my behavior of sobbing and, in turn, reinforced my conviction that I couldn't possibly go to work the next day.

My husband's question snapped me back to reality: "What would you ideally want to do?" Without missing a beat, I replied, "Stay home with the kids." This was the exact response that jolted me out of my spiral. I adore my

---

[2] Learn more about the Positive Childbirth Cours at www.lifenlabor.com.
[3] Cognitive Behavioral Theory, developed by Aaron T. Beck in the 1960s, focuses on identifying and changing negative thought patterns.

kids, but staying home full time has never been my dream. My thoughts weren't reflecting my truth.

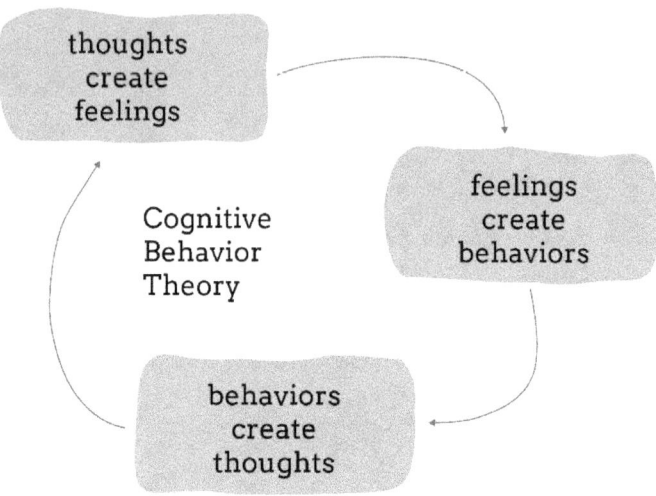

MINDFULNESS: A TOOL FOR TRUTH

This realization brought me back to one of the key lessons from my Positive Psychology studies: mindfulness. Jon Kabat-Zinn defines mindfulness as "awareness that arises through paying attention, on purpose, in the present moment, non-judgmentally." That last part, non-judgmentally, is crucial.

The average person has somewhere between 12,000 and 60,000 thoughts per day, and in a culture full of misinformation, it's no surprise that many of our thoughts might be false as well. Yet, our brains believe everything they say. Your thoughts originate in your mind, and your brain trusts them implicitly.

In that moment of clarity, I asked myself:

Are these thoughts true?

Are they helpful?

The answer to both was a resounding no. While the culture at my job was challenging, there were many things I loved about it, like the flexibility, my salary, and generous benefits.

Now it's your turn to catch the spiral: the next time you feel a thought spiral taking over, pause. Notice the thoughts without judgment and ask yourself if these thoughts are true or helpful.

If they aren't, choose a narrative that serves you better. Over time, you can recondition your mind to avoid creating a crisis out of unverified "facts." Remember, "Between stimulus and response there is a space. In that space is our power to choose our response. In our response lies our growth and freedom."[4]

By practicing mindfulness and challenging your inner narrative, you'll find it easier to shift from despair to clarity and maybe even reclaim a little peace in the process.

HABITS

Once you begin to recognize your thoughts, the next step is to transform those positive thought patterns into habits. With thousands of thoughts per day, we have thousands of opportunities to shape how we experience life. That's a lot of potential for change!

As I prepared for my first childbirth experience, I discovered mindfulness and meditation, which were life-changing during labor and early motherhood. Once my baby arrived and I became a working mom, I abandoned those healthy habits and reverted to old coping mechanisms: working late into the night, sipping wine, and doom-scrolling.

Rinse and repeat with baby number two.

Feeling overwhelmed as a new mom of two, I connected with a mindfulness coach and explained my dilemma: I had experienced the benefits of mindfulness but couldn't stick to it because I was too busy.

STARTING SMALL

My coach reminded me that mindfulness doesn't have to mean dedicating 30 minutes to meditation each day; it can start small, really small. Today, right now, I'm inviting you to start small, just as she generously encouraged me to do with this simple practice: breathe in a blessing, breathe out gratitude.

---

[4] Often attributed to Viktor Frankl and reflective of the themes in *Man's Search for Meaning*.

That's right, it takes less than 10 seconds. Take a deep breath in and think of a blessing from your day. It could be that warm cup of coffee, a smile from a stranger, or a moment of peace. Then, as you exhale, breathe out gratitude for that blessing.

This is simple. It's easy. And it works!

You can do it first thing in the morning, while waiting for a meeting to start, or even in the middle of a chaotic workday without a single person noticing you're doing it. As habit expert B.J. Fogg says, *"The easier a behavior is to do, the more likely it will become a habit."*

Our brains have 86 billion neurons, connected by 100 trillion neural pathways. The more you repeat a thought or behavior, the stronger that pathway becomes. This tiny practice of mindful breathing strengthens your positive neural pathways, rewiring your brain for gratitude and calm instead of anxiety and stress. Studies show that regularly reflecting on things you're grateful for can reduce anxiety and depression, enhance well-being, and help you respond to stress more calmly.

My invitation to you is simple: be intentional about doing this one small task each day, just 10 seconds.

When I began the new year with a focus on incorporating this practice, I realized how often my neural pathways defaulted to negativity. By starting my day with gratitude, I began to notice the ripple effect of this small mindfulness habit and how it was changing my subconscious programming. It reminded me of this wisdom:

> *Watch your thoughts, for they become words.*
> *Watch your words, for they become actions.*
> *Watch your actions, for they become habits.*
> *Watch your habits, for they become character.*
> *Watch your character, for it becomes your destiny.*
>
> – Mahatma Gandhi[5]

---

[5] Often attributed to Gandhi, though unverified, the quote reflects his mindful philosophy.

RELATIONSHIPS

The week I peed on a stick and found out I was pregnant with my first child, I got a call to interview for a high-pressure role that promised a grueling 18 months of long hours. I wasn't sure if I should even interview given my news.

As I met with a mentor for guidance, he congratulated me on the opportunity and said, "Go for this before you have kids because once you have kids, your career will be over. You won't want to climb the corporate ladder anymore."

I didn't share the pregnancy news with him that day, but his words stayed with me. I interviewed for the position anyway, and got the job.

THE POWER OF SHARED EXPERIENCES

Looking back, I realize how unseen and defeated I felt after that conversation. It wasn't until I attended my first Society of Women Engineers (SWE) national conference that I experienced a major perspective shift.

Imagine walking into a space filled with over 21,000 technical, smart, ambitious women engineers. For the first time, I didn't feel like the only woman in the room. It was overwhelming in the best way. Listening to these women's experiences and being able to relate on such a deep level reminded me that I can get a whole hell of a lot further in a supportive environment.

That experience was a wake-up call. I had always had mentors who were men, mostly because that's who dominated my field. But being surrounded by women who shared my values and experiences made me realize I needed to be more intentional about my support network.

When I got home, I took stock of my mentors. I didn't ditch the men (they're not inherently bad mentors!), but I did reassess. I sought out women in leadership positions whose balance I admired. I reserved conversations about work-life challenges for people who shared my values and could offer guidance that resonated with me.

FINDING RESOURCES

If your company offers resource groups or employee networks, especially women's groups, get involved. These communities provide powerful spaces to connect with others walking similar paths. If your company doesn't have one, maybe you could be the person to shine a light and help others feel more welcome.

Consider what other resources might be available to you. Does your company offer coaching, therapy, or other support services? I've personally worked with both coaches and therapists who have helped me slow down, gain clarity, and recognize the roadblocks I put in my own way.

You might be thinking, "but Karli, I'm the only woman in my company/group/etc." We hear you. That's why we wrote this book. You now have a Rolodex of strong women in STEMM. Connect with us. Add us on LinkedIn. Share your story. Ask for help. You're not alone, and you don't have to be.

When I look back at that night, crying into my pillow, I realize what I had forgotten in the months leading up to that moment: I have an extensive network of mentors, organizations, and resources I can lean on.

Don't sit alone in your own stuff like I did. Look around. Who can you reach out to? Where can you find connection, inspiration, and support?

Reflections | Relationships

Take a moment to think about your current mentors:

Who do you turn to for advice or guidance?

Do they share your values and understand your goals?

Are there gaps in your network where you could benefit
from different perspectives or shared experiences?

INSTINCTS

Fellow nerds, let me take you on a journey into our favorite realm: complex systems. Imagine your body as an advanced aerospace system.[6]

---

[6] Stay with me here; this will make sense!

Just like a high-tech aircraft, your body has a network of subsystems, sensors, computers, feedback loops, all working together to keep you soaring.

Now, when something goes awry in an aircraft, a Built-In Test (BIT) code pops up. This code alerts the crew that something is wrong and directs them to check the database to figure out what's going on and how to fix it. Ignoring that BIT code? Bad idea. The longer it's ignored, the greater the chance of catastrophic failure.

Guess what?

Our bodies send us BIT codes every. Single. Day.

If you're like me, you've probably been ignoring your own BIT codes for way too long. Maybe it's the tightness in your chest during a certain meeting, the blush that creeps up your neck, or, for me, the shoulders that I realize are next to my ears as I pack up to leave work.

It wasn't until I merged my understanding of systems engineering with positive psychology that I realized I had a problem: I wasn't paying attention to the BIT codes my body was throwing at me.

YOUR BIT CODES

Your BIT Codes are your body's subtle (or not-so-subtle) ways of telling you something is off. But we can't fix what we don't acknowledge.

The good news? Once you acknowledge them, there's a fix so universal that it's used in yoga classes, by boss ladies in high-stakes meetings, and by Navy SEALs prepping for battle. It's called Box Breathing:

- Breathe in for a count of four.
- Hold your breath for a count of four.
- Exhale for a count of four.
- Hold your breath for a count of four.

And repeat.

Simple but highly effective, Box Breathing helps activate the parasympathetic nervous system, which counteracts the body's fight-or-flight response. By focusing on your breath, you slow your heart rate, calm your nervous system, and give yourself space to respond thoughtfully instead of reacting instinctively.

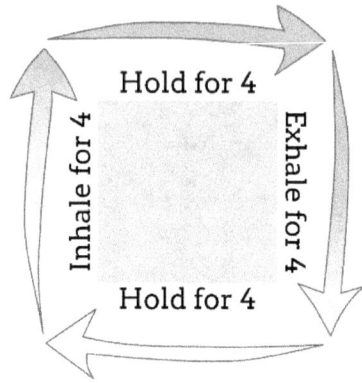

When you take the time to pause and breathe, you're creating space to:

- Notice the BIT codes your body is sending.
- Recognize thought patterns and emotional triggers.
- See the bigger picture instead of spiraling into a reaction.

Don't ignore your BIT codes. Much like an aircraft, you can't afford to keep flying without addressing the warning signals.

The next time your body sends you a BIT code, pause and try the Box Breathing exercise. Listen to your instincts, they're there to help you course-correct before something catastrophic happens.

Your body is the most advanced system you'll ever operate. Treat it with the care and attention it deserves.

Reflections | Instincts

What BIT codes has your body been sending you lately?

When was the last time you paused to notice how
your body feels?

What would it look like to intentionally slow down in
moments of stress?

VALUES

Stepping into senior management, my values were put to the test as I received 7:30 a.m. calls every Tuesday and Thursday.

My peers were all men: some with kids in college, some with kids out of college, some with a stay-at-home wife, and one with young children and a working wife. I had a 3-year-old, a 6-month-old, and a husband who traveled frequently for work. My mornings were pure chaos, dropping the baby off at 7:00 a.m., rushing the preschooler to drop-off at 7:30, stumbling with my phone on the drive to join my first meeting virtually by 7:35, with my frazzled butt in the seat next to my counterparts (mostly men) at 8:05. And this was when all cylinders were firing and no one had forgotten their damn water bottle.

When both my husband and a mentor suggested hiring help, I didn't feel relief but rather a sense of compression. The time spent navigating those messy mornings mattered to me. It wasn't just about getting the kids dressed or out the door, it was our time, time that I recognize as a working mother is already so limited. Those small moments, even with the chaos of screaming "other foot, other foot!" as I wrestled with their shoes, were what I valued.

Instead of outsourcing my mornings, I communicated my situation to my team. As a result, the meetings were pushed to 8:00 a.m. It wasn't perfect, but it gave me breathing room, and it also helped the man on my team with young kids, who quietly thanked me for advocating for the change, because now he too was able to drop his kids off in the morning.

WHAT ARE YOUR CORE VALUES?

Values act as your internal compass, guiding you toward decisions that align with who you truly are. They're deeply personal and unique. What matters most to me might not matter as much to you, and that's okay.

When we're clear on our values, our decisions feel purposeful. Without that clarity, we're more likely to react impulsively or make choices that leave us feeling disconnected or unfulfilled.

On the following page you'll find a Wheel of Life tool to reflect on how satisfied you feel in different areas of life today, and how you'd ideally like those areas to look in the future.

You are invited to consider:

What's your current satisfaction in each category?

How does it compare to your personal desired state?

Once complete, find the area that feels most misaligned. What's one action you'd like to take today to live closer to your values? Maybe it's communicating a morning conflict, picking up a religious text you've been meaning to read, or calling a loved one you've been missing.[7]

Intentional steps, no matter how small, help you realign your lived life with your deepest values.

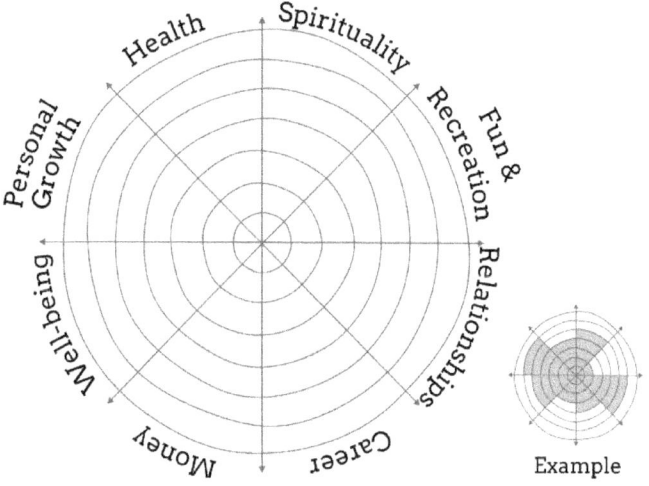

Wheel of Life tool to support reflection on current state and future goals across many aspects of life.

ENVIRONMENTS

As I stepped into my office that dreaded first day back at work, I had an "aha" moment as I was greeted by dead plants, a dirty floor, scratched walls, and leaky ceiling tiles, a space that mirrored how I felt inside.

---

[7] Printable versions of the *Wheel of Life* are available to download at elmmcoaching.com/press.

These spaces can either support or sabotage our efforts to live in alignment with our values. When we feel uncomfortable or out of sync with our environment, we're more likely to remain in survival mode and far from thriving.

Sometimes, small adjustments can create a ripple effect of positivity in your environment:

> **Surround yourself with inspiration.** I have since strategically placed books like *You Are Not Stuck* by Becky Vollmer, *Untamed* by Glennon Doyle, and *STEM Moms* by Cassie Leonard in my eyesight at my computer so that as I worked, I get visual reminders of my strength, my worth, and my ability to make a change to things that no longer serve me.
>
> I bought and placed a Japanese Maneki-Neko lucky cat, which greets me and reminds me daily that good fortune comes to those who are purposeful, passionate, and persistent.
>
> **Revive your space.** Repotting plants brought life back into my office and became a metaphor for self-care. Each time I watered my plants, pruned dead leaves, or moved them to a location that better served them, I reminded myself to nurture my own growth in the same ways.
>
> Go full Marie Kondo on your office or workspace and keep only the things that bring you joy. Not sure how to tell if something sparks joy? Pick up the item, ask yourself, "Does this spark joy?" Notice how your body responds, and take the appropriate action.
>
> **TL;DR:** *Throw the clutter away!*

Sometimes, little changes aren't enough. In a particularly toxic workplace, my therapist suggested creating a "Bingo Card" for the things I couldn't control that were driving me nuts. Each square held scenarios like "Request for COB data after 5 p.m." or "Mandatory meeting set up less than one minute before start." It was a humorous way to remind myself that these issues weren't mine to fix, and to release the undue pressure I put on myself.

Instead of being pissed that someone requested complex data from me five minutes before their meeting with a Vice President, I got excited that I had a new mark on my Bingo card. I started looking forward to the frustrations so I could treat myself to a Bingo win.

If small tweaks and coping tools aren't enough, it might be time to consider a completely new environment. You are valuable, you are needed, and you have the power to make a change. The narrative in our society is that change is hard and takes a long time. However, change can be instant, and we might lose nothing, instead, we could gain. Remember your worth.

> **Invitation.** Go back to your workspace and find one thing that doesn't bring you joy, serve a purpose, or feels like clutter. Declutter and donate it to someone who might find value in it. Remove it entirely and enjoy the spaciousness this one act provides you.

Once you notice the spaciousness this one act provides, you're more likely to examine the other environments in your life and identify what helps you thrive and what pulls you down into negativity and survival mode.

Remember, it's like the advice from an airplane safety briefing: put your own mask on first. By prioritizing your environment, you're creating the conditions to thrive, not just for yourself, but for those around you.

SURVIVING TO THRIVING IN STEMM

Did implementing the THRIVE framework have me walking into work on January 2nd with wind in my hair, the sun shining, and all the assholes suddenly less... *assholier*?

Not exactly.

But it did give me a powerful reframe. It shifted the way I viewed the negativity I had been drowning in and reminded me of something essential: I am in control.

The THRIVE framework isn't about pretending life's challenges don't exist or glossing over the hard stuff. It's about building resilience, not to avoid the fall, but to soften the impact when it happens.

By intentionally optimizing your thoughts, habits, relationships, instincts, values, and environments, you can take ownership of what's within your control. In doing so, you set yourself up to navigate the chaos and thrive, no matter how messy work or life gets.

Section 2

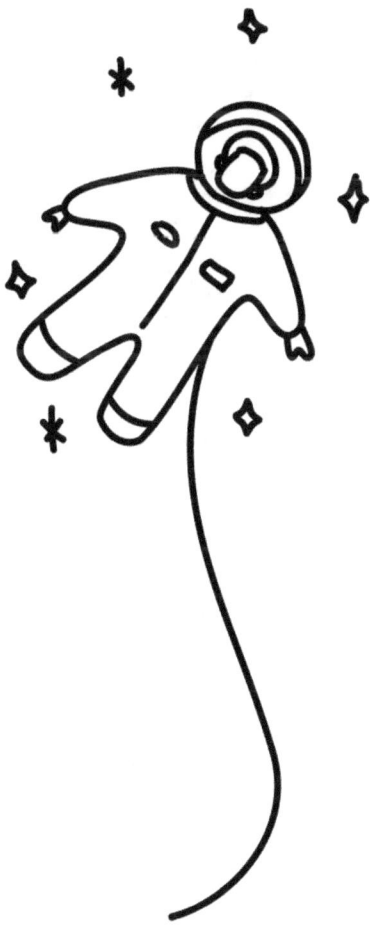

Six

Burnout

REIMAGINING STEMM AS A SUSTAINABLE SPACE

by Belinda A. Di Bartolo, recovering academic, STEMM strategist, and mum navigating careers, chaos, and everything in between.

Over a year ago, I realized that I had just overcome burnout.

It hit me after returning from the Christmas holidays, when I noticed that I was finally sleeping well again. Before Christmas, and for the previous two to three months, I had been sleeping more than nine hours a night but still waking up tired and grumpy every single day. I was deeply unhappy with my job, a situation that has not changed much since then.

At the time, I was a mother of two (now three) children and a postdoc in the U.S., originally from Europe. Many factors contributed to my burnout, beyond my research project not going well. As an EU expat in the U.S. on a visa tied to my job, I felt immense personal pressure to excel in my role, knowing that my position needed to be renewed annually. The stress of trying to balance work, home life, and personal well-being while striving for perfection became unbearable.

– Eleonora Grandi
Research Scientist Mom of Three

Did you know that nearly 60% of academics, 50% of senior-level women leaders in the public and social sectors, and 42% of senior-level women in corporate report experiencing burnout at some point in their careers? In STEMM, the numbers are even more staggering, with mid-career professionals facing the highest risk due to a relentless "publish or perish" culture and the increasing demands of leadership, caregiving, and innovation.

But... burnout doesn't just sneak in; it is built into the system. For many, it is the silent weight carried behind closed doors, whispered about among colleagues, and only truly acknowledged when it is too late to ignore. This chapter is a call to stop whispering.

HI, I'M BELINDA AND I'M A RECOVERING ACADEMIC.

As someone who spent almost 20 years navigating the academic world while raising a family during the second half of that time, I understand the relentless demands of a career in STEMM. I have felt the pull of trying to balance professional ambition with personal responsibilities, often at great personal cost. When I eventually hit my breaking point, I realised the system wasn't designed for sustainability, and most certainly not for women juggling multiple roles.

Once a research scientist, I now work to help others recognise their worth and redefine success, both within and beyond the walls of academia. I'm here to share what I've learned, not as someone who has all the answers, but as someone who has lived the questions and found a path forward.

This chapter explores burnout not as an individual failing, but as a systemic issue deeply embedded in the culture of science and academia.

Burnout is more than exhaustion; it's a sign of structural dysfunction that we have been conditioned to accept as normal. Through this chapter, we'll explore:

> **What burnout is,** understanding the different forms of burnout and why it manifests in STEMM.

> **Why mid-career professionals are especially at risk.** We'll examine the unique pressures that push capable, passionate individuals to the brink. Particularly caregivers, but not limited to.

How we can shift the narrative, moving from individual blame to systemic solutions that can sustain careers and well-being.

By the end, my hope is that you'll not only feel seen, but also free to advocate for change, whether for yourself, your colleagues, or the next generation of STEMM professionals. *Burnout is not inevitable.* Change begins when we recognise its roots and start reimagining what success looks like.

BURNOUT: A DEFINITION AND CONTEXT

Burnout is "the exhaustion of physical or emotional strength or motivation, usually as a result of prolonged stress or frustration." It also describes "a person who is worn out from overwork or dissipation." My personal favourite, especially for the engineers reading this, is "the cessation of operation of a jet or rocket engine, usually due to the depletion of fuel."[1]

Sound familiar?

Physical and emotional exhaustion? Absolutely. The relentless pace and expectations siphon off every ounce of energy you have. Worn out from overwork? That's practically a requirement for surviving in STEMM. And as for rockets running out of fuel? Let's just say you can feel like you're perpetually firing on all cylinders until the tank is bone dry.

According to the World Health Organization (WHO), burnout is "a syndrome conceptualised as resulting from chronic workplace stress that has not been successfully managed." It is characterised by three key dimensions:

Emotional exhaustion. Feeling consistently overwhelmed by work demands.

Cynicism or depersonalization. A sense of detachment from one's work or colleagues.

Reduced personal efficacy. A feeling of inadequacy and diminished accomplishment.

---

[1] Burnout, as defined by Merriam-Webster.

I like definitions; after all, I am a scientist. What interests me more, though, is that as we move through life, we sometimes misconstrue those definitions. And in the case of burnout, we often place the blame on ourselves.

These definitions capture the multidimensional toll of burnout: it's not just physical or emotional; it isn't caused by the individual. It's systemic. Burnout is what happens when we pour everything we have into a system that too often gives little, or nothing, back, leaving us wondering if we are the problem.

Spoiler: *It's not you; it's the system.*

WHICH TYPE OF BURNOUT ARE YOU EXPERIENCING?

Burnout is not a one-size-fits-all experience. Researchers have identified several distinct types across a range of personalities and spectrums, each with its own characteristics and causes. Understanding these can help us better recognise and address burnout in ourselves and others.

> **Overload burnout.** This is the classic image of burnout: pushing yourself to the limit to meet relentless demands. It's fueled by long hours, high pressure, and an inability to disconnect. Overload burnout often stems from environments that glorify overwork, where success is measured by how much you sacrifice.

> **Under-challenge burnout.** Less obvious but just as damaging, under-challenge burnout arises when you feel unfulfilled or stagnant. It results from monotonous tasks, a lack of meaningful work, or not being given opportunities to grow. Over time, this can lead to feelings of frustration, apathy, and disengagement.

> **Neglect burnout.** Neglect burnout occurs when you feel un-supported or helpless in the face of challenges. Whether it is due to unclear expectations, poor leadership, or systemic obstacles, this type of burnout leaves you doubting your abilities and feeling as though nothing you do makes a difference.

> **Habitual burnout.** This is burnout at its most chronic stage. When stress and exhaustion become ingrained in your life, they

lead to habitual burnout: a state where feelings of depletion, detachment, and ineffectiveness become your norm. It is the result of prolonged neglect of your mental and emotional well-being.

Burnout, in all its forms, erodes our ability to thrive and connect with what matters most. Recognising these variations allows us to better understand the diverse ways burnout manifests, as well as the systemic and personal factors that contribute to it. Each type offers clues about the underlying issues that need addressing, whether it's a toxic work culture, lack of challenge, or chronic stress.

> *I wish more people would talk about burnout as a common experience and be more supportive of those going through it, especially those in positions of power.*
>
> – Eleonora

What is Burnout in STEMM?

The Unspoken Reality

Burnout is the word whispered in hushed tones during coffee breaks, texted late at night to a trusted friend, or spoken aloud only when a breaking point has been reached. It's not just a feeling of being tired; it is the overwhelming realisation that something has to give, even if that "something" is your career, health, or sense of self.

In STEMM, burnout is everywhere. The reasons for this are clear: relentless productivity demands, precarious funding, long hours, pressure to continually self-improve outside of work commitments, and a culture that glorifies overwork. For women, the burden is even greater, as they navigate caregiving responsibilities and the invisible labour often demanded of them in their roles.

Burnout in STEMM isn't about working too hard.

Burnout in STEMM is about working in a system that doesn't work for you. It is about environments that demand more than you can give while offering little in return.

Many professionals enter STEMM because they are passionate about discovery and solving complex problems. But somewhere along the way, the system asks them to trade those values for metrics: journal impact factors, grant funding, or leadership roles where the focus is administration and not science. This creates a constant tension between what you believe in and what you're asked to prioritise.

The result? A sense of detachment.[2]

THE SYSTEMIC ROOTS OF BURNOUT

Here's the truth: burnout stems from structural issues that have nothing to do with individual resilience. These include:

> **Overwork culture.** The "publish or perish" mantra in academia forces relentless productivity, leaving no room for rest or recovery. This comes on top of the expectation to take on multiple demanding roles simultaneously: research, teaching, and administration.

> **Precarious funding.** Insecure funding creates perpetual anxiety, with researchers often balancing multiple projects and grant applications at the same time.

> **Lack of support for caregivers.** Caregiving duties, both at home and in the workplace, disproportionately fall on women, but ultimately, both men and women experience this lack of support.

> **Gender inequities.** Women in STEMM are often assigned tasks that are critical but unrewarded, such as committee work or organising events. These efforts do not count towards promotions but are expected nonetheless.

BURNOUT AMONG WOMEN IN STEMM

Burnout among women in STEMM is not just about long hours or heavy workloads; it's a consequence of navigating systems that were never designed with them in mind. Academia, in particular, was built on a foundation that assumed its members had minimal responsibilities outside their professional

---

[2] Not just detachment from your work, but from yourself.

roles. Historically dominated by men, the system was shaped with a single-career household in mind, where the "ideal worker" could devote their entire life to their career, supported by a partner managing all domestic and caregiving duties.

Fast forward to today, and women in STEMM are expected to meet those same unyielding expectations while juggling caregiving responsibilities, systemic inequities, and the pressure to represent in fields where they are still a minority. The system hasn't adapted, but the demographics of those who participate in it have.

THE WEIGHT OF INVISIBLE LABOR

Women in STEMM often carry the burden of invisible labour, both at work and at home. Research shows that women in academia disproportionately take on tasks such as mentoring students, organising events, and serving on committees. These are essential responsibilities, yet they are often regarded as housekeeping duties that don't count towards tenure or promotions. These roles are critical to the functioning of institutions but are rarely recognised or valued in performance evaluations.

At home, the disparity continues. Studies consistently find that working mothers shoulder the majority of caregiving and household responsibilities, even when they are the primary earners.[3] This "second shift" leaves women with less time and energy to devote to their careers or their own wellbeing, exacerbating burnout and reducing their ability to compete on equal footing.

A SYSTEM NOT BUILT FOR MOTHERS

The structural design of academia reflects assumptions that fail to account for the realities of working mothers. Consider the timing of tenure evaluations, which often coincide with prime childbearing years. Women who take maternity leave or reduce their workloads to care for young children risk gaps in their publication records, which can derail tenure applications or promotions.

---

[3] Working mothers today spend just as much time with their kids as stay-at-home mothers did in 1975. Unchecked, the expectations our society pushes on us create and/or add to the guilt. Whatever feelings we have about whatever thing not going right due to time pressure, the guilt and expectations get stacked on that making it feel so much worse.

Additionally, conference schedules, late-night grant writing, and expectations for international collaboration often clash with the demands of parenting. Fathers in academia are more likely to have a partner who manages these responsibilities, while mothers are less likely to have the same level of support at home. This further widens the gap in career progression.

> *I worked alongside a male colleague who bragged that he spent the whole week locked in his study writing his grant application - while his wife (a homemaker) looked after their 4 children. I was writing an application for that same round - too bad I was also looking after 3 children while my husband was working. Where's the equity? The system doesn't account for this.*
>
> – Anonymous

Even policies meant to support parents, such as maternity leave or tenure clock extensions, can backfire. Many women report feeling judged or penalised for making use of these options, facing implicit biases that question their commitment to their careers. The very policies designed to support women often end up reinforcing the systemic inequities they are intended to address.

CULTURAL EXPECTATIONS AND REPRESENTATION FATIGUE

Beyond systemic barriers, women in STEMM face the additional pressure of representation. Often the only woman in the room, or one of very few, they are expected to serve as role models, advocates, and diversity champions. While this work is vital, it adds to their already significant workload.

In addition, there are expectations from students, and sometimes colleagues, that women in academic settings will be more nurturing and available for emotional support or pastoral care compared to men. This increases the burden of mental load and can penalise women who do not conform to this stereotype.

There is also the ongoing need to prove themselves in male-dominated fields in order to be perceived as equal. Women often take on additional, behind-the-scenes work to strategically position themselves on an equal footing with men, further fuelling burnout. This phenomenon, sometimes referred to as the **prove-it-again bias**, forces women to continually demonstrate their competence in ways that their colleagues who are men do not.

THE CONSEQUENCES OF INACTION

These inequities are not personal challenges. They are structural failures with far-reaching consequences.

Women leave STEMM at disproportionately high rates, not because they lack passion or ability, but because the system wasn't built to sustain them. A 2023 study revealed that mid-career women in STEMM are nearly twice as likely as men to leave their fields, citing burnout, lack of support, and systemic barriers as the primary reasons.

This attrition weakens the entire field. Losing talented professionals and the diverse perspectives they bring limits innovation and reinforces the very systems that drive people out.

ARE YOU NODDING?

Did you feel exhausted simply from reading about how exhausted we all are? If you have felt drained, undervalued, or as though you're constantly falling short, it's not just you. It's the system. And the first step to changing that system is naming it.

Activity | Name Your Burnout

Take a moment to think about your current situation:

Which burnout(s) are you experiencing?

Which systemic root most resonates with you?

Name and shame your system.

*No one else is reading, go ahead and name it –
purely for personal satisfaction!*

A PERFECT STORM OF PRESSURES

> *I kept thinking, if I just push through this stage, it will get*
> *better. But every stage brought new challenges: balancing*
> *motherhood with lab work, securing funding while managing*
> *students, proving myself over and over. The goalposts kept*
> *moving, and I realized they weren't designed for me to reach.*

> – Belinda

STEMM professionals at the mid-career stage are especially vulnerable to burnout. By this point in your career, you are likely managing more responsibilities, such as mentoring, leading teams, or balancing administrative tasks, all while being expected to continue pursuing scientific excellence and publishing at an unrealistic pace.

Most of my mid-career clients talk about missing the science: the joy of an experiment working, or the thrill of the expected result. As you climb the academic ladder, you ultimately do less science and more administration.

It is not really the job we signed up for.

Burnout shows up in more than just academia. It also affects professionals in high-tech, medtech, and engineering. While some may miss the science, others, like me, always aspired to leadership roles. In a very real way, that *is* part of the job we signed up for. However, rising through the ranks comes with other intense pressures, including increased expectations and deeper political waters to navigate, which contribute just as significantly to burnout.

For women, the stakes are even higher.

The "leaky pipeline" means fewer women progress to senior roles, which increases the pressure to succeed and to represent those still in the game. Caregivers, in particular, are caught in a near-impossible balancing act, navigating between professional demands and personal responsibilities.

And it feels personal, something you could fix if only you worked harder, stayed more organised, exercised more, ate better, meditated, socialised with friends, found time for hobbies, and generally were superhuman. But this narrative is not only false; it is harmful. It shifts the blame onto individuals while letting the system off the hook.

Experiencing burnout taught me to be more mindful of both my well-being and my spouse's well-being. It made me more attuned to the signs of burnout and reminded me of what truly matters. While it was a difficult time, it was also an illuminating one, helping me realize the importance of prioritizing what's essential and understanding that my job does not define me at the end of the day.

– Eleonora

INDIVIDUAL VS. SYSTEMIC RESPONSIBILITIES

Burnout often creeps up on us slowly. It starts with exhaustion, whether physical, emotional, or both. Then comes detachment, a sense of going through the motions without really caring. Finally, there is a feeling of inefficacy, as if no matter how hard you work, it's never enough.

Take a moment to reflect:

Reflections | Burnout

Are you constantly exhausted, even after resting?
Eleonora talked about not feeling rested even after sleeping hours!

Do you feel disconnected from work you once loved?
Are you enjoying the trade of pipettes for pens?

Have you started questioning your abilities or value?

Is nothing exciting anymore?

If any of these resonate, it's not a sign of weakness. It's a
sign the system has failed you.

And while the root causes of burnout are systemic, individuals still have agency. This is not about 'fixing' yourself; it is about recognising your power to push back against the system.

Here are some ways to reclaim that power:

Name your burnout. I keep asking you to name things, but you will see that it shifts the power to you. Talk about burnout openly. The more we normalise these conversations, the harder it becomes for institutions to ignore them.[4]

Set boundaries. This isn't about saying "no" to everything; it's about being intentional with your "yes."

Lean on allies. Build a network of people who understand the challenges you face and can help advocate for change.

Activity | Set Boundaries

Make a list of all your professional responsibilities and tasks. *Are you laughing yet? Do you have enough paper?*

Now review the list. For each item, ask yourself: Does this bring value to me or my career?

Keep the yeses. Everything else? Let it go. *And sing the song while you do; it makes it better!*

A VISION FOR CHANGE

Imagine a STEMM environment where success is not measured by how much you endure, but by how well you thrive. A space where caregiving is valued, invisible labour is recognised, and systemic inequities are actively dismantled.

---

[4] Psychological Safety Moment: If you don't feel safe talking openly within your organization, consider who can you talk with to start normalizing the conversation for yourself.

This is not a utopian dream; it's a necessary shift for the survival of the field.[5] To move toward this vision, we need collective action:

Flexible work policies. From remote options to part-time roles, flexibility can help retain talent.

Fair funding models. Grants and awards should consider career breaks and caregiving responsibilities.

Visible leadership. Leaders must model healthy work habits and advocate for systemic change.

Share the load. Establish promotion criteria that include traditionally low promotability tasks.

ONE MORE ACTIVITY

Burnout isn't your fault, but change begins with you. Share your story.

Two key things helped me overcome that challenging period: expecting our third child and meeting people who became some of our dearest friends. Building a supportive network of people who understood our situation and with whom we could share our struggles was a game-changer.

– Eleonora

Speak up when you see inequities. Support others who are struggling. Together, we can shift the culture of STEMM from one that burns out its brightest to one that sustains and celebrates them.

---

[5] See more of my wonderful utopian dreams in Chapter 18, *Redefining Success.*

Seven

Imposter Syndrome

EXAMINING HOW SYSTEMIC BARRIERS ERODE CONFIDENCE AND CAREER PROGRESSION

by Ashley C. Wynne, experienced R&D leader who knows firsthand how imposter syndrome can persist, even with measurable success.

I've felt imposter syndrome in some capacity in every role I've held since the first day I started grad school. I moved from the Northeast to the Deep South, and not only did I have no cultural frame of reference for what I had gotten myself into, I also seemed to stick out like a sore thumb in every way, from clothing and regional terminology to the more academic challenge of feeling completely inadequate as I faced technically really freaking hard graduate-level coursework.

After graduation, I began my engineering career in a chemical plant. Everyday tasks, like trying to make decisions about a process that everyone else seemed to understand better than I did, left me certain that the guys I worked with must be talking behind my back about what an idiot I was.

Changing companies and moving into product development turned out to be a much better fit for me. Over a decade in that role has felt significantly more comfortable. So much so that when the opportunity came to go back to school part-time and finish a goal I had started over ten years earlier, earning a PhD, I took it.

But in my very first group meeting, as I listened to the other students discuss their work, I once again felt like I knew nothing. I did have something the other students didn't (as my boss reminded me when I expressed my feelings of imposter syndrome to him): over a decade of professional experience, plus two master's degrees. Still, I couldn't shake the feeling that I was in over my head and didn't deserve to be sitting in that room.

– Ashley

WHERE DOES IT END?

I think it's safe to say we've all felt out of place at some point in our lives. You feel awkward, incongruous, flooded with overwhelming thoughts that you do not, or are not, good enough to belong. You may even feel unwelcome.

This is the land of the dreaded **imposter syndrome**. It can come on quickly and can be all-consuming, damaging your confidence and impacting your contributions until you somehow, in some way, find a way out, which is often easier said than done. I can tell you from firsthand experience that I've encountered imposter syndrome in almost every professional role I've had. In some ways, I even feel it now, writing this chapter. *Who's to say I have anything profound to say about imposter syndrome?*

But that is exactly what we need to recognize. I am not a psychologist, but I am a woman in a STEMM career, and my experiences might help someone else begin to dig their way out of feeling like an imposter in their own story. Sometimes, that shared understanding is the very thing that helps someone feel like they belong.

Imposter syndrome can strike at any time, in any role in our lives. The focus here will be on professional circumstances, but recognizing the signs and learning ways to overcome the feeling that you don't belong can be applied across the board.

Imposter syndrome has been widely discussed across various platforms: scientific studies, business-focused publications, LinkedIn, it's everywhere! A resounding theme throughout these sources is that imposter syndrome, defined as feelings of incompetence and fears of being exposed as a fraud, disproportionately affects high achievers who struggle to accept their accomplishments. Studies dating back to the original 1978 research on imposter syndrome have shown that women, especially those in STEM fields, are particularly affected by it. This phenomenon has been attributed to the social conditioning of women to appear modest and to credit their successes to luck rather than to their credentials and experience.

Why can't we recognize leadership and accomplishments in ourselves? We see it in each other, but not in ourselves.

There are several experiences I can reflect on that illustrate this, but a more recent one came during a conversation with my PhD advisor. We were talking about some of my professional experiences, and I said to him, "I've been lucky." His immediate response was something like, "No, you have not been lucky. You've worked hard. Don't diminish your accomplishments."

Imposter syndrome is not just a personal problem. It is a byproduct of systemic issues.

Part of my professional achievements and experience can admittedly be attributed to being in the right place at the right time. Sometimes, reaching work goals is influenced by the projects you're assigned. What we need to remember, though, is that while some opportunities may come in part by chance, earning trust and credibility is very real. So yes, some of my projects may have offered a range of experiences that others didn't have access to, but I earned those opportunities because I had proven myself to be a reliable executor with a reputation for getting things done.

Women often struggle to identify themselves as experts and to fully take credit for their expertise. So, what do we do about it?

Is imposter syndrome rooted in our own insecurity?

Or are external factors reinforcing and amplifying our self-doubt?

Instead of internalizing those doubts, what if we reframed the narrative: *Is the very thing that makes me feel like an outsider actually what sets me apart?* How can you look inward and begin to see these differences as strengths, unique qualities that serve as powerful differentiators?

I believe there are several ways we can begin to mitigate or counteract feelings of incompetence and inadequacy. Some of the more commonly recommended ways to combat imposter syndrome include avoiding the comparison trap, discussing feelings with a mentor, and accepting that mistakes are natural.

While these are all legitimate tactics for addressing imposter syndrome, they often feel like "easier said than done." So, what can someone do when their self-confidence begins to crumble?

I offer the following strategies, not quick fixes, but intentional steps. Each one includes practical guidance and carries the potential for real, measurable impact.

Start With a Work Friend

One of the most valued people in my life started out as a coworker and has become one of my closest friends. She no longer works at the company where I'm still employed, but I remember many conversations with her where we were able to candidly express our work frustrations and insecurities.

When I made a mistake, I felt like I could go to her without fear of judgment or criticism, even when I had clearly made the wrong decision. She was a constant source of encouragement and gave feedback in a way that genuinely helped me improve, not to highlight what I had done wrong.

Having a relationship like this with someone at work is invaluable. We were each other's allies in the workplace. Being able to be authentic with each other, and helping one another see what we couldn't see in ourselves, got me through the real growing pains of being a technical professional. While valuable feedback can certainly come from a mentor or manager, the authenticity of friendships can lead to more sincere encouragement and honest insights. The dynamic between friends and managers is simply different.

Individual action. Intentionally find a constructive friend at work.

- Start by noticing who you naturally connect with at work; someone who listens well, shows up authentically, and doesn't judge. It might be a teammate, someone in another department, or even someone a few steps ahead of you in their career.

- Invite them for coffee or a walk. See if the conversation flows. Peer allyships often grow from small, honest conversations.
- Build a habit together of regularly connecting and sharing.

GET COMFORTABLE ACCEPTING PRAISE

AND BUILD A CULTURE OF CELEBRATING EACH OTHER

Scientific fields can be incredibly competitive. People are constantly vying for limited resources such as funding, promotions, publication opportunities, intellectual property rights, and project assignments. It's easy to view others as threats to your own success, and this culture of competition can intensify feelings of inadequacy and self-doubt.

I can't say I've never felt competitive. I've been frustrated by project assignments I didn't get or leadership roles I wasn't chosen for. I've experienced those moments of self-doubt, asking myself, *Why wasn't I selected for this opportunity? Is it because I don't [insert insecurity here]?*

But when I changed my mindset around opportunities, everything shifted. I stopped focusing so much on what others were doing, and what I wasn't. That mental shift created a real, almost physical sense of relief. I began to find joy in the opportunities I did have, and in working with people rather than seeing them as competition. Before long, new opportunities appeared, ones I would never have had the capacity to take on if I had been chasing roles that were never meant for me in the first place.

It turns out that a collaborative and celebratory mindset can also set you apart as a leader. It differentiates you from other technical experts. And when you collaborate with others and genuinely celebrate their successes, the whole team wins.

Individual action. Intentionally build a celebratory culture

- Take the time to promote each other's accomplishments and recognize a job well done. Celebrating good work is a simple but undervalued way to lift someone up and recognize their contributions and make them feel valued

- Interrupt the performative culture of *you vs. them* when you see it by reframing competitiveness as collaboration and naming shared goals. This can diffuse unspoken tension and prevent people from getting too far into their heads with thoughts of inferiority.
- Graciously accept complements and recognition of your own accomplishments. This goes a long way to modeling the culture you want to see. Not sure how to start? Consider a simple (and uncompromising) "Thank you."

The reality is, if we don't address the competitive culture in STEMM, the challenge of improving diversity in technical fields is only going to get worse, not better. We need to cultivate confidence within our technical workforce to avoid losing the brilliance of their contributions. And we need to build workplace cultures that prioritize collaboration over competition to help prevent, well... the leaking pipeline.

BUILD YOUR CAPACITY FOR CONFIDENCE

Capacity for Confidence, *noun:*

A person's ability to build, access, and sustain self-assurance,
especially in environments that may challenge or erode that belief.

We need to stop telling women, to *just be more confident*. It is not that simple. As we've discussed, systemic barriers actively erode confidence. Instead of offering useless advice, let's create meaningful opportunities for people to build their **capacity for confidence**.

Give people opportunities. If you manage or mentor someone, offer them chances to present, lead challenging projects, demonstrate their expertise, and gain experience through responsibilities they might not otherwise have access to.

I can say with confidence that the experiences I had as an early-career engineer gave me valuable opportunities to learn from more experienced colleagues, gain exposure to a variety of processes and product lines, and build a network of people I could collaborate with to execute increasingly complex technical work. The more opportunities someone has to learn, develop skills, expand their network, and demonstrate their competencies, the more their confidence will grow over time.

And when you do give people opportunities, stay with them. Offer mentorship and guidance when needed, and give them space to try out their own ideas. Continue to express your confidence in them and celebrate the wins along the way. Consistent affirmation can help them begin to see themselves as you see them, and may just be the key to countering persistent self-doubt.

> **Systemic action.** Intentionally create opportunities for capacity for confidence growth
>
> - As a leader or mentor, create opportunities for others to grow their professional experiences. Then stay close: guide, encourage, and celebrate them as they learn and lead.
> - As a growing individual, say yes to stretch opportunities, especially when they come from trusted leaders, even if you don't feel fully ready. Each challenge you take on expands your capacity for confidence.
> - At the organizational level, build a culture where early- and mid-career professionals regularly gain exposure. Structure projects to encourage cross-team collaboration, establish rotation pathways, and connect emerging leaders with mentors who actively champion their development.

CREATE AN INCLUSIVE WORKPLACE INFRASTRUCTURE

This final strategy ties back to the importance of diverse and inclusive workplace cultures. Given that you've chosen to read this book, it's likely you already recognize the value of diverse spaces.

Today, both research and media consistently highlight how inclusive cultures, and organizations that foster a climate of **psychological safety**, can effectively mitigate feelings of imposter syndrome. Leaders who promote and sustain psychologically safe environments create workplaces where employees feel empowered to challenge the status quo and comfortable sharing ideas and suggestions without fear of negative repercussions.

Psychological Safety, *noun:*

The belief that you can express yourself, sharing ideas, concerns, questions, and mistakes, without fear of punishment or judgement.

These organizations benefit from collaborative innovation, diverse perspectives, and the ability to adapt to changing landscapes. Leaders who demonstrate supportive and consultative behaviors help promote psychological safety and foster positive, inclusive team environments.

As discussed throughout this book, women are more likely to experience microaggressions and stereotyping, which can significantly affect how others perceive their credentials and expertise, and often how women perceive themselves. Frequent interruptions or the misattribution of their ideas to others can discourage full participation. Constantly having to advocate for oneself becomes exhausting and can ultimately deter women from contributing as fully as they might otherwise.

What does this have to do with imposter syndrome?

Workplaces that feel supportive and make employees feel that their ideas are valued have a direct impact on an individual's internal sense of belonging. When the fear of being wrong is removed, the thoughts that often fuel imposter syndrome can be significantly reduced.

Leadership exists at all levels, and the way we choose to interact with one another and contribute to workplace culture shapes how each of us perceives and experiences the workplace.

Individual action. Intentionally build an inclusive and safe culture.

- Find opportunities to invite input from others, encourage dialogue, and show your team that their perspectives matter.
- Model vulnerability, being willing to say, "I don't know, but I'll go find out." You don't have to have all the answers today, and neither do they.

FINAL THOUGHTS

Imposter syndrome is a feeling that can, and often does, affect nearly all of us at some point in our lives. It's not a fun experience, but we're not powerless. By enlisting the support of trusted friends and mentors, sharing our own experiences, and normalizing moments of self-doubt, we create space for relief and connection.

But this is not just a personal problem.

Imposter syndrome is a byproduct of systemic issues.

To move forward together, we must also shift workplace cultures. This means rejecting environments where competitive behaviors thrive and building cultures that celebrate diverse perspectives and shared successes.

We can help one another overcome self-doubt and create space for all of us to show up as our most authentic selves.

What can you do when panic strikes during a high-stakes moment at work?

I've had extreme bouts of imposter syndrome hit at the worst possible times, even walking away from a critical program review when I felt a full-blown panic attack coming on. My Rejection Sensitive Dysphoria (RSD), which causes small criticisms to feel like end-of-the-world rejection, sent my anxious brain into hyperdrive and had me convinced I'd be fired because our team had overlooked a requirement's impact.

Since then, I've discovered a few tricks to manage these moments without fleeing the scene or visibly unraveling.

First, I ground myself, almost literally! One of my common "stims," repetitive behaviors that aim to calm my nervous system, is to cross my legs onto my chair and bounce my feet against my hands. This behavior isn't exactly conducive to a round table review with executives and customers, so when subtlety is needed, I place both feet flat on the floor, yoga's mountain pose style, to remind myself I am on earth.

Next, I anchor myself with my "why." For me, that's my kids. I want to show them what is possible when you work hard at something you love. I have a special ring I wear with my children's birthstones. In tough moments, I touch that ring to remind myself of why I do what I do, a subtle movement, but a powerful mental tool.

If you feel panic rising, try to ground yourself, both physically and with your why. Change your body position. Choose something to keep with you as a reminder. Or repeat a word to snap you out of the big feeling.

It can be anything, as long as it works for you.

– Megan Wendell

Eight

A Labyrinth of Identities

WOMEN IN STEMM AND THEIR INTERSECTIONAL PATHS

*by Manpreet Kaur, Ph.D., engineer, mother, American,
Indian, Sikh, and many other identities.*

The first time I remember feeling "other" was when I was 10 years old, and my family was pulled aside for an additional security check because of our religion.

The next time I felt "other" was in engineering school, when I couldn't find the ladies' room on the first day, because there wasn't one in that building! In graduate school, I was excluded from a team activity because, as an immigrant, I did not understand baseball. And once again, in my first job, I was labeled as culturally submissive because I was "too agreeable," a judgment attributed to my being South Asian.

The story continues. Like many individuals, I am a product of my diverse identities. Each of these aspects has contributed to my experience of "otherness" and, together, they form a unique intersectional perspective that has deeply shaped my life and career path.

– Manpreet

Imagine a world where the brilliance of STEMM is equitably shaped by the hands of both women and men, unburdened by biases related to gender, race, sex, class, or national identity. Despite the progress we've made, the journey for women in these fields often resembles navigating a labyrinth, complicated further by both visible and invisible aspects of identity.

At the heart of understanding these complex experiences is the concept of intersectionality, which acknowledges that initiatives aimed at promoting equality have disproportionately benefited women who do not also face additional barriers related to race, sexual identity, or other intersecting factors.

Let's explore the intersectional experiences of women in STEMM and examine how these layered identities shape their career journeys.

The term **intersectionality** was brought to life by Kimberlé Crenshaw in 1989. Picture a crossroads where different aspects of identity, race, gender, class, and more, intersect to create unique experiences of discrimination or privilege. It's like a tapestry, where each thread contributes to the overall pattern, and removing even one thread changes the entire picture.

In STEMM fields, intersectionality functions like a hidden undercurrent that influences everything. Women in STEMM often face compounded biases, not just because of their gender, but also due to race, ethnicity, socioeconomic status, physical appearance, and other identity markers, such as wearing makeup. These intersecting identities can result in different treatment, varied access to opportunities, and unequal career progression.

PIONEERS AND TRAILBLAZERS

To understand today's landscape, we must travel back in time. Historically, STEMM has been a realm dominated by men, with women often left standing at the gates, knocking for entry. Those few who did make it inside faced a harsh reality of marginalization. This long history of exclusion has left behind a legacy of systemic barriers that continue to persist today.

Yet, against these odds, many women have carved their names into the annals of STEMM.

> Think of **Marie Curie**, who immigrated from Poland to France in 1891. She braved bias against both women and immigrants to pioneer research in radioactivity. Her work, which ultimately cost

her life, made her the first woman to win a Nobel Prize. And then she won a second.

Or **Ada Lovelace**, who overcame disability and illness to become a mathematician and scientist who imagined the first algorithm for Babbage's Analytical Engine.

Then there's **Katherine Johnson**, an African American mathematician whose calculations were critical to the success of NASA's space missions. Her contributions were relatively unknown until the release of the best-selling *Hidden Figures*, half a century later.

These stories are inspiring, but they also highlight the extra hurdles these women had to overcome, despite what some might call the "luck" of receiving recognition in their lifetimes.

In the world of engineering, consider **Emily Warren Roebling**, the unsung hero behind the Brooklyn Bridge. She managed the construction after her husband fell ill, all while serving as his primary caretaker. Despite skill, knowledge, and rapport with the construction team, she had to continuously sell the illusion that her husband was still in full control.

Hedy Lamarr, an actress of Jewish descent whose husband had ties to the Nazi regime, invented frequency-hopping spread spectrum technology with the intent of helping the Allies during the war. Her invention paved the way for modern wireless communication.

Their stories shine a light on the brilliance and resilience required to break through societal biases and barriers.

Fast forward to more recent times, we meet **Dr. Fei-Fei Li**, a trailblazer in Artificial Intelligence (AI). Her work on ImageNet revolutionized deep learning algorithms. As an immigrant who began on the lower rungs of economic success, she is a staunch advocate for diversity in the tech industry and for the development of human-centered AI that benefits people in positive and benevolent ways.

Or take **Dr. Mae Jemison**. In 1992, she became the first African American woman in space, breaking through both racial and gender barriers. Despite numerous obstacles, she earned a degree in chemical engineering and went on to join NASA. Her journey serves as a powerful example of both the challenges and the triumphs that women of color face in STEMM.

These pioneers continue to shape the world through their innovations and leadership. But there are so many more stories. Many women who persisted in the face of extreme othering have not received credit for their work.

Cecilia Payne-Gaposchkin, who immigrated to the U.S. in 1923 to pursue a career in STEMM, was the first to propose that hydrogen is the most abundant element in the universe. Her groundbreaking discovery was initially dismissed as "spurious" and later credited to others.

...and it continues to this day.

CONTEMPORARY CHALLENGES

Despite these inspiring stories, women in STEMM today still face a maze of challenges. For women of color, LGBTQ+ women, women with disabilities, and those from lower-income backgrounds, these challenges are often even more pronounced. Intersectionality helps us understand these layered barriers.

In researching this chapter, I spoke with several women who shared their stories, and I have interwoven their experiences along with my own in this section. Whether reflecting on my own journey or those of my interviewees, I see that we are a diverse group of women facing a wide range of individual experiences and challenges, yet there is meaningful overlap among us.

This chapter includes my journey as a Sikh, immigrant, overweight mother and wife navigating both academia and the tech world; Ana's journey as a stay-at-home mom returning to the workforce and a first-generation American of Hispanic heritage in the semiconductor industry; and Rose's experience as a first-generation American of South Asian descent who faced several challenging years as a young field engineer in the energy industry.

Whether it's the lack of properly sized equipment and uniforms or the absence of proper disposal options for menstrual products in the field, barriers show up in ways both large and small.

We've been denied challenging projects based on the belief that women don't belong in certain spaces, on construction sites, on rigs, or in remote industrial settings.

Some of us have been judged as "unprofessional" based on physical appearance, whether because of the color of our hair or being dismissed for our youth when a client asked for someone with more grey hair.

We've been asked to take on roles with less technical leadership and more emphasis on soft skills.

At times, we've been critiqued for the accents in our voices.

And we've faced the all-too-common social presumption that the career of a wife and mother is somehow secondary to that of her partner.

We have all lived the experiences this chapter highlights.

Microaggression, *noun:*

Everyday words, behaviors, or environmental cues, intentional or not, that convey dismissive, negative, or demeaning messages rooted in bias against marginalized identities.

Gender bias and discrimination in STEMM are like invisible walls. They can range from overt sexism to subtle **microaggressions**, like being asked to take notes or being silenced in meetings. Women often find it difficult to rise to leadership positions and struggle for recognition, as shown throughout this book. These biases impact hiring, salaries, and advancement opportunities.

When intersecting identities are added to the equation, the situation becomes even more dire.

> **Women of color** in STEMM often face a **double bind**, a tangled knot of racial and gender discrimination. This can leave them feeling isolated and undervalued, needing to work twice as hard to prove themselves. Research shows that women of color receive less mentorship and sponsorship, which are crucial for career development.

For LGBTQ+ women, the journey in STEMM is like walking a **tightrope**. They may face bias and a lack of inclusivity, navigating both professional and personal challenges. The intersection of gender, sexual orientation, and STEMM creates a complex landscape, one that requires thoughtful and deliberate navigation.

Women with disabilities and neurodiversity face unique hurdles, often related to accessibility and accommodations. This applies to permanent, temporary, and situational disabilities, especially in a culture where pregnancy is often treated as a short-term disability! These barriers can significantly limit participation and hinder professional growth.

These are just a few examples.

Intersectionality sheds light on the multiple layers of discrimination that women too often experience, affecting their career progression. However, this is by no means a comprehensive list of all intersectional challenges, which can also include religion, national origin, and much more.

CAREER ASPIRATIONS AND CHOICES

The intersectional barriers women in STEMM face shape their career journeys in profound ways. These barriers influence educational choices, career aspirations, job satisfaction, and retention in STEMM fields.

Imagine the educational path as a winding road with many turns, off-ramps, and speed bumps. Often, the lack of role models is as harmful as a lack of signage on that road. Intersectional factors like socioeconomic status can limit access to quality education, while cultural stereotypes and biases may discourage girls from pursuing STEMM in the first place. Intersectionality helps us understand how different identity factors merge to shape these educational experiences.

Career aspirations for women in STEMM are often deeply influenced by their intersecting identities. Feeling like no one at work would understand their family background, hiding how they were raised, minimizing their religion, or pretending everything is fine adds to the mental load and can chip away at confidence, ultimately affecting career choices.

We hear stories of girls avoiding certain fields because they're seen as "a man's job" or "women don't do that." We hear stories of women not taking a role because of motherhood expectations. Not taking a leadership role because of a coworker. Feeling unwelcome because of the workplace dynamics. Feeling stuck because of the consistent promotion of men over women. As a result, women may opt for paths perceived as more welcoming, even when their passion lies in STEMM.

Retention and advancement in STEMM can feel like trying to drive a difficult road up a steep mountain in a blizzard. Intersectional barriers contribute to higher dropout rates, as many women leave STEMM careers due to a lack of support and opportunity. Organizational culture and policies play a critical role in both retaining and advancing women in these fields.

STRATEGIES FOR CHANGE

So, what can we do to straighten this path? Addressing intersectional challenges requires a multifaceted approach. We need to create inclusive environments, promote diversity, and provide targeted support for underrepresented groups. Equally important is the willingness to share our journeys, our roads to success, and the challenges we've faced along the way.

Organizations must implement inclusive policies that meet the diverse needs of women in STEMM, creating environments where everyone has the opportunity to thrive. This includes flexible work arrangements, pay equity, and accommodations for disabilities. Many organizations need to critically examine their recruitment and hiring practices to uncover and eliminate hidden biases. Reviewing representation data, promoting diverse leadership, fostering open and inclusive communication, and encouraging allyship and advocacy are all essential steps.

Mentorship and sponsorship serve as both the GPS and the fuel in the tank for women navigating STEMM careers. Organizations should establish formal peer groups and mentorship programs that connect women with peers and experienced professionals for guidance and support. Sponsorship, where senior leaders actively advocate for women's advancement, is equally vital for career progression.

True cultural change within organizations is necessary to address intersectional barriers. It requires recognizing and supporting intersectional experiences and openly acknowledging their impact. This includes challenging stereotypes, promoting diversity and inclusion, and building a culture rooted in respect and equity. Training programs on unconscious bias and cultural competency can further support the creation of a more inclusive environment.

CONCLUSION

Intersectionality provides a valuable framework for understanding the complex experiences of women in STEMM. By acknowledging and addressing the intersecting barriers they face, we can create more inclusive and equitable environments that support their career journeys.

The success of women in STEMM is not just a matter of social justice, it is essential for driving innovation and progress in these critical fields. I encourage all readers to take the ideas from these chapters and find opportunities to share, discuss, debate, and reflect with as diverse a group as possible within your own communities.

Let's use this opportunity to talk openly about bias, our own and others', and grow from those conversations, so that no one is left feeling misunderstood or like they don't belong.

Together, we can continue dismantling the labyrinth, so the brilliance of STEMM can be shaped equitably by all who choose this journey.

	Actions	Considerations
Institutions	Implement inclusive policies.	Create safe feedback channels to assess cultural climate.
		Adapt policies based on employee feedback and lived experiences.
	Review recruitment and hiring practices to remove hidden biases.	Use blind resume reviews or structured interviews to minimize bias.
	Track and analyze representation data to guide equitable practices.	Regularly assess metrics and make data-driven adjustments.
	Promote diverse leadership and ensure inclusive decision-making.	Review who is missing from leadership, and why?
	Establish formal mentorship and sponsorship programs.	Ensure these programs are resourced, visible, and well-matched.
	Provide training on unconscious bias and cultural competency.	Make it ongoing, not one-time; include leadership participation.
Individuals	Share personal journeys, including challenges and successes, to normalize diverse experiences in STEMM.	Be vulnerable in sharing to encourage authenticity in others.
	Participate in mentorship and peer support, both as mentees and mentors.	Offer your experience generously; ask for help without hesitation.
	Engage in allyship and advocacy to support underrepresented voices.	Use your voice in meetings and platforms to lift others.
Policy Makers	Create and enforce policies that promote diversity and inclusion in education and workplace settings.	Mandate inclusive practices through legislation and incentives.
	Support funding for research and initiatives addressing systemic bias and intersectional challenges.	Fund scholarships, fellowships, and inclusive research projects.
	Encourage accountability and transparency through data reporting requirements and compliance audits.	Tie funding to measurable equity and inclusion benchmarks.

Mental Wellness Moment | The Importance of a Diagnosis

You may already know that mental health struggles can begin long before adulthood. Many conditions begin to present in childhood and can leave kids and their caregivers searching for answers. The path may seem simple, get a diagnosis, follow a treatment plan, but even getting the diagnosis can prove challenging, especially for girls. Many of the criteria in the DSM-IV were largely qualified based on how conditions present in boys, making it much harder for girls to be evaluated and, if evaluated, receive an accurate diagnosis.

I have experienced this firsthand. In retrospect, I showed symptoms of neurodivergence in elementary school. But because I was a high achiever, it was brushed off as just part of being "gifted." When I was eventually diagnosed with depression, I thought that everything would be solved because now I had the answers for why I felt different and a clear course of treatment. Or so I thought.

I spent the next two decades bouncing between therapy and medication options that would work for a while and then plateau in progress or even backslide. The problem? I had the wrong diagnosis. I was treating the symptoms, not the cause. And I'm not alone: 61% of women with ADHD are not diagnosed until adulthood, often when career demands, motherhood, or grief make it impossible to keep up the masks we wear to exist in a neurotypical world not meant for us.[1]

What can STEMM women and working parents do if they or a loved one is struggling? Follow your gut

If something isn't right, talk to a medical professional. Push for diagnoses and treatment paths that feel right. Advocate fiercely and don't allow any diagnosis, or lack thereof, define your limits. You deserve the personal and professional life you desire.

– Megan Wendell

---

[1] Compared to 40% in men.

Nine

Navigating Motherhood Alongside Career

THRIVING—ONE BOLD MOTHER AT A TIME

by Emily L. Bishop, engineer, mom, and guide for ambitious, purpose-driven mothers.

"Your position has been terminated."

The one sentence that changed the game for me. I was a Project Engineer with a Professional Engineer designation for a multi-national manufacturing company, a wife, and a mother of two children under the age of four. I thought the door to my career had been shut forever. Little did I know, it was only the beginning.

I received a phone call late one night from a trusted mentor telling (yes, telling) me to send her my résumé. She was having drinks with the CEO of a local manufacturing company and thought I would be the perfect fit. Turns out, she was right.

I re-entered the workforce as a production manager, arguably the most grueling of all manufacturing jobs, balancing management expectations and the people who make the product. While the learnings were invaluable, this wasn't the job that had me leaping out of bed in the morning.

Armed with the motto "keep walking through open doors," I decided to wedge my way into the sales world. I continued to say yes to every opportunity to get in front of our customers and sales team.

Today, I'm part of the Senior Leadership team, travelling all over Canada representing our product and, most importantly, our culture. I am thriving! I credit the ability to do this to my support team: my husband, my children (now eight and ten), and my dad. I also very unexpectedly lost my mother during this transition, and I cannot tell you how much strength and determination I drew from that experience. *Look at me, Mom, I'm in a book!*

If you feel you're at a crossroads in your professional life and want to make a change, you can do it.

Get loud with your goals.

Get loud with your partner and "home based" support team so they know what you need from them to succeed.

Get loud with your coworkers and mentors so they can help open doors for you.

Get loud with your boss so they understand your motivation and commitment.

Don't keep your goals in the dark from the people around you who are critical to your success.

You deserve to go after exactly what you want in your career.

And motherhood? It might just be the catalyst that fuels your drive, resilience, and unshakable determination to redefine success on your own terms.

– Katie Wilson
PEng, Product Manager

What do you do when the dedicated nursing room is locked—not by another mom, but by someone on a personal call?[1]

Or when a critical meeting runs long and your body temperature rises as you tally childcare late fees... again.

For mothers in STEMM, balancing work and motherhood often means navigating the unexpected and the uncomfortable. From storing breastmilk in a colleague's bar fridge to pumping in the Flight Test Debriefing Room, these aren't just anecdotes; they're daily realities for women trying to excel in fields that were never designed with them in mind.

As one of 14 women in a mechanical engineering class of 200, I always saw myself as one of the boys. There was nothing they could do that I couldn't. But birthing my son revealed a transformation most of my peers in STEMM would never experience. And despite growing up hearing I could do anything, the workplace hadn't yet caught up to truly support mothers in thriving, both professionally and personally.

My experience shaped the path I walk today—guiding mothers to lead with purpose, not in spite of motherhood, but because of it.

The traditional workplace was not designed for women—and certainly not for mothers. This is especially true in STEMM, where male-dominated environments persist. Despite the advances women have made in the workforce since the 1950s, there is still a lot to be done to build workplaces that truly support mothers. So, if balancing motherhood and a STEMM career feels like an uphill battle, know that you're not alone.

This chapter offers strategies you can explore to support yourself and others while striving for progress. We'll dive into three key themes:

- Embracing your identity as a mother at work.
- Leaning on your village for support.
- Giving yourself grace through the transformation of motherhood.

But first, let's talk about the **motherhood advantage**.

---

[1] This may also be called the Lactation Room, Expressing Room, or Mothers Room.

MOTHERHOOD ADVANTAGE

Motherhood isn't a professional setback; it's a powerful upgrade. While balancing a STEMM career and raising a family is challenging, it equips us with skills that enhance how we lead, collaborate, and solve problems.

We troubleshoot toddler meltdowns before 8 a.m., then bring that same calm, creative thinking to a test failure or team breakdown by noon. We juggle school runs and deadlines, sharpening our time management and forcing us to prioritize what really matters. When projects go sideways, we adapt, because we do it every day.

We become better communicators, reading tone and body language instinctively. That emotional intelligence helps us lead with empathy and navigate complex interpersonal dynamics. We advocate for our kids in doctors' offices and school systems, then bring that same clarity and confidence to meetings, negotiations and reviews.

Motherhood broadens our perspective. Whether building tech, analyzing data or conducting research, we work with a deeper purpose, knowing that our impact reaches far beyond the office.

So, if you ever wonder whether motherhood is holding you back, remember: it's leveling you up. These aren't soft skills. They're leadership skills, and they matter.

This chapter is for moms and moms-to-be in STEMM, drawing on real experiences of mothers around the world who have shared their challenges, insights and victories. I write through my own lens as a married woman and a biological mother living in Canada, while acknowledging that motherhood is

deeply personal and varied. Support systems and circumstances differ. This is a nuanced conversation, and wherever you're coming from, you are welcome here. I hope these perspectives help you thrive in both work and life, because you deserve to. Alright, let's dig in.

EMBRACING YOUR IDENTITY AS A MOTHER AT WORK

We often try to keep our work and personal lives separate, aiming to always appear professional and capable (see Deloitte's 2024 report on **covering**).[2] Then we get pregnant, and at some point, despite our best efforts, it becomes impossible to hide that life is about to change in a big way.

I want to pause here to acknowledge miscarriage and infertility. Infertility affects 1 in 6 women globally, and 10–20% of known pregnancies end in miscarriage. These experiences carry immense emotional and physical weight, often compounded by the pressure to maintain a career. Though rarely spoken about, they are deeply felt. If this is part of your story, know there is space for you here. You are seen, and your experience matters.

When I returned to work after having my first baby, I felt an immense internal pressure to show up exactly as I had before motherhood. That pressure was only reinforced externally. No alternatives were offered, not even a conversation. I had just grown, birthed and nourished a human who relied on me entirely for their survival, yet I was expected to walk into the office on Monday at 8 a.m. as if nothing had changed.

And I did, because honestly... I had no idea what I was in for.

There were no policies for gradual return, flexible hours, or part-time options. And I felt a heavy pressure to perform, to prove I was still capable. But maintaining the illusion that I had everything under control unraveled quickly. Daycare bugs, medical appointments, and strict pickup times made it impossible to keep my work and mom life separate or to meet the impossible demands of both.

STEMM workplaces need more examples of mothers showing up as their full selves and giving others permission to do the same. That starts with

---

[2] Covering refers to "ways in which individuals downplay known disfavored identities to blend into the mainstream."

honesty. Be open about what's happening in your life and what you need to succeed at work.

When I was pregnant with my second son, I was running a dual-fluoroscopy (X-ray) research study and had to share the news much earlier than I wanted to. Fortunately, I had a strong relationship with my supervisor (also a mom), who made accommodations and kept the information confidential. I know not everyone has that kind of support, but your needs are valid, even if they don't fit neatly into a policy.

Pregnancy and motherhood take a significant toll. A 2024 *Science* study found that pregnancy requires 50,000 extra calories over nine months, while breastfeeding can take as much time as a full-time job during the first year. Yet workplace support remains inadequate. The transition into motherhood impacts your energy, cognitive load and overall well-being. So, while I know that advocating for flexibility, time off, or even basic acknowledgment can feel daunting, this isn't a luxury. It's essential for sustainable success in both work and life. And it's time we start demanding it.

Ashley works in a technical role and spends a lot of time in manufacturing plants. Announcing her first pregnancy at work felt vulnerable, especially in such a demanding environment. When she shared the news, her boss responded with genuine congratulations and clear safety modifications. He checked in regularly and gave her the autonomy to voice what changes or accommodations she needed.

> *Balancing motherhood with a technical career that includes travel and irregular hours isn't easy. But having a supportive manager has made it possible.*
>
> – Ashley

The trust and flexibility didn't end with her leave. Today, whether it's a school event or a sick day, she's supported in both her roles: engineer and mom. Ashley's story is a powerful reminder that you deserve to bring your whole self to work.

Advocating for your needs isn't a weakness; it is leadership.

When we speak up, we support ourselves and pave the way for others to follow. And when workplaces make space for that, moms in STEMM don't just survive. They thrive.

Take a moment to think about your current workplace:

Reflections | Motherhood at Work

How would it feel to ask for a private, comfortable space
to pump at work if one doesn't exist?

How would it feel to tell your boss you're leaving early
because your child needs you?

What is something you could do this week to show up as your
full self at work?

LEAN ON YOUR VILLAGE

They say it takes a village, but for many of us, that village is nowhere in sight. Parenting in isolation has become normalized in Western culture, but it's far from natural.

For 95% of human history, communities raised children together, supported by networks of 10 or more caregivers. Today, in modern economies, this level of communal care is nearly nonexistent. The way our lives are structured makes it difficult, if not nearly impossible, to find the village we were meant to have.

The result is incredible pressure on parents to do alone what entire communities once shared.

So, what's the solution? If the village isn't there, we have to build it. And I know that's easier said than done, especially as a working mom, but the research is clear: building a support system benefits both parents and children.

I'm no expert, but here's what's helped me: knocking on a neighbor's door to ask if their teen babysits, introducing myself to other parents at daycare, arranging casual playdates, or dropping off food for a family having a tough week. These aren't grand gestures, just intentional acts of connection.

Sanchari went from co-parenting to being a single mother. While living in Denmark, far from her family in India, she recalls a night during the pandemic when her pulse spiked dangerously high. The next day, she needed urgent medical tests, but with hospital delays and her daughter's pickup time approaching, she was stuck. Two Danish friends, though miles away, stepped in to help.

> *It was like having a home away from home. It gave me strength knowing I could form a village in a different country.*
>
> – Sanchari

Eleonora moved from Italy to the Netherlands for her PhD, got married, and had two children there. She found the task of building a new social network from scratch daunting, but she persevered with the help of social media and existing connections to make it happen. Later, with a third child and now living in the U.S., they turned to the expat community to find mutual support.

> *Through persistence and trust, we formed strong friendships and found support. We learned that asking for help is crucial when family isn't nearby—and that most people are more than willing to lend a hand.*
>
> – Eleonora

Like Sanchari and Eleonora, you're not meant to do this alone, especially as a working mom. Trying to manage everything on your own can take a toll on your well-being and overall quality of life. Your support system isn't just a nice-to-have; it is vital for both you and your family.

And remember, support can take many forms. Yes, it includes family, friends, and neighbors, but it can also mean paid help such as childcare, cleaning, or grocery delivery. Sometimes, outsourcing is part of building the village.

Even with support in place, the demands on working moms today are intense and continuing to grow.

Let's look at the data:

- In 2000, working moms spent as much time on focused childcare as stay-at-home moms in 1975.
- By 2021, they were spending more time working *and* more time parenting than in 2003.

Life as a working mom is busy, and it's only getting busier. In my own journey, I often felt that if everything went to plan, our family would be okay. But one small thing, like a sick child, a car repair, or a surprise meeting, and everything fell apart. Sound familiar?

> **Take sick days.** Kids get sick frequently. The mental load of rearranging everything at the first sign of illness is heavy and all too familiar. Talking about this ahead of time with your partner or support system, building a backup plan, and having a short list of people to call can make a world of difference when those inevitable sick days come.
>
> **Open communication with your partner or support system** is essential as a working mom. Regular, honest conversations about schedules and responsibilities, while not always easy, have made a big difference for me. There is a lot of invisible work in raising a family. Naming it and dividing it in a way that feels right for everyone is key, while allowing it to shift and evolve over time. Both the book and game 'Fair Play' are a great resources for navigating these sometimes confronting but necessary conversations.
>
> **Let go of the need for control.** I'm definitely guilty of thinking I had my son's bedtime routine perfected. When I finally let my husband take over, it wasn't a disaster; it just looked different. As a recovering perfectionist, trust me, I get it. But kids benefit from different approaches, and so do we.
>
> **Get your kids involved in household tasks early.** It may take longer at first (one sock at a time into the washing machine), but I'm told it pays off. It nurtures their natural desire to help and reinforces their role as valued contributors in the family. Plus, chores are amazing for kids' mental health.

You do not have to, and should not have to, do it alone. Speak your needs. Accept help. Hire support if you can.

Building your village is not optional; it's essential for the well-being of your family and your ability to thrive.

Take a moment to think about your current support network:

Reflections | Your Village

What's one small thing you can do this week to expand or nurture your village?

MOTHERHOOD IS TRANSFORMATIVE

The moment a child is born, the mother is also born. She never existed before. The woman existed, but the mother, never. A mother is something absolutely new.

– Osho,
Spiritual Teacher

Motherhood is transformative, and we now have a word for this evolution: **matrescence**. Lasting two to three years, matrescence reshapes a woman biologically, psychologically, socially, politically, and spiritually. The term was coined by Dana Raphael in the 1970s.

Matrescence, *noun:*

The physical, emotional, and social transition
of becoming a mother.

Yet this transformation is rarely acknowledged, especially in the workplace. Many mothers, myself included, find themselves trying to fit back into a career and life designed before kids, and wondering why it feels so hard.

Becoming a mother is not just a series of new skills or behaviours,
it's a complete reorientation of a woman's identity, her values,
and how she makes her way through the world.

– Jessie Harrold
Coach, Doula and Author of Mothershift

No amount of planning in advance can fully prepare you for what lies ahead. What can help is learning to embrace change, letting go of perfection, and giving yourself grace. Of course, that is easier said than done, especially in STEMM fields, where traits like precision, planning, and high achievement make it difficult to accept the messiness and unpredictability of motherhood.

Give yourself permission to re-evaluate your priorities, values, and goals as you evolve. An identity crisis in motherhood is a challenge many moms face but rarely discuss openly, especially among women in STEMM, whose identities are often deeply rooted in their professional success. Adding the demands of motherhood while striving to balance them with career aspirations can feel like a significant challenge.

And there it is, the word that haunts so many working moms: *balance.* Every mom I talk to wants it, but between work and parenting, it feels impossible to achieve.

What if, instead of chasing balance, we strive for alignment with our values, our authentic selves, and what matters most in this season of life? It's not about doing it all; it's about doing what matters most.

That whole 'you can have it all'
—nope, not at the same time; that's a lie.

– Michelle Obama
Former U.S. First Lady and Advocate for Women's Rights

My invitation to you is to get clear on what truly matters now. Motherhood is *supposed* to reshape your values.

Let it. And then, let the rest go.

SHOULDS

It's so easy to get caught in the swirl of *shoulds,* from society, social media, and even well-meaning friends and family.

Should you send out perfect family holiday cards? Volunteer for every school event? Coach the sports team? Bake homemade cupcakes for fundraisers? Plan Pinterest-worthy birthday parties?

Should your kids be playing instruments, attending summer camps, and participating in every spirit day?

The truth is, you don't have to do any of it if it doesn't align with your values.

Comparison only fuels pressure and self-doubt. Every mother's journey is unique. Life will ebb and flow; sometimes parenting will take priority, and sometimes work will. Keep checking in and adjusting to stay aligned.

Take a moment to think about your current commitments:

Reflections | Your Shoulds

Is there anything you're currently doing, big or small,
that doesn't align with your values?

Get curious (without judgment) about why.

How would it feel to say no and reclaim that time and energy?

SELF CARE

And don't forget to take care of yourself. When life gets busy, self-care is often the first thing to go, but it is actually the key to managing everything else. The deadline, the toddler tantrum, the messy house. They are all more manageable when your own needs are met first.

Feeling overwhelmed by the mental load is a signal, not a personal failure. Slowing down to care for yourself is productive. A regulated nervous system supports focus, creativity, calm, connection, and compassion, both at work and at home.

Reflections | Self Care

What would it feel like to carve out a small window of
intentional time for yourself this week?

When will you dedicate time today to slow, mindful breath?

How will you celebrate yourself for following through?

Kids learn by example. When we care for ourselves, we show them self-love in action. So the next time you catch yourself pushing through, take a moment to pause. Take just five minutes.

Take a deep breath. Inhale through your nose, fill your belly with air, and sigh it out through your mouth.

5 *things you* SEE

Ground yourself with a five senses exercise. Shift your aware-ness intentionally, starting with five things you can see.

4 *things you* FEEL

Take a short walk.

A small reset can return tenfold in calm, clarity, and the ability to handle whatever comes next, both at work and at home. Give it a try.[3]

3 *things you* HEAR

PRACTICAL STEPS FORWARD

2 *things you* SMELL

For women navigating parenthood and STEMM, consider these suggestions for practical steps forward on your personal journey.

1 *thing you* TASTE

---

[3] See Chapter 5, *From Surviving to Thriving*, for another breathwork technique: Box Breath.

This week, do one thing that brings you joy: a quiet bath, a peaceful walk, or a hot cup of coffee, uninterrupted. That renewed energy will ripple through your work and home life.

This month, take inventory of the invisible work at home. Share the load with your support system in a way that feels fair, and outsource where possible.

This quarter, revisit your values and priorities. Where are you spending time on things that no longer matter? What do you wish you had time for? Start shifting your energy toward what truly matters to you.

For everyone looking to create change in this space, consider if you could:

Start sharing the mental and physical load at home.

Stop assuming what pregnant and working moms want or need. Ask, listen, and give her the choice.

Continue celebrating working moms at every stage. They are leaders in STEMM *and* raising the next generation. That is pretty incredible.

If you're a STEMM mom, you're likely juggling a lot right now. Here's what I hope you've taken away from this chapter:

- Don't hide your motherhood at work. Own it, and let others know how to support you. Your future self and future generations will thank you.
- You're not meant to do this alone. Find your village. It is time to say goodbye to martyrdom in motherhood for good.
- You're transforming too. Motherhood doesn't just birth a baby; it also brings forth a new version of you. Give yourself permission to change, to reassess, and to grow.

And remember: You have the motherhood advantage.

This framework is long overdue—Mothers have led since the dawn of time, and it is time they are formally recognized as the leaders they are.

Mother-Leader Intuitionship is an emerging leadership theory that seeks to define and honor the often-overlooked leadership qualities inherent in motherhood, similar to the *motherhood advantage*, which we call the "magic of moms." The phenomenon that mothers are natural, capable leaders is rooted in the research we conducted throughout our doctoral studies.

Halfway through our leadership studies, we, both mothers of four children, became acutely aware that the lived leadership experiences found in motherhood were largely absent from the literature. This omission was striking, given that for the majority, mothers are our first teachers and first leaders. It is imperative to address this, particularly given that there are more mothers participating in the United States workforce than ever before and yet remain significantly underrepresented in leadership roles. While current statistics do not specify leader-parent ratios, it is estimated that 30% of college presidents are women and only 10% of Fortune 500 CEOs are women. It is reasonable to infer that even fewer of these individuals are mothers; a striking lack of the magic of moms.

> *"Becoming a mother has encouraged me to*
> *start my own successful business."*

Our culture is happy to benefit from the highly skilled labor of mothers in the home. And instead of being recognized for the remarkable competencies cultivated during their time away, mothers are met with questions about skills gaps and time off when it comes to re-enter the paid workforce. As we learned more about leadership and shared our personal stories, we came to realize that mother-specific research could address that leaky pipeline. Essentially, if we could show that mothers develop leadership competencies through maternal experiences, these could and should be accounted for in the paid workforce.

> *"Reading through this survey has provided a welcomed*
> *recognition of the myriad ways being a parent has increased*
> *my interpersonal and leadership skills."*[1]

---

[1] All quotes are from our ten in-depth interviews or our anonymous research survey (n = 954).

In our first-of-its-kind research, nearly 1,000 mothers responded to our survey exploring the relationship between traditional leadership competencies and maternal competencies. The results were more promising than we ever imagined. We found significant connections between the leadership skills cultivated in motherhood and those recognized in the labor force. Over 87% of respondents reported becoming more discerning and insightful, more tolerant and empathetic, or having greater kindness and warmth since becoming a mother. They also reported an improved ability to understand and communicate with others, an increased capacity to develop alternative approaches and help others build their strengths, and a stronger tendency to consider the needs of the group. Our research demonstrates that mothers have already developed the strengths organizations strive to teach their talent.

"Paying attention to an evolving child allowed me to become a better listener and honed my negotiation skills."

When given the opportunity to share additional thoughts, mothers overwhelmingly connected their motherhood skills to their paid leadership roles, even if they had not previously considered that relationship:

"I wish that people would acknowledge and appreciate the brilliance and resilience of Motherhood, it truly is a beautiful thing."

Through in-depth research, it is clear that maternal experiences enhance leadership capabilities; a phenomenon that is currently lacking in traditional leadership frameworks. We propose a new leadership theory that expands existing theories to include the experience and wisdom that mothers bring to the leadership conversation: meet *Mother-Leader Intuitionship.*

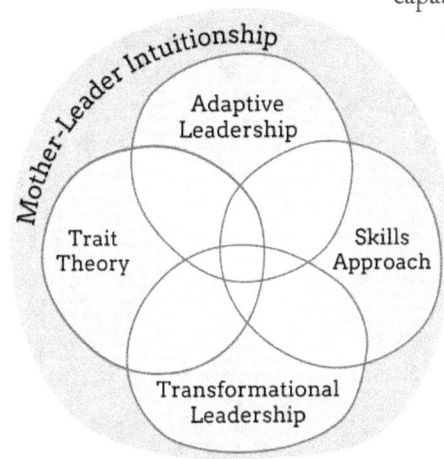

– Dr. Laura Marie Rivera
& Dr. Mindy Ursino

Ten

Stay-at-Home Parents

STEPPING OUT OF AND RETURNING TO THE STEMM WORKFORCE

by Jennifer G. Christensen, designing systems and designing a life of adventure. Industrial engineer → household CEO and chaos manager → innovator in start-up engineering → chief home strategist.

I grew up in a small town with working parents and did not know many stay-at-home parents (SAHP). My mom took a few years off when I was young but returned to work after my sister was born. My parents coached sports, attended athletic and musical events, and chaperoned. As a result, staying home was not something I considered or planned to do.

After graduation, I moved across the country and started my first job in a challenging work environment. A manager once joked that he wouldn't have hired a pregnant employee if he had known, and he often offered patronizing advice. One woman who had young children left for a better work-life balance.

I didn't consider how working in that environment with kids could affect my own career growth, since having children was then a future prospect.

The culture valued long hours and visibility, expected the company to be your top priority, and required annual commitments to relocate if asked or risk career stagnation. Despite having fantastic leadership, supportive coworkers, and career advancement, I left the company before starting a family, partly because the culture seemed incompatible with raising children. I went on to work for an early-stage startup.

Later, after two years of trying, we were thrilled to be expecting our first child, and I felt a deep emotional connection to our baby. After he was born, I was determined to stay home with him. Following another long journey, we welcomed our second child. We had hoped for more, but after years of trying, we decided to embrace life as a family of four. Thanks to our savings and my spouse's income, I continued to stay at home. I am grateful for that choice, though I sometimes wonder how life might have been different if I had returned to work.

After a decade as a SAHP, a newly formed startup offered me a part-time position, which eventually grew from 15 to 30 hours per week. The experience was positive: it boosted my confidence and reminded me that I was more than "just a mom," (for my kids too!) and that I could make a difference within a company. After a few years, I left startup life and am once again a SAHP while I determine what comes next.

– Jennifer

Parenting is a time full of joy, tears, comedic moments, unmeasurable love, loneliness, and every other emotion. Maybe you dreamed of staying home with your kids, never considered it, or perhaps landed somewhere in between.

Deciding to become a stay-at-home parent involves weighing a range of personal and family factors—finances, flexibility, relationship dynamics, scheduling, and more. This chapter serves as both a window and a mirror into life as a STEMM SAHP, offering insight and wisdom from those who made the choice to step away and later return to the workforce.

TO STAY OR NOT TO STAY HOME

Insights gathered from a global community of STEMM mothers highlight the diverse experiences of stay-at-home parenting. Kathy, BS in Engineering, U.S., took company-paid parental leave but didn't intend to become a SAHP. Another U.S.-based structural engineer shared that she was "advised by women in the office not to take any more time than provided or to go part-time because it would be 'career suicide.'"

Other mothers returned to work as primary earners, some transitioned to part-time roles, and others left the workforce altogether—each navigating their own mix of personal, professional, and cultural influences.

An Unpaid Yet Rewarding Job

Being a SAHP is an unpaid, around-the-clock job. You may not know when you'll return to your professional role or a full salary again. A stay-at-home mom (SAHM) works an average of 106 hours per week, based on the Salary.com calculator.

> In my city, 106 hours at the median salary would be $247,192 USD per year!

That figure brings a sense of pride for the formidable work I've done at home, while also serving as a reminder that, in reality, the job lacks a monetary paycheck. However, SAHPs receive invaluable "paychecks" in the form of baby smiles, toddler hugs, flashes of teenage happiness, and countless memorable moments.

Financial factors often play a key role in a woman's decision to stay home or return to the workforce, but they are not the only considerations. Other important criteria for evaluating the decision to stay home include:

> **Budget considerations.** Does taking time off fit your household budget? Have you considered the impacts to retirement savings?

> **Career and parent goals.** What are your career aspirations? What are your goals as a parent? How will extended time away affect both of those? Could a part-time role support these goals?

> **Professional topics.** How long can you take leave before you are behind changes in technology? Are there any certifications you need to keep active?

Support systems. Do you have childcare available to you? Are there healthcare insurance options for you? Are there local resources or places to connect with other parents?

Women surveyed shared the following to illustrate their decision to stay home:

I did not plan to stay home, that still surprises me. I graduated with my master's, finishing my capstone project overseas... when the U.S. economy tanked. I came back to no work and was over-educated but under-experienced. I pieced together contract work for months, then moved to clinical research and then social services... We had great benefits through my husband, so I quit, took a few weeks off, and planned to go back to the public health field as an unpaid intern. Then I found out I was pregnant, surprise! I knew too many folks who were passed up for jobs or promotions due to pregnancy, so I decided to stay home with my son for one year and then go back to work. Eight months after he was born, surprise, I was pregnant again. So, I kept staying home.

– Jen M.
BS Biology and MSPH Tropical Medicine, U.S.

I definitely wanted to be a SAHM, and was excited about the opportunities that I could "be my own boss," choosing how to use my time each day with my kids. I remember being excited about being able to contribute more to our community... Our decision for me to quit work came while I was pregnant with our third child, due to the financial reality of my paycheck not being able to support three children in daycare.

– Tamara O.
MS in Industrial Engineering, U.S.

Angela, BS in Cellular and Molecular Biology, U.S., spent 25 years as a research scientist working in both industrial and academic research in immunology. She wasn't able to take time away when her kids were little, but when her family's financial situation changed, she took time to be a SAHP with two teenagers.

Beth, MS in Aerospace Engineering, U.S., worked part-time for three years. "I wanted more time to be with my kids and see them grow while they were young. I enjoyed volunteering at their school, and having one day off a week allowed for that. I didn't seek to be a SAHP, but it worked out right where I was."

Staying home or resuming a career both come with their own obstacles and rewards. Embracing your choice and finding fulfillment along the way can help you appreciate whichever path you take.

ADDITIONAL PARENTAL LEAVE DYNAMICS

While taking time away from the workforce, you may benefit from having a partner with access to family leave. According to the global data source Organisation for Economic Co-operation and Development (OECD), "all but one OECD country (the U.S.) offers paid maternity and paternity leave around childbirth at the national level, but countries differ markedly in the duration, payment, and uptake of these policies." On average, paid maternity leave lasts for 18.5 weeks, while paid paternity leave lasts for 2.3 weeks.

Note that "men and women use parental leave differently. They're judged differently for it, too," as a *TIME* magazine article of the same title asserts. They found that men are more likely to use their leave away from the household, engaging in leisure or professional networking. Women, are more likely to use parental leave in the home and for childcare activities.

Adding a child to the family is an ideal time to discuss the distribution of household responsibilities. Don't assume your roles, plan them. Schedule leisure time intentionally. If your partner needs to stay connected while on leave, set clear boundaries around work tasks. Establish flexible expectations that can adapt to your family's changing needs, both during leave and after a return to work.

Embrace creativity and adaptability. If a plan isn't working, reassess and make adjustments. Achieving a sense of balance at home often depends on sharing childcare and household tasks, while also ensuring that both parents have time to rest and pursue their individual passions.

YOU'VE MADE THE DECISION TO STAY AT HOME

HARNESSING YOUR STEMM SUPERPOWERS AS A SAHP

"Enjoy the time, it goes so fast."

Have you heard that piece of wisdom? I personally relate to Gretchen Rubin's quote: "The days are long, but the years are short." The older my kids and I get, the more it resonates with me.

Being a SAHP can be challenging, with moments of doubt and feelings of overwhelm or underappreciation. In those moments, remember how much the hypothetical SAHP salary is worth, and remember the immense value and lasting impact your visible and invisible contributions have on your family.

From infancy to toddlerhood, to teens and beyond, each stage brings unique challenges and joys. Staying at home with babies revolves around constant needs and care. Toddlerhood introduces mobility, boundless curiosity, and the early signs of independence. School-age children begin a journey of academic, physical, and emotional development. It's truly amazing how each stage builds on the one before it!

While your routine as a SAHP may differ from your previous professional life, you can use your skills to create fun and meaningful experiences with your kids. STEMM parents, for example, often excel in math and science and can explore a wide range of exciting topics. Seize the opportunity to introduce your children to the fascinating world of STEMM!

Engage your child in what you love, choose topics you're comfortable with, and remember that children of all ages are capable of understanding complex ideas when those ideas are scaled to their age and ability.

There is research to support the idea of sharing complex topics with kids. As the National Association for the Education of Young Children (NAEYC) explains, "young children are capable of engaging in, at developmentally appropriate levels, the scientific practices that high school students carry out."

Encourage your young ones to observe, predict, experiment, and make sense of their findings. This creates space for everyone to practice engineering habits, including "systems thinking, creativity, optimism, communication, collaboration, supported persistence, and attention to ethical thinking," even during free play.

As a fearless STEMM mom, you have an added opportunity to show that women are resourceful, amazing, strong, smart, trailblazing, and so much more. Your influence on your kids is powerful and lasting!

Engage	Ways to integrate STEMM with children of all ages
Read	Find STEMM-themed children's books or listen to audiobooks and podcasts.
Volunteer	Spend time at school for math, science, makerspaces, or reading programs.
Explore	Consider nature walks or visiting science museums and aquariums.
Play	Incorporate STEMM into imaginary play and block play.
Watch	Share time together watching science educators and documentaries across various media platforms.
Get curious	Encourage "outside-of-the-box" thinking and questions by asking "What do you think?" or "Why might that be?" Highlight STEMM design principles, emphasizing the importance of accepting and learning from failures.
Be creative	Build a home environment where STEMM topics are openly discussed, including current events.

Share your love for STEMM. Your excitement is contagious!

MEASURING YOUR SUCCESS

Full-time parenting is rewarding and filled with positive moments, but it lacks formal performance reviews or bonuses to counterbalance the rough days. Negative feedback is inevitable—kids might not like dinner, the house may be dusty, dishes can pile up, or your activity choices get dismissed. My teens went from loving activities with me to responding with eyerolls, but our conversations have become deeper and more interesting.

Allow your definition of success to evolve as you and your kids grow, and take time to celebrate the small wins you notice along the way.

FEELING ALONE - NAVIGATING PURPOSE AND COMMUNITY

Being a SAHP can feel isolating, which is why forming even a small community is immensely valuable. Building connections with other parents takes effort, but it's worth it.

Initially, my core village consisted of four women and our toddlers. We met weekly for songs, art, stories, playtime, and adult conversation. The group eventually dissolved when the kids entered different schools. Later, classroom parents took turns watching younger siblings so others could volunteer. Now, with teens, I connect with other moms at activities and through their friends' families.

When my younger child entered school, I embraced more volunteer roles, from leading art lessons to heading the parent group. When the math club dissolved, I created a during-school STEAM program. For seven years, I ran this 90-minute program, choosing topics I loved and blending critical concepts with fun, engaging projects. Although the preparation was substantial, it became one of my most cherished volunteer efforts. Sharing my love for science, engineering, and math—while fostering resiliency and inspiring kids—was incredibly rewarding!

If school volunteering isn't for you, that's okay! Pursue opportunities that bring you joy: coaching, starting or joining activity clubs, singing in a choir, participating in a book club, attending a gym, or connecting through professional organizations. These experiences can build community, develop skills, and expand your network. Alternatively, consider exploring part-time work while your kids are in school if that suits your lifestyle better. What fulfills your heart and gives you a sense of purpose?

STEMM mom Lindsey, BS in Mathematics, U.S., shared, "Volunteering is what gave me a purpose and an identity outside of 'mom.' It gave me a community and network and friends."

Try to get what *you* desire out of your time as a stay-at-home parent.

This season of life is temporary.

TAKE CARE OF YOU

Make time for yourself, even with a busy schedule. I understand the hesitation to add "one more thing," especially with all the responsibilities moms carry—kids, work, extended family, and more—often putting their own needs last. You may need time to rest and recover, exercise, binge-watch a show, or do something you love to recharge. If longer breaks aren't possible, even squeezing in 5 to 10 minutes for breathwork, listening to music, or taking a short walk can offer a much-needed pause in the whirlwind of motherhood.

TIME FOR WORKFORCE RE-ENTRY

The decision to return to the workforce can be just as complex as the decision to stay home in the first place.

Moms, whether in the workforce or at home as SAHPs, often carry the majority of household responsibilities, both mentally and physically. During the COVID-19 pandemic, as highlighted in a *Scientific American* article by Mothers in Science, many mothers were "forced to quit their jobs or reduce working hours to juggle homeschooling and caregiving."[1]

WHAT WE WISH WE KNEW BEFORE RETURNING TO THE WORKFORCE

STEMM moms who were surveyed shared a variety of tips for returning to work. While not all advice will fit every situation, consider how each piece of wisdom might inform and inspire your own unique journey.

> **Document your skills.** Creatively update your resume and connect your SAHP experiences to professional skills.

> **Maintain and build connections in your network.** Some women surveyed re-entered the workforce by leveraging previous professional relationships. Stay connected with former colleagues, professional organizations, and even other parents. Consider finding a mentor who can offer guidance, support, and insight from a career or professional perspective.

> **Signal your interest.** Let your network know that you're seeking job opportunities. Getting your resume noticed can be challenging. Tapping into your connections may help you reach decision-makers more effectively. Using social media platforms can also boost your visibility and open doors to new opportunities.

> **Expand your skillset.** Learn new programs and technologies through online courses, educational websites, or in-person classes. Use job descriptions and role expectations to identify

---

[1] See Chapters 4, *Ideal Worker vs. Ideal Parent,* and Chapter 9, *Navigating Motherhood Alongside Career,* for more.

which skills to develop or strengthen.

Know your worth. You are not new to the workforce and your work as a SAHP is valuable, even if you have not been getting paid!

Express your needs. Can you build flexibility into your schedule? If you need to pick up your kids from school, could you work from home in the afternoon? Can you or your partner adjust your workday, starting earlier or later, so you can share before- and after-school care? If your job is inflexible, is there someone in your network you can ask for help?

Explore re-entry programs. Research and contact companies and women's groups who offer resources and opportunities for SAHPs returning to work.

Decide on childcare. Determine your family's childcare solution before accepting a position. If possible, implement the arrangement in advance of your return to the office. This will give you time to prepare for the job and help your child adjust gradually to the new routine.

Practice stress management. Develop habits that help you manage stress as you prepare to return to the workforce. Schedule mini-breaks throughout the day or plan longer breaks when possible to rest, recharge, and re-energize.[2]

BE PREPARED FOR REALITIES

While a SAHP hopes for a smooth transition back to work, it's wise to be prepared for unforeseen realities by considering the following:

Adjust expectations. Caroline, BASc in Mechanical Engineering, U.S., shared, "When I returned, it was never quite the same. I took a big step back in my career. That being said, I would not have changed staying home." Jane D., PhD in Biomedical Engineering, Canada, reflected, "Sometimes the effects of time

---

[2] See Chapter 5, *From Surviving to Thriving*, for stress-management techniques.

away can take a while to come out—for example, that career advancement piece was really delayed for me."

Be ready for new challenges. Coworkers may not fully understand the scope of your parental responsibilities, such as caring for a sick child or coordinating vacation time around school breaks. Jen, PhD in Computer Science, U.S., shared, "It was hard when my kids didn't sleep and I came to work the next day with headaches, or when they got sick, or daycare was closed. That time felt like a treadmill of dual demands."

Consider how you will handle pressure. Jane D. spent time in academia and felt intense pressure to be productive upon returning. "This is especially detrimental to academics who need to 'produce' after grad school if they want a hope of getting funding and becoming a professor or running a research lab. While I knew I had technical skills that didn't disappear and, if anything, certain transferable skills were strengthened at home, I did not continue to develop the maturity and intuition that I would have if I'd stayed in the workforce."

Seek support if you encounter bias. As a mother, you may face discrimination. One mom, despite having 20 years of previous work experience, found that the title of "Mother" impacted her re-entry into the workforce more than simply being a woman. If you encounter discrimination, seek support from company resources, mentors, or your professional network.

Refresh family norms. Determine your priorities and accept that you can't do it all. Give yourself grace when routines shift or expectations change. Maybe your kids start buying school lunch, you miss a sports practice or piano lesson, or you're only able to volunteer for part of the science fair, and that's okay.

Negotiate household duties. Once again, reassess and redistribute household responsibilities. Take your new family schedule into account and put an updated plan into action. Adjust your standards and expectations to align with the demands of both work and parenting. Remember, your plan can and should evolve as new routines take shape.

Ask for help. Rely on your support network and be creative in managing your time and responsibilities. Consider options such as hiring a house cleaner, participating in a nanny share, seeking help from extended family, delegating tasks, or arranging carpools. You might also explore public or company-sponsored transportation, which can turn commute time into productive time.

Offer yourself grace. There will be days when you feel like an amazing employee, mom, and partner—and other days when you feel like you're falling short in every role. One mom shared, "The guilt of leaving my babies, along with the constant balancing act of work, pumping, and finding time to be with them, made it one of the most difficult periods of my life."

Advocate for others. Once you're settled, look for ways to support other women and moms navigating similar challenges. Help someone find a pumping location, advocate for a flexible or hybrid work environment, offer understanding to those facing parental struggles, and share helpful tips and tricks. As you advance professionally, avoid "pulling the ladder up." Instead, extend a hand to support those coming up behind you.[3]

Embrace the return. I loved working toward new goals, having fresh conversations, feeling a different kind of energy, and collaborating as part of a team. One mom shared, "My team asked me if it was hard to be back at work—one might have even said 'back from your time off.' I laughed. We were literally sitting around talking, drinking coffee that was still hot, and no one was crying anywhere. Work is easy. Less rewarding, but much easier in terms of total energy consumed."

---

[3] See Chapters 20 and 21, *Advocacy* and *Allies*, respectively, for more.

Continue to trust yourself. There is no single path for re-entering the workforce. It will be challenging at times, but trust in your ability to succeed. If returning to work doesn't go as planned, take time to reassess your goals or adjust your path. Keep networking, stay open to opportunities, and continue moving forward on your journey toward where you want to be.

Navigating the Path Forward

From the moment you're expecting a child to holding a newborn for the first time, everything changes. Parenting brings shared decisions—some instinctive, others learned through trial by fire. Regardless of how long you are a SAHP, and whether or not you return to the workforce, your unique journey will include both triumphs and challenges.

Trust your instincts. Continually evaluate and balance your priorities and goals, keeping your family's needs in mind. Embrace this phase as you shape a life that fulfills your family. It's okay to be a little selfish. Don't let go of your dreams.

Adapt, compromise, and pivot as needed to create your own path forward.

It was a daily 20-minute battle to get my son to read six sentences. School placed him in a reading intervention group, but it was just more of the same. He hated reading too much to try.[1] ADHD medication helped for a while. Not even his favorite video game could motivate him to read text. Audiobooks were the only bridge that bypassed reading to build essential comprehension skills.

When I asked the school what else we could try, the answer was "more of the same." As someone with ADHD myself, I knew that "trying harder" wasn't the answer. I turned to our Employee Assistance Program (EAP), but most specialists referred us back to the school until one finally told me the secret insider's code: Request a special education assessment in writing. Legally, the school had to respond within 15 days.[2]

Despite more pushback from the system, we pursued the testing. The result? A clear orthographic processing deficit, a form of dyslexia. With that diagnosis, everything changed. The school offered an Orton-Gillingham curriculum and accommodations. We were moving forward at last!

A year later, I saw my son walking toward me, nose in a book.

"Who is this kid?" He's reading something, voluntarily!

He's now thriving, smiling in photos, and full of confidence. We've traded medication for supplements, and reading practice no longer feels like a battlefield.

The takeaway: Trust your gut and keep moving forward. If something's not working, troubleshoot. Advocate for yourself and those you love. And remember: a label isn't a limitation, it can be a lifeline.

– Anonymous

---

[1] Hating reading is very common for dyslexic kids and warning sign that they need help.

[2] I learned later that to automatically trigger an assessment a student must be two years behind grade level standard. Ironically, all the effort we put in kept him above that threshold.

Eleven

Charting Your Own Course

NAVIGATING BEYOND TRADITIONAL STEMM ROLES

by Jaymi T. Cormier, engineer turned scientist, turned mom of three, turned entrepreneur—curious and daring enough to chart her own course.

> There is freedom waiting for you,
> On the breezes of the sky,
> And you ask "What if I fall?"
> Oh but my darling,
> What if you fly?
>
> — Erin Hanson

Sailing has been an important part of my life since I was about ten years old. My family had never owned a boat, but one summer, my parents decided to register me and my three brothers in a sailing camp so we could give the sport a try. I was immediately hooked.

I loved that a boat offered a direct connection to the natural world: you can actually feel the sails harness the power of the wind as the energy is translated into forward acceleration, carrying you across the surface of the water. You move with the rhythm and sound of the waves, birds soaring overhead as the warmth of the sun embraces you. It is truly an ethereal experience.

One day, when I was about 18, I was crewing on a 30-foot yacht off the coast of Nova Scotia, Canada, on our return home from a race. We were several hours into our journey and could see land on the horizon off the starboard side. All was well. Then the fog rolled in.

It happened rather quickly, and we suddenly found ourselves completely engulfed in an opaque blanket of cool mist. Beyond a couple of meters in any direction, all visibility was lost. Staring into fog makes your eyes ache with strain, as there is nothing on which to set your focus. In the dampness, the chill slowly begins to set in. Worst of all, you become immediately disoriented, stripped of all external landmarks with which to mark your position.

Respect the elements indeed.

The helmsman and owner of the boat was unsure what to do. As luck would have it, a good friend of ours, who had a great deal of experience with sailing and navigation, had joined us for the sail home. He quickly went below, pulled out a nautical chart and plotting tools, and within minutes called out our heading. With the use of the steering compass and a few regular check-ins with our chart, we were able to navigate ourselves home with no visibility.

I learned a valuable lesson that day: a bit of knowledge, a few basic tools, and the right team around you can help you determine your course when you find yourself without a visible path.

– Jaymi

This chapter is written first and foremost for women who, for whatever reason, decide it's time to venture off a clearly defined career path in STEMM. Perhaps the decision is to leave STEMM altogether, or perhaps a new route can be found that allows for better alignment with values and priorities.

There is no shortage of reports highlighting the exodus of women at each stage along both academic and non-academic career paths in STEMM. Many of these reports note that the occurrence is more common for women in STEMM compared to other professions, more prevalent for women than for men, and not solely a response to parenting or caregiving responsibilities. Indeed, the drivers of this phenomenon are complex and multifaceted.

Many of the contributors to this book have shared the experience of needing to chart a new course. We offer our reflections, along with some strategies that helped us navigate this transition, in the hope that it makes your journey a little easier.

What Do You Want to Be When You Grow Up?

The question "What do you want to be?" sets us up to plan our entire future by forcing us to select a "job," a pre-defined construct. By extension, we become fully aware of the external expectations imposed upon us. We now have a target and a clear set of indicators against which to measure ourselves. I suppose this kind of forecasting eases the brain's inherent drive to make predictions and supports planning and decision-making to ensure our survival. It is not altogether a bad thing. This clarity certainly brought me great peace of mind, knowing I had a well-defined destination and a path to get there.

Importantly, however, the selection of a "job" establishes a set of binary conditions, especially in academia: you are on the path, or you are not. You fit in the box, or you do not. This can create a very challenging situation if, for any reason, the job you once chose no longer feels like a good fit.

In my journey to become a tissue engineer, having completed a bachelor's degree in engineering, I found myself at the end of a master's degree needing to make my first course adjustment. I was married at the time, and the decision to move and pursue my dream job was no longer one I could make on my own. Life had become more complicated.

Despite my initial aspirations to work in industry, when an opportunity at my current institution presented itself, I agreed. This path would also satisfy my partner's needs, and I set off in pursuit of a doctorate degree. With the chance to work in industry or academia, I could still clearly see potential destinations; the path had simply taken an unexpected turn.

Unfortunately, I had forgotten how quickly the fog could roll in.

With a one-year-old in tow, I managed to write and defend my thesis. With a perfect 4.0 GPA, 12 peer-reviewed publications, a book chapter, a patent application filed, and a solid track record of prestigious scholarships, there was nothing but opportunity on the horizon. Through all the handshakes, shoulder pats, and congratulations, I finally had to confront the big question: where would I pursue my post-doctoral fellowship?

With a Master's and PhD from the same institution, I knew that to "level up" and be taken seriously within the academy, I would have to move away to pursue a post-doctoral fellowship (or two) at another institution, ideally abroad. I was an excellent budding scientist, full of potential to maybe one day become a leading scholar in my field. And yet, with a babe in arms and a husband firmly rooted, his sights set on his own career ambitions, I was not convinced that this was a path I could follow. Despite my initial conviction to become a tissue engineer, a quick glance at industry job postings did not offer much more inspiration. Full-time work with travel commitments did not align well with my desire to stay close to my new little one.

When I finally had the nerve to say out loud that I would not pursue a faculty career path, something very unexpected happened: everyone evaporated. All momentum and promise for the future, my future, was gone. There was no debrief, no interest in where I might go or what I might do, and no council on alternate career paths I might consider. I was left standing there alone, and for the first time in my life, I had no path in front of me, only fog.

The trick is to find what you are passionate about and do that.

Academics are trained, groomed, and indoctrinated to prove they are experts in their work. The perfectionism and fear of failure that are cultivated can have devastating consequences when a traditional faculty career path is, for whatever reason, no longer an option. It would seem that this feeling of isolation, of being lost in the fog, "rudderless" as one of my co-authors described it, is unfortunately not unique. In fact, Belinda, another co-author of this book, makes her living as a coach for people looking to leave the academy.

In sailing, dead reckoning is the most basic way of estimating your position using your last known location, your course, and your speed. What indicators do you have to determine where you are in your life? How will you know if you are moving in the right direction? In my experience, there are a few tools that are invaluable in helping you find your way.

Tool 1. Lean into your intrinsic gifts to establish your position

> Perhaps instead of asking, "What do you want to be when you grow up?" we should be asking, "Who do you want to be?" What are the values and principles you would like to live by? What are your gifts? Your passions?

I was introduced to someone who became a mentor during my transition to starting my own business. He offered me two pieces of advice that became the nudge I needed to make the terrifying leap to founder and business owner. We'll discuss the second piece further below, but the first was this: *you might be good at a lot of things; the trick is to find what you are passionate about and do that.*

When you depart from a well-defined path, where there are clear external indicators and expectations of your professional identity, progress, and success, there is an opportunity to pause, shift your gaze inward, and *remember the things that bring you joy.* Then, *look for ways to weave these gifts into your profession. Your passions can become the foundation for how you bring value to key interest parties in your ecosystem.*

The process of deep reflection and writing allowed me to see the common threads woven through different life experiences that brought me joy. It allowed me to articulate my passions. I found the *The Lightmaker's Manifesto* by Karen Walrond very insightful. I worked through the prompted reflections from the book, and in the process, learned that I love connecting with people and am deeply activated when I have the opportunity to create, strategize, and problem solve.

Harnessing these gifts became the foundation of my consultancy. I engage with collaborative teams to facilitate the development of compelling and impact-focused research initiatives. Together, we build new ideas, strategize, engage partners, and map pathways to impact. In this way, I work with scientists to ensure their research can have a positive effect on the world.

Inspired by *The Lightmaker's Manifesto*, I've included a set of reflection questions to help you do the same. Considering what you are passionate about can become a powerful tool as you begin to chart your own course and determine your position.

Reflections | Your Joy

Consider what brings you joy—both at work and at home.

With deeper reflection about what it was that sparked
the joy, common themes can start to emerge.

Give it a try. Go write it down. You might be surprised
with the patterns that begin to emerge.

COURAGE OVER CONFIDENCE: NO PINK POWER SUITS

During my PhD, I was invited to participate in a number of public education initiatives focused on the research our team was leading. In doing so, I discovered that I have a knack for communicating science in a way that is accessible and intriguing to broad audiences. Since I had made the decision not to pursue a post-doctoral fellowship abroad, I turned to the research institute I had been working with during my graduate program and noticed a gap I might be able to fill.

I was good at building partnerships and communicating science beyond the academy. What if I could do that on behalf of the researchers in the institute? What if I could help get others excited about the work we were leading? Maybe I could help mobilize the research in new ways, reaching users and beneficiaries outside the academic sphere.

I pitched the idea to the institute director, who agreed that this would indeed be quite useful. Over five years in this new role, I catalyzed partnerships, led public engagement initiatives, and helped secure funding through grants and philanthropic collaborations.

My subsequent position at a new university unfolded in much the same way. I had the opportunity to pitch the idea for a role that would support research teams with partnership engagement and knowledge translation, and I was delighted when this was again met with enthusiasm. I worked in this role for five years and, in addition to supporting teams with knowledge translation planning, I created a new framework for engaging multidisciplinary teams to proactively build collaborative, impact-focused research initiatives.

Leaning into my passions allowed me to see the research ecosystem through a new lens, and I began to notice how my gifts could bring value to others. With no existing path, no predefined job title, and a little serendipity, I had found a way to build my own position.

Luck is what happens when preparation meets opportunity.

– Seneca
Roman Philosopher

I loved my work and deeply valued the opportunity to engage with the research community. Unfortunately, new and ill-defined positions can be tricky within a very traditional and hierarchical system that thrives on clear boxes and strict processes.

As it turns out, I don't do well in a box.

I am a creator, an innovator, a builder. I seek opportunities to connect people in new ways and to inspire new ideas. This often involves working outside "my lane," and, needless to say, it was soon time for me to decide once again: do I mould myself to fit into the trifling box laid out in front of me, or do I take the leap and chart my own course?

Answering this one question was anything but simple. It led to months of rumination and turmoil. I felt caught in a storm, again. I was now a single mom of three and not in a position to take on significant financial risk or face unemployment. But I also knew I could no longer stay where I was, because the storm there was real too.

As I alluded to above, I had the immense fortune of being introduced to someone who is highly regarded in the higher education ecosystem. To my surprise, this individual offered to be my "wingman" and generously made time in his busy schedule to meet with me almost weekly, as I timidly and painstakingly began the journey of starting my own business. I knew that my gifts and skills brought value to the research ecosystem. My concern was whether I could succeed independently. Me, a founder and CEO, running a business on the sidewalk in front of the ivory tower.

I was not convinced.

My mentor's second piece of advice was this: *This journey has no rearview mirror. Don't look back.* He encouraged me to follow through despite being afraid.

By now, I hope you can appreciate that the fear is real. I still have it. Will my clients find value in my services? Will the projects dry up? Will I make a difference in the world? Will I mess up my corporate taxes? Can I actually lead a business? As one of my co-authors put it, *"I am so sick of hearing that all I need to do is put on a pink power suit and just be confident."*

Tool 2. Gain speed through courage.

> Departing from a well-defined path to chart your own course does not require confidence, or a pink power suit for that matter. But it does require a great deal of courage.
>
> *The fear is real, and it might always be there.*

However, fear should not be the only reason you don't proceed. You can feel the fear, carry it with you, and if the next move seems logical, strategic, or it just "feels right," you can still step forward. Each time we push ourselves to move forward through the fear, each time we take a step despite being afraid, we build confidence.

I did it once. I can do this again.

And if it doesn't work, I know I can figure it out.

CREATING YOUR OWN INDICATORS TO MEASURE SUCCESS

Graduating with an engineering degree from a Canadian university grants you the privilege of attending an iron ring ceremony. Closed to all except those with iron rings, it is a ceremony where new engineering graduates are presented with their rings and affirm their commitment to the conscientious practice of their profession.

Despite the sweat and tears I had poured into my engineering degree, about a year after the ceremony, I stopped wearing my iron ring. Since I hadn't followed the traditional path to become a professional engineer, I felt I wasn't really an engineer. And in choosing to depart from the faculty career path at the end of my PhD, I now felt I wasn't really a scientist either. I had more than a decade of post-secondary education behind me, but, feeling alarmed and far too young for an existential crisis, all I could think was, well, what the heck am I?

I was recently invited to participate in a panel discussion. It was organized by graduate students, and the intent was to bring people together to discuss the meaning of failure, redefining success, and how to evaluate success when breaking away from the traditional academic career path. One of the questions I was asked to prepare for was: "With all that you have learned, how do you evaluate your success?"

My answer is simple: with my own yardstick.

Cheeky, I realize, but the point I hoped to make was that when you decide it's time to chart your own course, you are left without an external framework against which to measure yourself. Although this can be unnerving, it can also be an opportunity.

As mentioned earlier, clearly defined parameters and boundaries create the illusion that you are either in or out. And if you are out, the lack of definition often leads us to a default conclusion of: "I failed." I have now come to a place where I try my best to take a blended and balanced approach to assessing my own success. I know what indicators matter to the research ecosystem, and I certainly incorporate some of those into my self-assessment. But I also measure non-negotiable elements that matter to me, such as:

- Time investment in my mental and physical wellbeing.
- Time spent with my children and family.
- The portfolio of projects I choose to engage with and whether I believe they can have a positive impact on the world.
- Clients that value my services and feel they have benefited from working with me.

For me, joy, fulfilment, recognition, and even revenue are all outcomes of making conscious and intentional choices that align my actions with these indicators. I don't get it right every day, but on average, over time, I strive to keep these indicators in balance. Like my dad always said, "Don't chase success. Do good work, the success will follow." And with my own yardstick, I get to decide for myself what success means.

Tool 3. Chart your course using your own indicators.

The transition away from a predetermined career path offers an opportunity to pause and reflect on what "success" means to you.

The reality is, no matter what our career choice, we will be professionally measured against imperfect sets of indicators created by others. However, we can remind ourselves that we are so much more than a job title, and give ourselves permission and space to reflect on and define what success looks like for us. These personal indicators can help us understand whether we are headed in the right direction. For any given "job," they can also be combined with some external measures to create a more personalized and balanced set.

It takes courage to advocate for what we need in a world where we have been conditioned to seek external validation through frameworks we did not design. But the practice of identifying our own indicators and assessing ourselves against those can help ensure we are moving in the right direction, aligned with our own goals and values, especially when we lack a clear path.

Remember that there are tools that can help you chart your course toward clearer skies, and there are people out there who genuinely want to see you succeed.

There have been several iterations of the following quote, attributed to different people: *You can't control the wind, but you can adjust your sails.* We will all encounter the fog and the storms at some point in our journey. And the degree of difficulty in navigating this turbulence will often be influenced by the privilege granted by one's race, gender, sexual orientation, able-bodiedness, education, or economic status. The key is to remember that there are tools that can help you chart your course toward clearer skies, and there are people out there who genuinely want to see you succeed.

And, in case you were wondering, I started wearing my iron ring two years ago, when I decided to start my own consulting practice.

I haven't taken it off since.

Key Take Aways

To mid-career women who are curious about charting their own course:

- Remind yourself that "jobs" are predetermined constructs, not your identity. You can choose to chart your own course and define a career that is better tailored for you. You can establish your own definition of success. It won't necessarily be easy, but it will be rewarding. A colleague of mine who has since become a confidant and friend once said to me: "If you don't feel that you are in a good situation, then you go, and you shoot for the stars."

- As another of my new mentors stated so cleverly, "You see Jaymi, you jumped but you wouldn't have fallen. You had your *NET-work* to catch you." I had not appreciated the value that my network offered until I set off to start my own business. Invest time in your relationships through an approach built on reciprocity and mutual benefit. This network of teammates becomes an invaluable asset in your personal and professional journey, especially if you decide it's time to chart your own course.

- Good mentors can be hard to find, but they are out there. People will not do the work for you, but there are people all around you who genuinely want to see you succeed and will help you on your journey.

- Remember: you might be good at lots of things. Figure out what you are passionate about and do that.

- The fear is real, but it shouldn't be the only reason why you don't proceed. Taking small steps despite the fear can help build confidence and growth over time. Do your homework and bet on yourself. As Cassie says: "I realized that if I started my own company, my first employee would be a great one!"

Twelve

Academia

MOVING EQUITY FROM MARGINS TO MAINSTREAM

by Jessica G. Borger, Aussie immunologist, equity crusader, and mum juggling STEMM, family, and smashing glass ceilings.

After completing my PhD in immunology, I began my career as a junior academic researcher in a biological field where women equal or possibly outnumber men. At first, the gender inequities I encountered seemed limited to the usual but problematic societal norms. For example, a senior leader once 'French' kissed the women as they arrived at the Christmas party. Apparently, in France, you receive a kiss on each cheek. Fascinating, but we were not in France; we were in Scotland.

However, as I became more senior, the landscape shifted dramatically. I experienced what it felt like to be a minority: being misunderstood in lab meetings and needing a man to repeat my words to be heard, only to watch silently as he was given, and accepted, credit for the ideas; being excluded from collaborations because the boys made those decisions at the pub; being overlooked for conference invitations because I had just returned from parental leave, so how could I possibly travel, as the umbilical cord must still be attached; and being omitted from publication authorships to avoid cluttering the list of senior men. I still remember a tokenistic email I received, inviting me, verbatim, to chair a symposium as "a woman is needed to ensure gender equity." There was no mention of my expertise or outstanding skillset.

Yes, I have been the only woman in the room. Yes, I have had to slam my laptop shut and state that it was my turn to be heard. And yes, I have had to ask men on more than one occasion to please take a seat because I felt intimidated by them standing over me at my desk.

Despite these challenges, I am proud to be a woman in academia. I refuse to let the system push me out of my chosen career. I will only leave if I choose to, and on my own terms.

– Jessica

An academic in STEMM conducts research within their area of expertise, publishes scientific findings in peer-reviewed journals, applies for grants to fund their research and secure a salary, collaborates with other researchers to tackle complex scientific challenges, and presents their findings at scientific meetings. I relished, or rather, I used to relish every aspect of being an immunology researcher, hoping that my hours spent in the dark, looking down a microscope, would in some part contribute to the advancement of my field and be leveraged to provide benefit to society.

But I left research to become an educator.

If every part of what it takes to be a researcher in STEMM made me thrive, could I be so privileged and yet still not happy?

CHALLENGES IN ACADEMIA

Let's first discuss the peer review process, which has been the most important mechanism for quality control in science for decades. Groups of scientific experts, including peers and colleagues, judge the work of other scientists to allocate research funding, identify manuscripts with high scientific merit for publication, confer award recognitions, evaluate job applications and promotions, select presentations for conferences, and, more recently, investigate cases of scientific misconduct.

The peer review process has the potential to be equitable, if inequities did not already exist within the system. For example, a "Daversity" problem persists in STEMM, with men named "David" in Australia having been awarded eight times more grants than those with the most common women's names.

Metrics that solely measure scientific rigor, such as research publications, have not overwhelmingly been shown to exhibit gender bias. However, peer review processes for grants, hiring, and promotion are unblinded and specifically judge the researcher's academic profile and leadership. This paves the way for reviewer biases to influence outcomes. Reviewers' decisions are susceptible to systemic biases based on the information available to them, such as the applicant's gender, race, or affiliated institution. Funding agencies report lower success rates for women researchers, as well as for non-white applicants.

The **Matilda Effect** captures a well-established tendency to undervalue women's scientific achievements, so it must be assumed that gendered stereotypes will influence their experiences. Returning to our initial question, how could I not be happy as a researcher in STEMM, we should reframe it as: "How could I not be happy as a 'woman' researcher in STEMM?" Even then, it remains a challenging question, as each woman's experience in STEMM is uniquely shaped by her intersectionality.

Matilda Effect, *noun:*

A form of bias in which women's scientific achievements
are misattributed to colleagues who are men.

How Did Academia Get Here?

Girls and women have made tremendous gains in education and now make up around half of the university-educated academics entering STEMM. However, inequities within STEMM remain. Men continue to far outnumber women in engineering and mathematical fields, including economics and computer science. In contrast, women are overrepresented in the life sciences and psychology, although those numbers have remained largely unchanged for nearly 30 years.

Exactly where do these inequities start in an academic's career journey?

THE SCISSOR SHAPED CURVE

Regardless of the STEMM field, a significant gendered divergence emerges in career trajectories, commonly referred to as the **scissor effect**. At the mid-career stage, which is a pressure point perfectly aligned with the moment academics are forging their independence, women's careers markedly diverge from those of men. This stage often coincides with family-building years. It is at this point that women begin to leave the system in increasing numbers, particularly as seniority and leadership increases.

Indeed, fewer than 30% of the world's STEMM professionals are women. Even those who continue to advance in their academic careers tend not to progress at the same pace, and far fewer reach the same level as men as their careers develop.

This is the leaky pipeline in action: mid-career women leaving academia and taking their expert knowledge and unique skill sets with them. As they depart, we're all left with diminished potential for diversity in scientific discovery and its benefits to society. The illustration on page 166 captures many of these prevailing influences along this journey.

Hopefully this book is showing you that the causes driving women from STEMM are far more complex than simply trying to fix that annoying, constant drip. We can't just tighten the tap. Before we begin to fix the system, (not the women), we must first investigate the water source. Let's explore more around what gender bias actually looks like in an academic STEMM setting.

GENDERED BIAS IN ACTION

Bias itself refers to the unjustifiable treatment of individuals based on specific characteristics; in our case, gender.

I remember, as an early career researcher, being grabbed on the ass at a Christmas party. But wait, it wasn't *like that*. It was only a "prank" by a technology facility manager I relied on to analyse my samples. He was "just" trying to make it look like his mate, an Associate Professor and Lab Head in my department, had grabbed my ass instead.

"Hilarious, that's fine," said *no* woman ever.

But bias does not always present itself sexually.

> I was once "reminded" by my supervisor how lucky I was that he had hired me. "Obviously," as a mother of a small child, he presumed I would probably have another soon, which he believed would delay *his* research program.

And bias can be far more subtle.

> I think every woman reading this has heard something like this from a man at work before: "How did you not know about drinks at the pub on Friday after work? We were all there."
>
> *We*, being the men.

Bias can also be far harder to call out as it's complicated.

"Relative to opportunity" is a section in grant applications where researchers list career disruptions that should be considered when evaluating publication frequency, grant success, and overall research impact. But the real question is: how do peer reviewers actually take this into account when comparing me to men applying at the same career stage?

> Indeed, a colleague's application for promotion was denied on the grounds that she was "unable to demonstrate sustained trajectory," as her capacity to work at a higher level had been "disrupted" after only recently returning from six months of parental leave to have a baby.
>
> I took 12 months of parental leave. During that time, no one worked on my research. I didn't write grants or publications (though I do remember breastfeeding a two-week-old in one arm while updating figures to address peer review questions for a submitted paper with my free hand). I didn't attend conferences or seminars. Over the next four and a half years, I accrued another 12 months of disruption because I worked four days a week.
>
> How are these two years of interruptions interpreted, measured, and reflected? How am I compared to men at the same career stage without two years of career disruption?

Unless a reviewer explicitly accounts for these factors, how do we know whether these adjustments are being considered appropriately?

	KEY INFLUENCES		
	Gendered Play	Access to Schooling, Access to STEMM Curriculum, Gendered Norms	STEMM Subject Availability, Gendered Norms

Peers

Role models

Educators

Relatives | Counsellors

Parents and Caregivers

KEY INFLUENCERS

CAREER GROWTH

| EARLY EDUCATION | PRIMARY SCHOOL | HIGH SCHOOL |

Key issues, and associated influences, that lead to increased rates of women leaving academic STEMM careers. All of which perpetuate the scissor effect.

UNDER-GRADUATE	POST-GRADUATE	EARLY-MID CAREER, RESEARCHER	PROFESSOR
STEMM Subject Availability, Course Requirements	Conferences, Publications, Workplace Culture & Practices, Policies, Funding Sources	Family & Caregiving Responsibilities, Work Flexibility, Recruitment Practices, Job Security, International Opportunities, Career Mobility, Funding Sources	Family & Caregiving Responsibilities, Work Flexibility, Promotion Practices, Recognition & Attributions, Re-Training Opportunities, Workforce Reentry Programs, Funding Sources

Employers

Senior Leaders   Sponsors

Networks

Mentors

The system acknowledges career disruptions on paper, but in practice, how often is the playing field truly leveled? The reality is that numerous reports highlight persistent inequities in funding success for women.

MORE GRANTS, MORE MONEY—IF YOU'RE A MAN

Women face many barriers in achieving a comparable track record to men at the same academic level. Numerous publications and reports from funding bodies confirm the prevalence of gender disparities that favour men in grant funding success.

I have written extensively on this topic. In 2022, I published an article on the gender bias present in peer review, specifically in relation to research funding.

When a national newspaper here in Australia republished the piece, many of the readers' comments, instead of being supportive, were filled with disgust, hate, and misinformation. Some readers suggested that women need to "stop talking about their gender when it has nothing to do with science" or claimed that "men receive more grants because they are simply better than women at science." Considering our brains are the same, perhaps some men *do* think with their dicks?

An analysis I conducted of gendered funding outcomes from Australia's largest government funding agency, the National Health and Medical Research Council (NHMRC), revealed that although overall success rates were similar, men were disproportionately awarded a staggering 20% more grants than women. This resulted in an additional AU$400 million in funding for men to continue and progress their research within just three years of the scheme's introduction.

And it is not only happening in Australia. More men than women are receiving funding across academia worldwide, from the United States to the United Kingdom and throughout Europe.

For women, receiving less funding leads to fewer first-author and senior-author publications, which in turn results in fewer citations than men. This further reduces women's chances of future funding success.

WHAT'S IN A NAME? LESS, IF YOU ARE A WOMAN

Women are less likely than men to get authorship on scientific publications. There can be insidious challenges to authorship.

> At the start of my postdoctoral career, when securing publications was critical for early-career fellowships and establishing my independent research, I was deliberately removed as a co-author from a publication by one of the senior authors. The reason given was that the authorship list should not be "cluttered." Rather than recognising my contributions in the lab and supporting my publication record, men who had contributed little, perhaps only by paying for a coffee while discussing the results, were included without question.

Academia is highly competitive for everyone. My supervisor chose to sacrifice my career progression for the sake of boosting her own citations and future grant success.

Authorship is not always fair, and it is rarely transparent. Even at the same career stage, women are less likely than men in their research group to be listed as authors.

END THE 'DEFAULT IS MAN' BIAS

The "default is man" or masculine bias refers to the tendency for stereotypically masculine traits, such as independence and assertiveness, to be valued or regarded as the standard.

Masculine bias is often more difficult to detect than overt discrimination because it is subtle and rarely questioned. For instance, differential treatment may involve the nomination of more men than women for awards or promotions. To counter this, some organisations have introduced self-nominations. Unfortunately, this can further disadvantage women, as self-promotion is typically seen as a masculine trait and is actively discouraged in many cultures.

Masculine defaults harm women in academic STEMM fields, as women are often not socialised to display these traits. This can lead to feelings of being unsuited to environments that prioritise them, contributing to imposter syndrome and self-doubt. When women do exhibit such traits and act assertively, for example by negotiating or standing up for themselves, they often face backlash because these behaviours defy traditional gender roles.

> I was once told I was too direct in a meeting, which, apparently, justified the chair of the committee raising the palm of his hand to my face to silence me mid-sentence.

My advice here—be yourself. Don't let them make you be someone else, or silence you.

Practise advocating for yourself and standing your ground. I share plenty of advice on what this involves and how to approach it in my chapter on advocacy. It can be scary to be the only voice speaking up, so surround yourself with a strong network that can help amplify your voice. This means surround yourself with allies.

SUPPORTING WOMEN IN ACADEMIA

NETWORK FRAGMENTATION

Moving from the UK back to Australia after completing a PhD and a successful five-year postdoctoral position made me realise how important networking opportunities are in academia, especially after taking career breaks or changing workplaces and homes. Even something as simple as having a cup of coffee with colleagues can make a real difference.

On my first day in my new academic position in Australia, I was introduced to the lab's whiteboard. My name was added, and I was expected to update it constantly with my whereabouts. *At least I didn't have to note bathroom breaks. Phew, lucky me.*

> "But never put down that you're on a break for lunch or coffee. You don't take breaks for those."

> Great. I'd put on a few pounds lately—
> *maybe this was their way of helping?*

I figured I'd at least get to meet colleagues at the weekly departmental meetings But to this day, I still have no idea when those meetings actually happened, because I never left the lab bench.

In that first year back in my home country, I had never felt so alone. Alone in what should have been highly collaborative research, and incredibly isolated in the workplace.

Receiving less grant funding, fewer grants, and publishing less leads to women becoming invisible. If you don't have the research output to talk about, you won't be invited to conferences, and you won't speak with potential collaborators or reviewers of your grants and publications. Your networks, and the associated benefits, start to fragment.

I'm a good writer. I'm also persistent, and I'd like to think my research was pretty awesome, if I do say so myself. Together, this meant I was very successful in applying for conference travel grants. You need to do this if you don't have your own funding, because your supervisor's budget usually can't be used to pay for your conference registration, accommodation, and flights.

Just after receiving my first fellowship in Australia, which was my opportunity to start my own independent research and enter the cancer therapy field, a dream 1 had held since my mum was diagnosed with brain cancer, later followed by breast, bowel, and pancreatic cancer, and following the recent death of my dad from lung cancer, I was awarded a significant international travel grant to go to France and network with researchers in my new field.

Each year, established academic women in STEMM are nearly 20% more likely to leave their careers than men.

Instead of congratulating me, my supervisor simply remarked, *"You're getting good at writing these."* She then told me I could not accept the funding because my research wasn't developed enough in the field. *Clearly, the peer reviewers who awarded me the grant must have missed that memo.*

This was the same supervisor who had employed me on a base-level postdoctoral (Level A) salary after eight years of experience, and at a lower rate than the men with PhDs who had graduated from her lab just a year earlier. Even when I received my fellowship, which had budgeted for a lecturer (Level B) salary, I never received that salary increase or, more importantly, the recognition.

I often wonder what it would have been like back then if I had the networks I have now.

I felt helpless back then.

I feel powerful now.

I have power in my voice. I have power in my actions. And I know I have options.

POWER POSITIONS

Academia is not only about the research. There is a huge power differential between those who have money (funding) and those who do not.

Those with funding can get away with the inequitable behaviours.

The bad behaviour.

They can get away with all the stories I have shared because universities and medical research institutes want the income. There are so many STEMM graduates coming through the system, far more than there are jobs available, that we are all easily replaceable. This is especially true for mid-career researchers, who can be replaced with cheaper, more junior versions. After all, we might go off, have babies, and delay ongoing research progress.

I guess your next question is: why did I put up with bullying, micromanaging, and inequitable pay? Because I needed the job.

I was, and still am, the main income earner and a sandwich parent, providing for and caring for both my son and my elderly mum, who also lives with us. I was afraid that if I spoke up, my one-year contract would not be renewed. These were people with broad, established networks. What if I could not find another job if I spoke up? They might end up as reviewers of my grants or papers and sabotage my chances of success.

But ultimately, we do not stay forever. Each year, established academic women in STEMM are nearly 20% more likely to leave their careers than men.

SAYING YES

Unlike men, women often face heavier academic demands, through implied obligations to serve on committees, explicit expectations to provide pastoral care, and expectations or requirements to shoulder larger teaching loads. These compounded responsibilities reduce the opportunities women have to focus on their research.

During my postdoctoral research, I was also a journal editor, participated in early career researcher and gender equity committees, contributed to teaching through guest lectures and tutoring, and became a well-known science communicator in my field. I appeared on STEMM panel events and career pathway seminars, was interviewed on the radio, and published in mainstream media.

Why did I say yes so often? Because I wasn't publishing enough, or winning grants, or attending conferences. I needed to fill my CV with other achievements to prove my worth. This was all extra, on top of the job I was actually paid to do. It was all unpaid work. It was done late at night, early in the morning, and on weekends. It took time away from my family, my friends, and myself.

Women often feel pressured to say yes to every opportunity. But it is just as important to say no, because every yes to something new is also a no to the time, energy, and priorities that truly matter.

LIFT HER UP, DON'T PUT HER DOWN

You may have heard of the term *Queen Bee*, but what does it really mean?

Too often, women are seen as competitors rather than allies, reinforcing the idea that there's only room for one at the top. This is especially true in academia, where limited funding and job prospects mean we are quite literally competing for grants and fellowships. We continuously compare our metrics and CVs against others across teams, departments, institutes, and oceans.

Sadly, women who do bully in the workplace, target other women 80% of the time.

> I've won a number of awards for gender equity. But the Vice-Chancellor's Award for Gender Equity from my university was my first-ever glass trophy. Big moment, right? So, I dressed up for the occasion in my classy electric blue jacket, black leather pants, and heels. Because, hey, this old gal still had it.
>
> But instead of a "Congrats," a postdoc in my department joked that they should just take a photo of me in that jacket, pretending to hold a trophy, since I've stood like that so many times before. Then, to save time, just superimpose the award on my posed picture.
>
> That was the last time I ever wore that jacket.

The big problem is that when there are few women in leadership, they are frequently compared to one another, creating unnecessary competition. This can cause women leaders to distance themselves from supporting other women in an effort to avoid the tug-of-war bias.

It's fair to say that some women have had challenging experiences with bosses who are women. I've shared some of my own experiences throughout this chapter. But we also need to remember that many women, including myself, have had supportive and inspiring women supervisors, just as we've encountered both good and bad bosses who are men.

It's important to create opportunities for everyone and to lead by example. Should I promote more women than men to help balance the system? I genuinely don't know. But the one thing I do know is that pushing other women down to bring someone else up is not the answer.

Too often, women are seen as competitors rather than allies, reinforcing the idea that there's only room for one at the top.

As long as women remain under-represented at the top, they will continue to be judged collectively and subjected to greater scrutiny. Instead of viewing women leaders through a single lens, we must recognise that leadership comes in many forms. By supporting and championing one another, we can break these stereotypes and create a workplace where women lead, mentor, and thrive together.

How Can We All Drive Change?

I guess you are wondering why we stay in academia.

We love what we do! We are STEMM researchers and we get to do really cool research. Really cool research we trained really hard to do.

Be The Leader You Want To Follow

Making a meaningful difference that shifts the dial is what motivates me as a leader.

Leadership is about trust foremostly, as I have seen firsthand what happens when it's lacking.

Flexibility in academia should acknowledge the long hours we put in, including the emails sent at five in the morning and the weekends spent catching up on work instead of being at my son's swimming lesson. Yet in a previous role, on top of late nights and weekends working from home, I was "mentored" with the advice that visibility equated to leadership. My supervisor told me I was expected to be physically present at the workplace for eight hours a day, five days a week, which meant I missed dinner with my family five nights a week.

In another role, passive-aggressive sticky notes were left behind with timestamps such as 9:40 a.m., marking when my supervisor came looking for me. There was no recognition that I was still at the microscope at 10 p.m. and not at home tucking my son into bed that night.

Leadership should never be about policing presence; it should be about trust, respect, and outcomes.

True leadership is about being the change you want to see.

Leadership is about building trust and supporting each individual's circumstances, whether they have children, elderly parents, or football practice with their mates. If the work is getting done, and getting done well, and if there is a culture of respect and trust, then success does not need to be measured by the hours someone clocks on and off.

LIVING THE CHANGE

I want to live the change I want to see.

I can't be part of the change if I am not part of the system. Although I left scientific research a few years ago, I still use my science training and networks as an executive member of university staff, serving as an Associate Professor and Director of Education. I also draw on my lived experience as a scientific researcher to continue advocating for systemic change.

The way I led at junior levels, through work in gender equity, advocating for peers, and building networks, got me noticed, earned respect, and enabled me to reach senior levels in academia beyond my scientific research alone.

No matter what career stage you are in, you can be a leader. Leadership is not just about what you achieve, it's about how you bring others with you and lift them up.

- Find your cheerleaders and be one yourself.
- Celebrate a colleague's win and share her achievement.
- Make introductions that can help her career.

Leadership is not about holding power; it's about lifting others as you climb.

Your small actions will create ripples that will transform workplace culture, and importantly your experience within it.

Thirteen

Rise and Shine

A WOMAN'S GUIDE TO SURVIVING AND THRIVING
IN CORPORATE STEMM

*by Monika McDole-Russell, senior leader in MedTech, passionate about
gender equity and helping women in STEMM thrive in corporate spaces.*

I am such a stereotype. Middle child of divorced parents, always trying
to prove her worth and get attention. Straight-A student, rule-follower,
people-pleaser, workaholic, Type A personality who isn't comfortable
unless she's achieving, succeeding, winning, or competing. I had my
first nervous breakdown from overwork at 22, and I was proud of it.
Every time I earned a degree, won an award, or got a promotion, I was
satisfied for approximately 30 minutes. Then I would set my sights on
the next accomplishment, begin mentally listing the ways I was
unqualified for my next coveted opportunity, and make plans to go
after it anyway.

Some might say I was custom-made to work in Corporate America.
Before my corporate STEMM career, I was a scriptwriter and
eventually a director and producer of corporate training videos and
mini-documentaries. Like STEMM, film production is a very male-
dominated field, and it was pretty much expected that any young
woman would endure a certain amount of "good-natured"
harassment: sexist remarks, come-ons, double entendres, and

"accidental" touching. Ironically, it wasn't the sexist environment that led to my departure from that industry. It was the desire for simpler things in life: a steady paycheck, a retirement account, and health insurance.

That's how I found myself in technical writing, first with the U.S. Forest Service, then at a large medical device company. I ultimately found my calling in the field of regulatory science for medical device development.

I found the corporate world to be my near-ideal work environment. I am a creature of habit and routine who also constantly seeks challenge and change, and the ebb and flow of the medical device development cycle within the security of a large corporate matrix provides the perfect mix of freedom and structure.

Fast forward two decades, and I have eagerly and purposely climbed the ladder, acquired an advanced degree, and now hold a senior leadership position. My role combines the best of all worlds: engineering, regulatory strategy, people development, and contributing to the growth and development of the business. It is my dream job.[1] To top it off, I know the work my team and I do brings much-needed technology to patients and physicians around the globe. It is complex and challenging work. It's not always fun, but it is always worth it.

This is important because, as others in this book have described, and as I will also expand on, being a woman in STEMM is not an easy path, no matter the role. If you are going to be successful, either your role or your ultimate goal must be worth staying the course.

– Monika

The current model of how women are represented in corporate STEMM is flawed. However, as we've learned, while all models are flawed, some can still be useful.[2]

---

[1] Or pretty close to it.
[2] See Chapter 2, *Values and Choice.*

Within this chapter, I've offered my model for corporate success. It's like a map through an obstacle course. When you reach the giant climbing wall, you still have to climb it, but you knew to expect it, so it's not a surprise.

Stranger in a Strange Land

In my career, I have worked for or with almost a dozen device companies, all espousing a dedication to fairness and equity in the workplace to varying degrees. I have witnessed brilliant successes in policy and laughable failures of the same, often within the same company. Some days, I feel invincible. Other days, I wonder why my entire career feels like a dumpster fire.

My goal is not to tell you how to fix what's broken in the system. It is to give you tools to navigate your way through an imperfect system without giving up who you are.

Almost 20 years in, here is what I can tell you: *working as a woman in corporate STEMM is hard.*

My job is by turns brutal and brilliant, enervating and energizing, cutthroat and collegial. I have been othered and ogled; I have been feted and feared. There is a better-than-average chance that, as a woman in corporate STEMM, you too will be harassed, bullied, intimidated, taken advantage of, and sometimes made an example of. There have been times when I have been lost in the wilderness of others' expectations.

But by keeping my *why* foremost, staying authentic, and embracing both vulnerability and resilience, I have forged a career that I can look back on with pride and forward to with anticipation. So much good has come of it, and there is so much more yet to accomplish.

When The Going Gets Tough

Women in STEMM are still, to a certain extent, seen as oddities. Especially on the lower rungs of the career ladder, the corporate experience for women remains uneven. Sometimes they are treated as equals, occasionally celebrated as examples of diversity or singled out for dream opportunities, and at other times held at arm's length out of fear or resentment.

What is a woman in this environment to do?

When the going gets rough, center yourself with questions like,

What brought you here?

What motivates you to do the job you do?

What gets you out of bed in the morning?

Keeping what drives you at the forefront of your mind will make the inevitable rough days more bearable.

On my hardest days, I take pride in what my team builds together. I reflect on what first drew me to this field: a love of problem-solving, continuous learning, and meaningful contribution. Leadership gave me a new lens, one focused as much on empowering others as on delivering outcomes. I lead by serving, guided by a belief that knowledge shared is knowledge multiplied.

My desire to lift and help others also has a downside. As the old Peter Gabriel song goes, I love to be loved. And the truth is, not everyone loves me, or even likes me, and some are quite forthright about it.

In my experience across a range of corporate environments, praise and compliments are like oxygen on Mt. Everest: harder to find the higher you go. Some days will be dark. The politics will be against you. The promotion will go to someone with a better network than yours. Or you will have to sit quietly next to a senior colleague while he proudly proclaims his "new idea," knowing it is actually the exact same idea your employee proposed to him a year ago, and he shot down as unrealistic. The list goes on.

In times like those, I open up a folder on my personal laptop titled "Props." That folder contains positive messages and feedback I've received from colleagues, friends, co-workers, and direct reports. It also holds quotes that inspire me. The contents of the folder help me refocus on the good in my job and in my life.

If you don't have something like this already, start one today. All praise is fair game to include: glowing words from a performance review; a heartfelt compliment from a colleague; quotes that keep you motivated; thanks from a mentee - anything and everything that reminds you of how amazing you are.

"I'M MY MOTHER'S GIRL"

I was raised to be a strong, independent thinker. I admire women like those portrayed by Barbara Stanwyck, Hedy Lamarr, and Lauren Bacall during cinema's Golden Age, the molls, dolls, and femme fatales, the whip-smart women who talked tough and often got the better of lesser men. I've also always been drawn to the retro 1940s cultural vibe overall, so it's no surprise that my corporate "uniform" consists of pencil skirts or tailored suits, silk blouses, and high heels.[3]

I don't dress that way to appeal to men; I dress that way because the look appeals to me. In some way, I believe that choosing to dress in a deliberately feminine way reclaims power from those who would objectify women. (Did I also mention I was raised a feminist?)

> *I'm my mother's girl.*
>
> – Lorna Moon, played by Barbara Stanwyck
> *Golden Boy*[4]

It turns out that the outspoken behavior part of the equation was better in theory. In reality, outspoken, opinionated women often stand out in the wrong way in a corporate environment. It is true that the more experienced and respected a woman becomes, the more her opinions and outspokenness are likely to be accepted, but only to a point! Once she becomes too experienced (read: old), these traits risk turning on her, reinterpreted as eccentricities that can stall her career where she stands.

Very early in my career, the men on the team referred to me as "the Scottish Pineapple" (because I was prickly when annoyed) or "the Sheriff" (because my role involved reviewing marketing materials and removing non-

---

[3] Because this style of dressing can be seen as provocative if not done properly, I have a very strict set of self-established rules I follow: all skirts worn with heels must hit below the knee; I only wear shorter skirts with opaque tights and flats. If I wear a form fitting top, I wear wide-leg pants. If wearing a pencil skirt, I wear a tailored or silk blouse. And I never, ever show cleavage.

[4] In the 1939 film "Golden Boy," when the mobster Joseph Calleia asks fight promoter Adolphe Menjou if Barbara Stanwyck's character, Lorna Moon, is his "new girl," she responds, "I'm my mother's girl."

compliant wording). I started getting feedback like, "You should be more cheerful," "You're too argumentative," "Don't be so critical in meetings," "Try to be softer and less intimidating," and my favorite: "Smile, sweetheart! It won't kill you!" Meanwhile, the men around me regularly insulted each other, raised their voices, and, as far as I could tell, didn't smile unless they damn well wanted to.

If your personality is like mine and you choose to pursue a career in the corporate sphere, it is more than likely that you will quickly learn, through well-meaning advice or "developmental feedback," what is expected of you to fit into a particular environment. I have found that, to a certain extent, it's true that if you want to play the game, you have to play by the rules. Sometimes that means moderating some of your traits and amplifying others.

> **Option 1.** If the moderations required feel unreasonable to you, maybe that particular environment isn't the right fit. *If so, move on.*

> **Option 2.** If it only requires a tweak or two here and there, and the goal is worthy (if the job is amazing, or the opportunity will set you up for future success), make the modifications and focus on aligning your persona to fit the environment.

In my case, success in the corporate setting meant learning to moderate my tone, dial back the sarcasm (which was probably a good thing anyway), adopt a diplomatic approach, and address conflict head-on, with a mediation mindset. The modifications I made to the way I show up professionally are just varying shades of who I already am.

If I had to significantly modify who I was every day, for instance, if I were forced to work in an environment where I had to be demure and deferential and run every decision by someone for approval, I know I couldn't keep it up for long without serious damage to my health and well-being. That behavior runs counter to who I am at my core.

Like me, you may find you have to adjust how you present certain parts of yourself in order to get where you want to go. But think of it more as choosing the right outfit for the setting, rather than reinventing your entire wardrobe.

I DIDN'T COME TO PLAY, I CAME TO WIN

I am unabashedly ambitious, driven, and competitive. I've disclosed this to every hiring manager in every interview I've had over the past 15 years, while also making it clear that my goal is not to achieve a certain title or salary. My goal is to further the mission of the business and elevate my teams to a level of excellence they didn't know they were capable of. By this point in my career, I know the title and salary will follow.

Have I paid the price for my ambition and drive? Yes.

Have I catapulted my career because of them? *Also, yes.*

There are women in STEMM who choose to prioritize work-life balance, who have made time for family and hobbies, perhaps they have suffered for it, perhaps not. I salute and support every single one of these women and every choice they have made.

But they are not me.

You are the captain of your career. You get to choose how far you are willing to go for your goals and dreams, and you have full control over when to adjust your sails or change course entirely.[5]

As a STEMM professional with strong problem-solving skills, if the incoming information indicates that a change is needed, be open to navigating in a different direction.

Here are the choices I've intentionally made in pursuit of my own vision of a successful career in STEMM:

- I work 50+ hour weeks because that's what it takes to get where I want to go in the company I have chosen to work for.
- I pursued an advanced degree because I wanted to feel like the equal to any peer in the room.
- I don't have children. I decided early in my life that motherhood wasn't for me. As I got older, although it wasn't a burning desire, I thought maybe it would be an OK experiment, but by then, it was biologically too late. Do I regret it? Not so far.

---

[5] See Chapter 11, *Charting Your Own Course*, for more.

- I never turn down travel, because face-to-face interactions are highly valued in my organization. I go whenever and wherever I'm asked. I offer to travel on nights and weekends when others may not want to. If I'm not specifically invited to a particular meeting or conference and I believe there is value in attending, I put together a persuasive argument for my function's inclusion and ask. As a mentor once told me, if you don't ask, the answer is always no.[6]

No one makes me do these things. I do them because I will do whatever it takes to achieve the goals I've set for myself. You may choose to do all of the above and more, to climb, to reach, and for the love of the game. You may do some or none of the above and still succeed. It all depends on your environment, your role, and your personal limits.

So find those limits. Test them. Try them. Know where they are, so no one can ever push you beyond them without your consent.

When You're Beyond Your Limits

I had a manager tell me that he hated women who hyphenate their last names because it was disrespectful to their husbands. But I've also had a leader who told me he'd never seen anyone read a room as well as I do.

A man on the executive team in my business once walked by a group of women leaders and said, "Don't anybody get pregnant this year; we have important things to accomplish." But I've also had a leader who trusted me to head meetings where things might get contentious because he knew I would bring everyone together and reach a consensus in a way he couldn't.[7]

So yes, I have had toxic leaders who tore me down. I've also had leaders who gave me opportunities to shine and prove myself. And I have lived

---

[6] I waited too long (in my opinion) to put myself out there as a subject matter expert, speaking at conferences, leading workshops, and joining webinars to raise my profile. Don't make this mistake. Market yourself now. It's good for your career, and It's good for your organization to have smart, visible people representing them at industry events.

[7] For once, that earned me a nickname I didn't mind: "The Diplomat." It also ultimately earned me a promotion, and I didn't mind that either.

through them all. Why? Because I focus on my end goal. I am here for a purpose, and no amount of sexism, misogyny, or othering will drive me away.

But there is a limit for everyone. If you cry every night, dread work every morning, and cringe when you have to interact with your boss, leave. Or make plans to leave soon. You have pushed, or been pushed, beyond your limits to an unhealthy extent. There is a distinction between persisting and suffering. You must learn where that line is for you. It's different for everyone.

SUPPORT AND BE SUPPORTIVE

In Chapter 5, Karli talks about the importance of connecting with other women in STEMM, and I couldn't agree more.[8] One way to do this is by joining STEMM-focused professional organizations for women, such as the Society of Women Engineers (SWE), the Association for Women in Science (AWIS), or MedTech Women. Don't discount the value of any organization for professional women, if one speaks to you, check it out. If your company has a women's network, join it and be an active member, not just a passive meeting attendee. Some of the best relationships I have were built through my company's women's network.

Whether through women's networks, professional organizations, Lean In Circles, or simply like-minded women you bump into at the company holiday party, make connecting with other professional women a priority. Seek out a variety of women with different life experiences, ages, and professional levels.

The importance lies in the connection and the relationship. Build a community of women who are, or have been, in the trenches with you, who can hear you out and build you up. Take time to maintain these connections. Some might require coffee once a month; others may only need an email check-in once a quarter. But it is critical to stay in touch.

The easiest way I've found to do this is to start with a list of your top 25 contacts and create a calendar, setting up reminders to check in with them at whatever interval makes sense for that relationship. Don't skip this step; it is

---

[8] See Chapter 5, *From Surviving to Thriving*.

so much harder to reconnect than it is to maintain regular check-ins with your existing connections.[9]

Finally, be bold and seek out women who are executives. Women are scarce at the top, and those who make it are often more than happy to share their knowledge and wisdom with you. All you have to do is ask.

So many women I talk to feel intimidated by these leaders and hesitate to approach them. So here's a simple guide I offer to help anyone get that first meeting:

- Research the top executive women at your company.
- When they are present at a company event, approach them afterward. Introduce yourself with your name, title, and function, and say something like: "I really admire what you've accomplished. Thank you for your contributions to [our company]. I aspire to reach your level one day. May I contact your admin to set up a brief 20-minute meeting to ask you a few questions about how you got where you are today?"
- Whether she says yes or no, thank her for her time and leave. *Don't hover.*
- If she said yes, contact her admin that day, explain you met [executive] at [event] and she agreed to a short meeting with you. Ask if they can help you schedule it and assure you will work around the executive's calendar.
- When you meet with the executive, be respectful of her time. Have a set of questions prepared that are tailored to her experience.
- Watch the clock and wrap up a minute or two early. If she invites you to reconnect with her occasionally on your progress, *do it.* She is giving you the gift of access to her time. Don't squander it.

One thing to remember: for this whole women-supporting-women structure to work, you have to do your part. As you rise, lift other women. Whenever possible, if a woman asks you for your time, give it.

We are so much less without each other.

---

[9] Even if brief and scheduled.

THE ENEMY WITHIN

One thing that can still come as a surprise, as it's often neglected in discussions about advancing women in STEMM, is that sometimes the enemy comes from within.

While women are quick to point out the ways in which men derail them, we are less willing to admit that some of our worst detractors can be other women. The top spots in leadership are so few and far between that competitive, ambitious women may turn on each other in the climb to the top.

I've had this happen to me, and I've also been guilty of doing it to others.

Now, with the benefit of years of experience, I can better see how destructive that is. It's like doing the patriarchy's work for it, focusing on infighting and politics until the lowest common denominator prevails and everyone is worse off.

Since coming to this realization, I've made a conscious effort to recommend women peers for roles and special assignments, and to seek out the input of both peers and younger colleagues far more than I ever did early in my career.

Not surprisingly, my career has been better off for it.

Here's the advice I wish someone had given me years ago: don't be the enemy in your own camp.

WITH GREAT POWER COMES GREAT RESPONSIBILITY

Even when women are all pulling together and supporting each other, we can still fall into the trap of becoming willing prisoners within the walls of misogyny. Especially early in our careers, women are often hesitant to push back or call out bad behavior.

Here is where I'll be controversial: I say they *should* hesitate. As a young woman with a fledgling career, you must look to your own interests first. At that point in your journey, this is not your fight. This is exactly why communities of supportive women are so important.

Throughout my career, there were times when I was protected and supported by more experienced women leaders who had the political capital to spend. In turn, as I have risen through the ranks, I've done the same, protecting and supporting women junior to me.

United we conquer; divided we fall.

Life Is Not Fair

My Aunt Vickie has the (perhaps dubious) distinction of being the first person to inform me of a truism I had not yet figured out. My tween self was sitting in her kitchen, complaining at length about some perceived injustice, when she turned away from the counter where she was peeling vegetables, put her hand on her hip, and interrupted me mid-complaint with: "Sugar, nobody ever said life had to be fair."

At the time, the little drama queen that I was sulked about how, well, *unfair* that was. Life! Not fair! To *me*! But oh, how correct Aunt Vickie proved to be. Life is not fair.

Unlike the fairy tales of old, there is no prince coming to rescue you. If you're of a younger generation than mine (Gen X), maybe your childhood stories didn't condition you to expect a prince or knight to save you, and you aren't even waiting to be rescued. Good for you! Because, fair princess, there are dragons ahead.

In Chapter 15, Kelly reminds us that "Understanding the invisible forces that shape people's perceptions of women can make them easier to tolerate since it isn't about you personally."[10] So know this:

> You will be told you're brash.
>
> You will be told you need to smile more.
>
> You will be seen as too young to know anything.
>
> You will be seen as too old to add value.
>
> You will be resented by some because you are tall and imposing.
>
> You will be pandered to by others because your voice is too high.
>
> You will be judged in ways men are not judged.
>
> You will see your peers who are men get away with things no woman's career would ever survive.
>
> You will see all of these things.
>
> *And yet.*

---

[10] See Chapter 15, *Glass Ceilings & Cliffs*.

You will adapt to or ignore these things, not because you accept them as valid, but because your vision encompasses so much more than someone's limited perception. You can see through the fog of opinions and judgments cast by others to the brass (or iron) ring that calls to you.[11]

BE THE CHANGE YOU WANT TO SEE

In the end, no job is perfect, and no company is ideal. But if you can find a good role in a company with a reasonably healthy culture, where you can put down roots for two years (or twenty) and gain the experience you're looking for, do it.

That "good enough" job might develop into an amazing job right where you are, or it might be the stepping stone to a stellar opportunity you haven't even imagined yet.

This is where senior- and executive-level women can be invaluable: by setting examples, acting as guides, and advocating for or sponsoring and supporting early- and mid-career women. Generally, once a woman reaches the Director+ level, she has built relationships and acquired political capital, not just in her current role or company, but across networks and professional communities. Now is the time to pay it forward, to reach down and pull others up the ladder, to reach out and address inequality when we see it, and to advocate for meaningful change.

The corporate climate for women in STEMM is improving. Perhaps not fast enough, but progress is being made. Still, it will take all of us, professional women and our allies, to truly turn the tide.

No matter what, if you stay true to who you are, stand steadfast in the value you bring, and seek to serve a greater good, you can confidently shoot for the moon. And even if you miss, as the saying goes, you'll land among the stars.

---

[11] See Chapters 3, *Inlet Forces*, and Chapter 11, *Charting Your Own Course*, for more on the Canadian Iron Ring tradition.

Fourteen

Pressured Out of Technical

"SHE CAN TALK TO PEOPLE?!"

by Kelly A. Seiler Vocke, engineer in robotics, sensors, and manufacturing, unapologetically technical and here to stay.

In high school, I joined the after-school robotics club. We designed small Remotely Operated Vehicles using 2A motors, foam for buoyancy, and a PVC frame. The controller was a series of switches mounted on a Tupperware container. We tested our robots in the pool and ran WD-40 through the motors after each session to prevent them from seizing due to rust.

It was so cool to build something from scratch, learn basic electronics (like SPST vs. DPDT switches, soldering, and series vs. parallel circuits), experiment with buoyancy, and learn to drive a machine we had designed ourselves.

As a strong writer, I ended up doing all the documentation for my group, and we won Best Documentation at the competition. As the lone girl in my group, that fits a pattern seen all too often. Girls are more likely to be strong in both liberal arts and sciences. This dual strength too often results in girls being assigned documentation tasks at the expense of their technical development.

My high school offered a lot of hands-on opportunities. I took an architectural drafting class, and while I had been considering architecture as a career before that, the experience ultimately helped me decide it wasn't the best fit. I was most interested in the problem-solving aspects, which turned out to be only a small portion of an architect's job.

Classes in computer science, computer hardware, advanced math, and physics prepared me well for my future career. Research shows that girls with engineering experiences are more confident in choosing their career paths, even if they don't end up choosing engineering.

I'm all grown up now, with 18 years of engineering experience across aviation, subsea sensor systems, and manufacturing. I'm married with two kids and a suburban home, the picture of the American dream. And yet, some of the things I experienced in high school are still happening.

I was thrilled during my interview for my current role to learn that the team had a group wiki, templates, and automation in place for common busywork, running reports, pulling document numbers, filling basic information into templates, and so on. I had set up similar systems in previous workplaces, and I was excited to benefit from them as a newcomer. Alas, this was all implemented, perhaps not surprisingly, by the woman in the group.

– Kelly

Women in STEMM are often pushed toward taking on a disproportionate share of documentation or coordination tasks, which can leave them without sufficient technical experience to be considered for promotion. As a result, it can seem like a natural next step to move into a STEMM-adjacent, soft-skill-intensive role, often at the expense of their technical development and long-term career growth.

This is problematic because roles further from the technical core are frequently seen as less prestigious, tend to be recognized with lower pay, and are often not the job the woman wanted to do in the first place.

I learned to always take on things I'd never done before.
Growth and comfort do not coexist.

– Ginni Rometty
Former CEO and Chairwoman of IBM

WOMEN BRING A VARIETY OF PROFESSIONAL SKILLS

In addition to having both strong liberal arts skills and strong technical skills, research shows women are also more likely to be good at **soft skills**.[1]

Soft skills, which are generally applicable across all professions, include critical thinking, problem-solving, public speaking, professional writing, teamwork, digital literacy, leadership, a professional attitude, strong work ethic, career management, and intercultural fluency. These skills form the centerpiece of effective leadership.

From here on we will be calling these **professional skills**, as "soft" anything often risks negative connotations in STEMM workplaces.

Professional skills are learnable, but our society has a tendency to let men off the hook, especially if they are seen as eccentric geniuses. When I asked a colleague how her leadership skills class was going, she mentioned that the class was mostly women, which was especially striking given that our company is male dominated, with even less female representation in leadership roles.

Perhaps professional skills are underdeveloped in male-dominated professions because they include elements that are culturally coded as feminine, such as communication, empathy, collaboration, and emotional intelligence.

Professional Skills, *noun:*

Skills that help you communicate, collaborate, solve problems,
work well with others, and manage your time, emotions,
and responsibilities. Formerly known as "soft skills."

---

[1] Apparently, the U.S. Army had noticed that leadership, administration, communication, and strategic thinking were key to success and developed training programs to develop these skills in its troops.

In my experience, niche technical skills can sometimes allow someone to opt out of soft skills and low-promotability tasks. Early in my career, I worked with an older man with a niche specialty. Despite being difficult to work with, slow to reply, never releasing his own documentation, and even outright disrespectful, he was never held accountable. His technical skills were considered too hard to replace.

At a leadership course, my instructor shared a similar story about an "irreplaceable" antenna design specialist who was eventually fired for losing his temper one too many times. The team didn't fail without him. Instead, they came together to support three junior engineers in filling the technical gap. While there was an initial schedule impact, team morale improved, and by the next project, they were performing better than ever.

Technical skills are often easier to measure than professional skills. You can quantify that a circuit is converting power correctly, that a bridge holds the weight of traffic, or that the required number of lab tests was completed.

Professional skills, on the other hand, especially when done well, are nearly invisible. Shutting down an unproductive side project in a meeting, getting people aligned behind the scenes, writing agendas, or taking notes are just a few examples of the work that makes projects run smoothly. A problem that is avoided is much less noticeable than one that brings a department to its knees.

WOMEN DRIFT

Too often, women with strong technical interests and skills drift into non-technical roles because they possess more well-rounded professional skills, doubt their technical abilities, and are more likely to act as team players. All three of these factors can be traced back to their upbringing.

From an early age, women are socialized to engage in prosocial behavior. Girls are often praised, and at times guilted, for their willingness to make personal sacrifices for the benefit of their families, schools, and other communities.

Girls' imposter syndrome is fueled by having their technical abilities questioned, a lack of role models, and persistent social messages that girls aren't good at STEMM. As adults, this self-doubt often follows women into the workplace, especially in environments where they face **prove-it-again** bias.

Math class is tough!

– Teen Talk Barbie
Toy Released in 1992

Women's stronger professional skills often position them to be the ones who communicate with other departments, recognize when people are miscommunicating, and identify gaps. They may also be the ones asked to take meeting minutes or organize the next team social event. *When you're the person best equipped to resolve an issue quickly, it seems only logical to step in, right?*

In a study aimed at examining gender differences in volunteering for low-promotability tasks, a significant proportion of men never volunteered, regardless of the circumstances. Even men who consistently volunteered for low promotability tasks in all-male groups did so less often in mixed-gender settings. All women groups tended to share the responsibility of volunteering more equally across the ten rounds.

The combination of stronger professional skills, self-doubt, and a tendency to be team players has resulted in women taking on more low-promotability tasks than men on average. Spending less time on technical work hinders career growth, leading to less critical technical experience and, ultimately, fewer promotions.

Common STEMM-adjacent roles that technical women often move into include technical writing, program management, sales, user research, advertising, human resources, and management. This shift is sometimes encouraged by well-meaning mentors or peers who notice them excelling in these areas and suggest making it their core focus. But I'm always cautious of that advice, it assumes women enjoy certain tasks simply because they perform them well. What's most impactful for your career and your goals may not align with what's most beneficial for the company.

To maintain control of your own career, the first step is to advocate for equitable systems in which responsibility is rotated among all team members.

If that doesn't lead to change, you may sometimes need to look the other way when major communication issues arise. Sometimes, the only way to create change is to let things break.

Certain problems only become visible when they escalate into pain points for the team. If you're always the one taking on invisible tasks or working extra hours to compensate for an unfilled position, nothing will change. This applies both to low-promotability tasks and to overwork caused by staffing gaps. Until a deadline is missed, others may not recognize the problem.

A third technique is to actively document and be prepared to defend your technical strengths. Marie found that even as a skilled structural analyst, her professional skills often stood out more than her technical work. When her manager was planning to rate her below average on technical skills, claiming he was "trying to differentiate scores," she was prepared with data. She countered with a stack of technical examples, including a special project she completed with her mentee in half the projected time, much to the customer's delight. *Measurable data for the win!*

Women leave STEMM fields at twice the rate of men due to failures to advance, sexism, and culture. While unintentional gender bias and societal conditioning certainly contribute to the challenges women face at work, there are also toxic workplaces that actively push women out. History has shown that when fields become female-dominated, both prestige and pay tend to decline.

Gatekeeping is real.

Thriving In the Technical Grind

If technical work is Type II Fun for you, this section is for you.[2] Thriving in highly technical roles is absolutely possible. Here are a few resources to help you land the roles you aspire to, and perform at your peak once you're there.

Interview Strategies

If you choose to stay technical and resist the drift, it's likely you'll need to interview from time to time. Here is my list of interview tips that have served me well as I've advanced to my role as a senior engineer.

> **Develop a story toolbox.** Look up common interview questions (*tell me about a time when you overcame a challenge*) and come up with five or more stories in the STAR (Situation, Task, Action, Result) format.[3]

---

[2] See Chapter 2, *Values and Choice*, for more on Type II fun.

[3] Pro tip from Cassie: "I always finish with a secret L (STARL). What did I *learn* from this experience. Works every time!"

Stay enthusiastic. Hold in the back of your mind throughout the interview how excited you are for the position, company, product, whatever. Do not over-analyze new data in real time.

Be strategic. Look through the job description before your interview and strategize what you most want the interviewer(s) to know about you. If it doesn't come up during the interview, bring it up yourself when they give you the floor for questions.[4]

Practice *riding the pause*. When you finish your STARL answer, let them talk next. Ride the pause. Time warps and it might feel like forever, but they are still processing. Do not word-vomit to fill the silence. It's fine to be uncomfortable.

Remember that interviews are a weird test. It's acceptable to share an example that's true, even if it's not the *whole* story. For example: "I'm looking to take the next step in my career." Translation: "I hate my job and feel trapped at this company," but don't say that part out loud.

I had a great manager in my first full-time position out of school, but I was so bored. I changed positions within the company and ended up with a terrible manager and semi-interesting work. It took me a long time to find another job. My confidence had been shaken, and it somehow leaked out during interviews. I felt like I was ineffective, that my technical skills were behind relative to my experience (imposter syndrome), and that I didn't know how to identify a healthy work environment.

I got to a better place by working with a career coach to get super clear on what I was looking for, practicing until the "why I was leaving" part came out neutral, and approaching interviews as a two-way street, interviewing them as much as they were interviewing me.

I have provided a list of questions I've used in past interviews, along with the intent behind each one. I choose to avoid direct questions designed to assess "cultural fit," as I find broader questions more useful. The responses

---

[4] Pro tip from Monika: "Applicants should research the company before interviewing. I can't tell you how many people I've interviewed who've said, 'So, what devices do you make here?'"

tend to reveal the fit naturally, rather than relying on someone's potentially biased opinion.

And be sure to use what you learned in your preparation research on the company to add thoughtful lead ins.

Questions to ask	What you *actually* want to know
What does a typical day or week in this role look like?[5]	Will this role work for me schedule-wise?
How do you set expectations for your employees? How do you measure success?	What's the leader's management style.
What is the size and makeup of this team?	How diverse is the team? Will your manager have time for you?
What major processes or projects would you expect a person in this job to improve or overhaul?	Will they give you enough control to be effective?
How do you train new hires? How will I access what I need to be successful?	Will I be mentored in my new role or left to figure it out on my own?
If you could change one thing about the [job/ department], what would it be?	Are there red flags to watch out for? Listen closely to what they say and how they say it.
What are the key business reasons for driving this position? Is this a new or replacement position?	Is there a potential for long-term job security?

DEEP WORK

Certain aspects of technical work require a more intentional approach, as they demand periods of uninterrupted focus, intellectual effort, and delayed gratification. Cal Newport refers to this as "deep work."

Awareness of deep work can help you perform at your very best, especially if you're committed to avoiding the drift, ignoring well-meaning but misguided advice, and staying the course as a technical expert.

---

[5] Option to follow-up with a question about when people tend to start, when they leave, or do they have a flextime policy.

Because of the nature of deep work, it's important to be mindful of how your work environment affects your ability to perform effectively. Interruptions, commonly in the form of meetings in the corporate world, can significantly impact your ability to meet deadlines and produce your best work. Take time regularly to carefully assess whether your work environment is conducive to deep, focused productivity, and make adjustments as needed. Many "should do" items are actually far more optional than you might think.

> *The biggest waste of time is to do something well that need not be done at all.*
>
> – Gretchen Rubin
> *Author and Renowned Happiness Expert*

Many individuals need to schedule blocks of time during the hours when they are sharpest in order to work on complex tasks effectively. A meeting scheduled at the wrong time can disrupt that flow and make it difficult to complete a highly technical task that day. The transition into and out of a focused state is often lengthy, and larger tasks require significant delayed gratification. You may not be able to determine whether your idea worked for quite some time, especially if prototyping or input from others is required.

It's also important to become aware of how imposter syndrome can create emotional blocks. For some, deep work feels riskier and more intimidating. The uniqueness or complexity of a task may require input from a mentor, particularly for junior professionals. The steep learning curve can give the impression that no progress is being made. If you find yourself avoiding the tasks that will ultimately give you the experience needed to reach your career goals, consider seeking support through career coaching, therapy, or self-help. Karli's *From Surviving to Thriving* chapter offers excellent guidance to help you get started.[6]

---

[6] See Chapter 5, *From Surviving to Thriving.*

KNOW THYSELF

You've probably heard the quote, *"Be yourself; everyone else is taken!"* I personally find it a bit annoying because it starts you at the finish line. Most people don't know what they truly like until they've had the chance to try out different options. Outside influences can creep in and distort your values. Things that are easier to compare and measure, like money or prestige, can unintentionally rise in priority above your more meaningful, closely held values.

What other people enjoy can be a good starting point. There's a reason something is popular, but until you try it for yourself, you won't know whether it actually suits your unique personality.

> *Do what you feel in your heart to be right, for you will be criticized anyway.*
>
> – Eleanor Roosevelt
> *U.S. First Lady and Champion of Women's Rights*

It can be all too easy to fall into doing what we're highly skilled at without stopping to consider whether we actually enjoy it. Additionally, some things we're good at come easily, while others require more effort and struggle. If you can find a job that hits the trifecta, high skill, enjoyment, and ease, at least half the time, you're lucky indeed.

I've also provided an array of questions to reflect on what you enjoy.[7]

When you discover what you truly enjoy, it's important to value it highly, because no one else will do it for you. If you're lucky enough to have found a passion, follow it!

---

[7] See Chapter 2, *Values and Choice*, for additional exercises to help bring clarity.

Consider	Self-reflection
What I Value	Is this part of my core job function?
	If I don't do it, can/will someone else do it?
	Does this work align with my career goals?
	Can I include this in my performance review?
	What will success look like, and can its impact be measured?
Visibility and recognition	Will this work be recognized or noticeable by others?
	Has this work been recognized before? By whom?
	How will I strategically promote the impact of my work?[8]
My skills	What are my unique skills?
	What skills come naturally?
	What do I genuinely enjoy doing, and what do I avoid?
	What am I passionate about?
Protecting deep-work time	Will this meeting advance my project?
	Will this meeting provide facetime that may lead to better projects or a promotion (if that is your goal)?
	Which meetings don't really need me?
Alignment at workplace social events	Do the "fun" things at work happen when I don't organize them?
	Am I ok with doing low promotability work to have these experiences?
	Does the stress of these activities overpower the enjoyment?
	Do I resent others' lack of participation?
	What is the minimum way I'd be happy participating?
Drift check	Conduct a quarterly review to prevent unintentionally drifting away from your personal goals.

[8] See Chapter 15, *Glass Ceilings & Cliffs*, for additional tips.

I've had ups and downs with self-acceptance around how my brain operates. For much of my life, I worried that my mental differences would keep me from achieving everything I wanted, personally and professionally. I thought that the things that made me different must inherently make me worse. But after years of therapy, I am learning to see those same differences as potential strengths that make me uniquely qualified for the ambitions I hold.

For example, I have a pretty high baseline level of anxiety. I am constantly in a state of overthinking or worrying, whether it's work-related, family-related, health-related, or something else entirely. Early in my career, my program manager witnessed me in a moment of tizzy and joked that I'd be good at risk management. At the time, I nervously laughed, unsure whether it was a compliment. But recently, I said the same thing to my current manager and truly meant it. Why should it be a bad thing that I can identify where something could go wrong? Or that, due to my internal hyperactivity, I naturally want to identify mitigation steps?

If you are struggling with self-acceptance of your neurodiverse presentation, consider how you might reframe what you are feeling as a strength.

Turn that thought into a mantra and repeat it to yourself regularly. Start with moments when it's easy to believe in yourself. Progress to the harder times when you need to hear it most. With time, this mantra will take root, allowing you to thrive in the ways that you, and your brain, were meant to.

– Megan Wendell

Fifteen

Glass Ceilings & Cliffs

"SHE'S JUST NOT LEADERSHIP MATERIAL"

by Kelly A. Seiler Vocke, senior engineer, redefining how we see leadership.

> Never be limited by other people's
> limited imaginations.
>
> – Mae C. Jemison

It felt like a dream. I was offered a promotion into cross-program leadership! Of course, I said yes.

I had been working for years to build a strong foundation of technical and leadership skills, and this must be my reward.

Never mind that this high-profile program was already over budget and behind schedule. Never mind that this senior leadership role came with all the responsibility and accountability for getting both the schedule and cost back on track, without granting me the all-too-critical missing piece: the authority to affect change in either area.

You see, while my title said that fixing the program's technical overruns was my job, my level was one tier below all the technical team leaders. Each of these men (they were all men) held Director titles. My promotion brought me to the title of Senior Manager, also known as a nuisance who was probably too young, too green, or too whatever to be taken seriously. I was set up to fail before I even started.

As I stepped into the role, I discovered the program was already in full crisis mode. Program leadership held me up as the solution, or rather, held me out. What I lacked in resources, title, and support, I tried to make up for with gumption, tenacity, and grit. Some days went well, some did not. And some days, I cried the whole drive home.

As the blame mounted, the attacks became more personal. My performance rating plummeted. Long-time executive mentors began to back away.

I looked around—up, down, and sideways—and realized I was all alone, standing on a precarious cliff. It was time for me to walk away from my dream job.

– Anonymous

According to the Women's Business Collaborative, women make up only 9% of CEOs of the largest 3,000 publicly traded companies in the U.S. In this chapter, we'll explore the **glass ceiling**, the **glass cliff**, the **glass escalator**, and other invisible social forces that shape how professional, leadership, feminine, and masculine identities intersect.

While women often face difficulty breaking into top leadership positions (the Glass Ceiling), they are also disproportionately selected for risky or precarious roles (the Glass Cliff). In addition, in female-dominated fields, men are more frequently chosen for leadership positions (the Glass Escalator).

Many people are unaware that they hold biases against women in leadership. However, research, historical events, and the lived experiences of older women leaders all suggest that such biases are common. Take politics, for example.[1] Polling on this subject shows that nine out of ten people believe women are well suited for

---

[1] Few US voters are willing to admit that they are uncomfortable with the idea of a woman President. According to the 2018 General Social Survey just 4% say they wouldn't vote for a woman, if she was qualified. The 2024 iteration of Gallup's longstanding survey of willingness to vote for Presidential candidates of differing backgrounds shows 93% would be willing to vote for a woman candidate, if she were qualified.

political office and say they would personally vote for a woman president. However, when it comes to an actual, specific, real life woman candidate... there don't seem to be any that are acceptable.

She has an authenticity problem. Too shrill.

– Hillary Clinton's Critics

Unrealistic and dishonest. Too divisive.

– Elizabeth Warren's Critics

She laughs funny.

– Kamala Harris's Critics

As a woman in STEMM, I find it incredibly frustrating that no matter how likeable or technically skilled a woman is, gender biases often prevent others from recognizing it. However, there is hope.

Understanding the invisible forces that shape people's perceptions of women can make those experiences easier to tolerate, since they aren't about you personally. We'll discuss strategies for navigating these barriers, and I'll share some personal reflections along the way.

We all contribute to these biases. People often assume that women in STEMM will naturally lift each other up, but that isn't always the case. We were all raised in the same society, shaped by pervasive gendered expectations. We shouldn't need to experience sexism ourselves to recognize the harm it causes—for all genders. I would love to see women have an equal opportunity to pursue (and get!) leadership roles.

THE TRADITIONAL LEADERSHIP MODEL

It's time to say the quiet part out loud: masculine and feminine stereotypes underpin how people view men and women in the workplace. One of the functions of stereotypes is to differentiate in-group (people like us) from out-group (others).

The following Venn diagrams highlight how historically established ideal leadership qualities tend to overlap more with traits traditionally seen as masculine. Stereotypically feminine traits, by contrast, show less overlap with traditional leadership traits.

Traditional Masculine Stereotypes		Ideal Leadership Traits
Independent Protector Provider Stoic Self-Reliant	Ambitious Assertive Confident Competent Competitive Risk-Taker	Adaptable Compassionate Empathetic Resilient Self-Aware

Traditional Feminine Stereotypes		Ideal Leadership Traits
Collaborative Emotional Gentle Intuitive Kind Nurturing Open Supportive	Compassionate Empathetic Self-Aware	Ambitious Assertive Confident Competent Competitive Risk-Taker Adaptable Resilient

This gives men an advantage in the workplace, as they are often perceived to already possess what is needed to lead simply by virtue of their gender. In many cases, feminine traits are even seen as being in direct opposition to the traits associated with leadership.

But can women just act more masculine?

Turns out, not really.

When women do not display personality traits that align with societal expectations of their gender, it can make others uncomfortable. That discomfort often turns into personal dislike. This phenomenon is known as the likeability versus competence **double bind**.

MODERN LEADERSHIP MODELS

What is considered "ideal" in leadership has thankfully begun to evolve. Several leadership models have emerged that embrace a more holistic approach to managing teams and delivering results.

EMOTIONAL INTELLIGENCE

There is a significant body of research that places emotional intelligence (EQ) above IQ or technical skill when predicting leadership success.[2] Success in leadership is only 20% dependent on IQ at the higher levels of an organization.

However, do not take this to mean that IQ and technical skills are not important in STEMM. You must have both. Emotional intelligence is critical when distinguishing who will become the strongest leader.

> *IQ washes out when it comes to predicting who, among a talented pool of candidates within an intellectually demanding profession, will become the strongest leader.*
>
> – Daniel Goleman
> *Psychologist and Author*

---

[2] Emotional Quotient, like Intelligence Quotient (IQ), is an indicator of potential for success.

Goleman's EQ theory comprises five core components: empathy, effective communication (or social skills), self-awareness, self-regulation, and motivation.

The first two are outward-facing skills, while the final three are internally focused. As discussed in my *Pressured Out of Technical* chapter, women are, on average, stronger in communication and social skills, while also maintaining strong technical abilities.[3]

Empathy is often seen, at worst, as a weakness and, at best, as a risky strength—even though research consistently links it to increased employee engagement, innovation, and retention. Despite its proven value, empathy remains undervalued in many leadership spaces.

Empathy and vulnerability are closely intertwined. Brené Brown, a prominent U.S. researcher, emphasizes that vulnerability is not a weakness but a strength. It allows us to connect with others on a deeper, more authentic level.

Fortunately, emotional intelligence is a learnable skill.

> *The ability to learn is the most important*
> *quality a leader can have.*
>
> – Padmasree Warrior
> *Technology Executive and Former CEO of NIO U.S.*

SERVANT & INCLUSIVE LEADERSHIP

The Servant Leadership model, developed by Robert Greenleaf in 1970, centers the idea that the leader serves the team. It focuses on sharing power with team members, fostering growth, building community, listening, demonstrating empathy, putting others first, and honoring others' experiences. An empowered team leads to improved outcomes across the organization.

> *Leadership is not wielding authority*
> *—it is empowering people.*
>
> – Becky Brodin
> *Professor at Saint Mary's University*

---

[3] See Chapter 14, *Pressured Out of Technical*.

The Inclusive Leadership model focuses on creating an environment where all team members' unique perspectives are valued and where there is equal access to opportunity. It was developed and championed by several organizations between 2005 and 2020.

Both leadership models emphasize traits traditionally associated with femininity, such as people development (nurturing and supportive), collaboration, intuition, empathy, self-awareness, and compassion.

What if leadership evolved into a more comprehensive model—one that values both "masculine" and "feminine" qualities and benefits all people, along with the organizations they shape? In this future model, traits like people development, collaboration, intuition, empathy, self-awareness, and compassion would stand equally alongside competence, ambition, assertiveness, confidence, competitiveness, and risk-taking.

> *Emotional Intelligence is critical in building and maintaining relationships and influencing others–key skills that help people throughout their career and wherever they sit in an organizational structure.*
>
> – Margaret Andrews
> *Harvard Leadership Instructor*

Destigmatizing qualities long associated with femininity, yet proven effective in strong leaders, could elevate the overall quality of leadership and create space for everyone to welcome women as leaders.

Vulnerability, often viewed as incompatible with legacy models rooted in stoicism, aggression, and expertise, might one day be recognized as a strength in all leaders. What if we could shift our collective perception of leadership?

> *Leadership is a series of behaviors rather than a role for heroes.*
>
> – Margaret J. Wheatley
> *Author and Leadership Expert*

THE GLASS CEILING

You've probably heard of the **glass ceiling**—that persistent refrain: *We would totally pick a woman, just not this specific one.* She's too aggressive, too shrill, too... whatever. You know, the same leadership qualities that, in a man, are seen as natural and normal.

> Maybe they even lament, I can't quite put my finger on it,
> *but I know I don't like her.*

A woman finally breaks through and... nothing. She's the only one. That shattering of the glass ceiling isn't the dramatic event we often imagine. It's more like a tiny crack appears, and through a mix of luck, timing, the support of a champion, and the woman contorting herself into the "just right" personality— walking that fine line to appear competent without completely sacrificing likability—she manages to break through and land that coveted position. If she's lucky, her personality was already close to what it needed to be: someone who values warmth, community, and holds firm but fair boundaries with humor.

People often believe they're already fine with women in leadership, so there's no collective realignment of what is truly possible. It just *happens to be* that a man is perceived as the best choice much of the time.

The sad truth is that in many organizations, there is a very narrow range of personalities that women are "allowed" to have in order to be successful. Women who don't twist their personalities to meet these expectations are often told to be more accommodating—or to stand up for themselves more— depending on the situation. But it's never quite right.

Rachel, an aerospace engineer, was once compared to an overly accommodating coworker during a project meeting: "Can't you be more like Lilah? Lilah doesn't have a problem." The unspoken implication was clear: Lilah's willingness to comply with anything asked of her had become the standard.

LOSS OF AUTHENTICITY

There is a significant risk in changing your style to meet other people's expectations of women and leaders. It can come across as inauthentic, which can damage people's trust in you.

Hillary Clinton is a high-profile example. In the 1990s, she softened her public image by baking cookies to downplay her career-oriented focus, aiming to be seen as an "acceptable" First Lady. Later, during her presidential campaigns, she underwent another transformation but was perceived by some as too aloof and out of touch with everyday people. Her many public reinventions likely contributed to perceptions of untrustworthiness.

CHANGING PERCEPTIONS

When many women break through a particular ceiling, we hope it brings us closer to the dynamic, action-packed image of shattering glass. Unfortunately, what often changes is our perception of the position—not our perception of how capable these women are.

Fields with many women at the top start to be seen as "women's work" and consequently the pay and prestige drops. For example, as women were forced out of programming, starting in 1984, the prestige and pay increased. In Russia, where medicine is a female-dominated profession, doctors are often underpaid and lack professional respect.

Research also shows that when a candidate pool includes many women or people of color, it becomes dramatically more likely that someone from that group will be hired, as people tend to conform to the perceived status quo.

THE GLASS CLIFF

When a risky career opportunity comes up, a woman is more likely to be chosen. This phenomenon is known as the **glass cliff**. Examples of tapping women for leadership in times of crisis:

> **Sallie Krawcheck** was appointed President of Bank of America's Global Wealth & Investment Management division in 2009, during the aftermath of the subprime mortgage crisis and a mass exodus of financial advisors. Lauded as 'the most powerful woman on Wall Street,' she held the role until her abrupt firing in 2011.

> **Carly Fiorina** became CEO of Hewlett-Packard in 1999, after a decade of decline following the death of the founders, making her

the first woman in history to lead a Fortune Top 20 company. However, according to CNN, "her fall from stardom was just as dramatic." When she ran for President in 2016 her tenure at Hewlett-Packard was criticized heavily.

Theresa May was elected Prime Minister of the United Kingdom in July 2016, following the divisive Brexit referendum. Faced with a deeply divided nation, she struggled to reconcile the pro-Leave and pro-Remain factions within her party and country. She resigned in June 2019.

Marissa Mayer was appointed CEO of Yahoo! in 2012 after years of decline, lackluster stock performance, and an uncertain future. As the fourth CEO appointed in a single year, she inherited a challenging situation, and when Yahoo!'s struggles continued, the responsibility, both professional and financial, fell squarely on her shoulders.

Hafize Gaye Erkan was appointed Governor of Turkey's Central Bank in June 2023 amid steep inflation and a depreciating currency, becoming the first woman to hold this position. Despite implementing proactive policy changes and receiving international praise, she resigned eight months later, citing a "major reputation assassination campaign."

Stephanie Pope was appointed President and CEO of Boeing Commercial Airplanes in March 2024, just two months after a door plug blew out mid-flight on a 737 MAX 9. Tasked with leading the recovery of the crucial and "troubled" plane-making division, she is navigating intense scrutiny while working to restore public trust.

HIGHER STANDARD OF ACCOUNTABILITY

Women also face a double standard for misconduct at work.

- While women are more likely to be appointed to CEO in times of crisis, they are also 45% more likely than their male counterparts to be removed, according to the Journal of Management.

- Harvard Business School tells us "Women caught in misconduct were 20% more likely to be fired and 30% less likely to find new employment."
- Women are prosecuted for white-collar crimes more readily than men. Research shows that, compared to men, women commit fewer white-collar crimes, yet they are prosecuted at a higher rate relative to the percentage of presumed crimes committed.
- Women face higher sentences for white collar crime in contrast to other types of crime where women generally enjoy lenient sentences.
- Women are held to a higher standard. Two high profile examples of this are Elizabeth Holmes and Martha Stewart.

OPPORTUNITY OUT ON THE CLIFF

The glass cliff is real, but fortunately, some women gather the support they need and are afforded the time and autonomy to navigate the terrain. Kate Swann led WHSmith for nearly ten years and orchestrated a stunning turnaround. Then she did it again at SSP. Irene Rosenfeld and Indra Nooyi also led major transformations—not because they beat the odds alone, but because they had time and trust.

While leading in a crisis is undeniably risky, it can also be an opportunity to demonstrate resilience, gain visibility, drive change, and shine.

For women whose upward career trajectory has stalled, it may be a rare shot at reaching the top of the organization. The key is to recognize the pervasive pattern, go in with eyes wide open, and have a strong support network behind you.

All of us can do better to support any leader willing to step up in times of chaos, regardless of gender, and to reject the notion that failure in a crisis confirms outdated assumptions that women aren't suited for top leadership roles.

SABOTAGE FROM WITHIN

Unfortunately, even female-dominated industries don't always see women as leaders. We were all raised in the same society, exposed to the same media messages, and attuned to how people are treated. It's easy to forget that if individuals haven't done the work to challenge their own bias, women can be just as sexist as the worst men. There is nothing about womanhood that inherently makes someone understanding or supportive of the challenges other women face.

Christina faced discrimination when she gave birth to her son while completing her MBA. Despite taking thoughtful steps to minimize disruption—working ahead on her portion of group projects and arranging to have her newborn nearby—she encountered unexpected hostility, particularly from other women in her program.

One project team member deliberately excluded her by scheduling meetings in locations where children were not allowed. Another peer regularly told her she should not continue her studies and even appealed directly to the Dean to have her removed from the program. Thankfully, with support from faculty and other classmates, and through her own determination, Christina safeguarded her place and successfully completed the program while navigating life as a new mother.

PERCEPTIONS OF POTENTIAL

Women are consistently considered to have less leadership potential and be less willing to self-promote despite higher ratings on current performance.[4] Women tend to only be promoted based on a proven track record of already performing the skills needed for the job they hope to move into.

Women tend to outperform men in key leadership skills such as coaching and mentoring, influence, inspirational leadership, conflict management, organizational awareness, adaptability, teamwork, and achievement orientation. These professional strengths enable women to be more effective in the workplace.

Learning to self-promote comfortably is vital to career advancement. For women, it can be challenging to self-promote without feeling at odds with stereotypical feminine traits. One effective strategy is to align self-promotion with those traits, presenting accomplishments in ways that feel collaborative and authentic.

---

[4] *"Potential" and the Gender Promotions Gap* found differences in potential ratings accounted for approximately half of the gender promotion gap at the company they were studying. *Overlooked Leadership Potential* found when it comes to getting promoted, men just need to show potential, while women have to prove performance. Multiple studies confirm that women are reluctant to publicize their achievements, while some highlight the backlash for high self-promotion at hiring depends on candidates' gender and age.

- Tap into collaboration stereotypes by sharing lessons learned. You might ask for five minutes at the beginning of a recurring meeting, present to another department within the organization, or host a lunch-and-learn session that highlights recent accomplishments.
- Remind people you're always happy to answer questions about your area of expertise.
- Phrase your strong traits as though they are repeated from others. For example, in interviews, saying, "My boss especially appreciated the trust I was able to establish with our customers" worked well for me.
- By owning your strengths and finding comfortably authentic ways to showcase them, you can rise above outdated and gendered perceptions of potential.

THE GLASS ESCALATOR

The **glass escalator** refers to the tendency of men in female-dominated professions to be promoted quickly and with less need for a proven track record. This phenomenon has been observed in fields such as nursing, education, libraries, and social work. While men may face prejudice from those outside their professions, they are more readily seen as leadership material by their colleagues, including women.

Although most women in STEMM work in male-dominated fields, women now graduate at higher rates than men in biology, and the healthcare industry is largely female-dominated.

THE MERITOCRACY MYTH

Meritocracy is the belief that a person's hard work and skill will lead to achieving their goals—landing a job, getting into college, winning an election, or succeeding in the stock market.

In politics, we often hear about candidates who are self-made and are told that people should "lift themselves by their bootstraps." Our society tends to believe that we have moved beyond bias and the lottery of social standing based on birth.

In the U.S., belief in merit as the primary driver of success is particularly strong despite the fact that our family of origin is a stronger predictor of success than other countries. Unfortunately, focusing solely on merit can lead to greater discrimination. Gender and social disadvantages often go unacknowledged, which allows bias to persist and even deepen. Research shows that believing in meritocracy can make people more selfish, less self-critical, and more prone to discriminatory behavior.

The other insidious impact of the myth of meritocracy is that when people do not benefit from their skills and hard work, they begin to doubt themselves. Turns out that imposter syndrome is meritocracy's fault!

> *In addition to being false, a growing body of research in psychology and neuroscience suggests that believing in meritocracy makes people more selfish, less self-critical and even more prone to acting in discriminatory ways.*
>
> – Clifton Mark
> *Business Data Journalist*

ACTIONABLE TAKEAWAYS

I hope this chapter has helped illuminate how gendered stereotypes influence perceptions and outcomes in the workplace. Below are two sets of takeaways: personal strategies for success in leadership and hiring strategies. Consider what you might add based on your own experience.

PERSONAL STRATEGIES

- Reduce the impact of the likeability-versus-competence double bind by focusing on warmth and visibility.
- Develop strategies to comfortably and strategically self-promote.
- Remember that you aren't alone. It's not you, it's the culture.
- Challenge your gender biases. If you have a strong reaction to something, consider flipping the pronouns—does it still makes sense?
- Consider reading a primer on feminism, such as the classic *Feminism is for Everybody* by Bell Hooks.
- Challenge your belief in meritocracy.

LESSONS FOR HIRING

- Challenge your belief in stereotypical leadership traits.
- Advertise jobs through diversity-focused organizations.
- Remove gendered language from job descriptions. AI can help.
- Reevaluate job requirements: are you advertising for the job's responsibilities, or simply replicating the resume of the person who just left? Eliminate 'nice-to-haves' (or move them to a section that makes it clear they are optional).
- Consider candidates with a career gap.
- Explore offering part-time or flexible roles.
- Challenge your belief in meritocracy.

Understanding the glass ceiling, glass cliff, and glass escalator is not just academic; it is critical to navigating your career strategically. Recognizing these systemic patterns of human behavior allows you to prepare, respond thoughtfully, and make choices that serve your long-term goals.

Sixteen

Menopause & Perimenopause

BREAKING THE 'MENO-MAZE' TABOO IN THE STEMM WORKPLACE

by Cassie Leonard, in full discovery mode, asking questions, digging into the data, and navigating perimenopause in real time.

I started experiencing brain fog and intense mood changes about five years ago, and it became increasingly difficult to hide both at work. I sought medical help because, as the sole income earner in my household, I could not let something as "simple" as perimenopause derail my career progress. I still haven't started menopause, but Hormone Replacement Therapy and medication are helping me appear "normal" when it counts.

Very few women in my company's women's network openly discuss the need for perimenopause or menopause support in the broader organization. Even fewer take action, because doing that would feel like raising your hand in a town hall meeting and saying, "I'm turning into an old woman!" Honestly, as long as the medical technology industry remains male-dominated, and as long as younger generations (yes, including the women) are willing to do anything to get ahead, I don't think anything will change. I expect to continue undergoing cosmetic procedures, exercising like a fiend, and hiding my age as much as possible until I retire.

Given that in Med Tech, any woman over 45 is considered "old," I have tried to keep my age a secret (as much as possible, given the internet) for more than a decade. And it's not just because of perimenopause. It would have been meaningful for older men and women executive leaders, including the CEO, who is in his 50s, to open a conversation on the topic and help normalize it. But because nothing is said, except in whispers among women during private conversations or in women-only meetings, I've felt an ever-present need to disguise the fact that I'm in perimenopause.

We, perimenopausal and menopausal women, are here, and we are legion. Just because someone doesn't say something about her experience doesn't mean she isn't living it, or fully supportive of yours. If you ever feel alone, like you can't talk about "the change," as my grandmother called it, just know that so many women are in your shoes. We're all trying to figure it out. It's just that no one wants to be the first to speak.

– MR
Senior Director in Med Tech

SPEAKING UP

Just recently, due to a sudden increase in fatigue, I've added naps to my routine for the first time since my boys were babies. I'm also experiencing irregular periods, brain fog, and mood swings.

This is perimenopause.

Frustratingly, I've become increasingly aware that this commonplace (and unavoidable) phase of my health journey is often shrouded in mystique, reduced to whispered side conversations, or even dismissed entirely.

As a 42-year-old woman, I recognize that I'm probably only experiencing the tip of this iceberg. I also know that I am professionally at the top of my game. With two decades of experience in engineering and leadership, a company to run, boards to contribute to, and books to write, this is an incredibly inconvenient time to need a nap!

MR captured the truth: "We're all trying to figure it out."

Perimenopause and menopause (PM/M), along with the challenges that accompany these natural phases of life, are experiences that all women and people assigned female at birth (AFAB) will encounter. These phases often coincide with the period in our careers when we are making our most significant contributions to our professional fields.

To truly begin a conversation about PM/M and its impact on women and workplaces in STEMM, I put out a call for voices. Throughout this chapter, you will find experiences and perspectives from twelve women, aged 40 to 57, who chose to speak up.

Some have had wonderfully supportive experiences integrating "the change" with their work lives. Others have felt isolated and misunderstood. Some see opportunities for positive change if we can simply get the conversation started, while others are concerned that mandatory menopause training could unintentionally hinder their ability to be taken seriously or to get the job done.

Alas, we may not have reached a consensus on one-size-fits-all solutions for women and workplaces in STEMM, but we do seem to agree on one thing: the conversation needs to get started.

> *There is literally nothing on the subject that has made its way*
> *into public discourse. I feel it coming soon, but we need it now.*
>
> – Anonymous

MEET PERIMENOPAUSES

You've probably heard of **menopause**, the biological process that "marks the end of a woman's reproductive life." But did you know that menopause is actually a single day? Yep, it's a milestone, exactly 12 months to the day after your last period. It's so finite that, with a bit of planning the week before, you could even throw yourself a party.

In stark contrast, **perimenopause**, also known as the menopausal transition, is a nebulous phase that can last five to ten years, or even much longer. "Peri" is the arduous journey leading up to the moment of menopause, during which estrogen and progesterone levels begin to fluctuate significantly, sometimes even within a single day. These hormonal shifts can trigger a range of new and mostly undesirable symptoms.

I always thought menopause was something I wouldn't have to worry about until my fifties. And that might still be true. But perimenopause? Perimenopause affects our lives much earlier than I expected.

A 2025 *Nature* study (n = 4,432) found that 55.4% of women in the youngest studied age group, 30 to 35 years old, were experiencing "moderate to severe" symptoms, using the established Menopause Rating Scale to measure burden. That's far younger than even the researchers anticipated. What might they have found if they had included women aged 25 to 30?

75% of women in the U.S. who seek medical care for perimenopause and menopause symptoms are left untreated.

Some women and people assigned female at birth (AFAB) meet Peri even sooner. Medical conditions and procedures such as hysterectomies can lead to the early onset of perimenopausal symptoms.

Engineer Vélez-Vega experienced her first hot flash at the age of 31. As part of her cancer treatment, she underwent a stem cell transplant that triggered an immediate entry into perimenopause. Fortunately, with her doctor's guidance, she was able to use birth control to, in her own words, "slow down the process and avoid further complications like osteoporosis at such a young age."

ACKNOWLEDGING THE TABOO

Fun fact: Perimenopause exists in your workplace today.[1]

---

[1] Yup, right now.

It is affecting many women and people AFAB between the ages of 30 and 55. These are the same experienced professionals who are moving into leadership roles, taking on customer-facing projects, stepping into the C-suite, and chairing boards.

So, why don't we hear about it?

Well, perimenopause and menopause are taboo.

The reasons why PM/M remain are taboo are endless and deeply personal. They are shaped by life experiences, culture, education, identity, whether someone has become a parent, or not. The list goes on.

While I could never capture every unique reason, I can offer data and share stories from our community to highlight three recurring themes that continue to fuel our resistance to discussing PM/M in the workplace.

STIGMA

In many cultures, particularly Western, menstruation is often loaded with stigma and shame. The end of our menses seems to be no different.

Thankfully, progress bringing menstruation to the mainstream is being made. For example,

> **Comedian and advocate Amy Schumer** partnered with Tampax in 2020 to destigmatize menstruation conversations through an educational campaigns that address common misconceptions.

> **In Seattle Public Schools** students are no longer separated by gender for sexual health curriculum. This means my sons are more informed, gaining an understanding of women's health. This helps a generation get in front of stigmas before they can even start.

Progress is encouraging, but I recognize that we still have a long way to go to fully break the stigma in STEMM. Many of our workplaces remain grounded in cultural norms that feel stuck in the 1900s, limiting our ability to speak openly about our symptoms and the support needed to protect our well-being.[2]

---

[2] As an 'Elder Millennial', I spent nearly two decades of my life in the 1900s, so I know it when I see it. And thank you to Iliza Shlesinger for coining this term.

CHANGES IN OUR PROFESSIONAL CAPABILITIES

As much as we may not want to admit it, if we're going to have an honest conversation, we need to be blunt, perimenopause and menopause come with real symptoms that impact our ability to function at the high levels we've come to expect of ourselves. Memory lapses and difficulty concentrating, commonly referred to as "brain fog," affect roughly 60% of women in perimenopause. This is a medical consequence of reduced estrogen reaching the brain's estrogen receptors.

> *We can't shy away from the fact that menopause does have certain negative effects on the brain.*
>
> – Anonymous

However, the reluctance to share these experiences, even with your trusted community, can have unintended consequences.

Yes, many of us will face brain fog and other disruptive symptoms. But if we all remain silent out of embarrassment or fear, we lose sight of the fact that these are real, valid medical conditions. Without open conversation and support, we're left to navigate them alone.

In isolation, the cost of PM/M grows, leading to the attrition of high-powered, highly skilled technical leaders and role models like you.

GENDERED AGEISM

If talking about periods and slower thought processes weren't already enough to derail the conversation, PM/M also intersect with gendered ageism, opening a Pandora's box of new concerns, biases, microaggressions, and stigmas to contend with.

As our senior director shared at the beginning of this chapter, some STEMM fields have a tendency to celebrate youth as essential to rapid innovation.

> *That would feel like raising your hand in a town hall meeting and saying, 'I'm turning into an old woman!'*
>
> – MR

According to a Harvard Business School study (n = 913), women in the workplace between the ages of 40 and 60 (note the close alignment with the typical window for PM/M) are prone to gendered age discrimination based on assumptions about family commitments and potential menopausal limitations. The study found that the perceived potential for distraction among women in this age range was frequently used to justify decisions not to hire or promote "middle-aged" women.[3]

It's true that discussing menopause in the workplace may inadvertently expose individuals to age- and identity-related discrimination, which carries significant risks. However, when approached mindfully and in environments where you feel psychologically safe, the potential benefits of opening the conversation may still outweigh the cost.

Only you can decide what's right for your situation.

OUTDATED WORKPLACE MYTHS

And then there are the assumptions. Many myths surrounding what menopause is, and isn't, persist in modern STEMM workplaces. Consider these four common myths and how they continue to reinforce the taboo surrounding PM/M.

Myth. This isn't relevant for our workplace.

Reality. Roughly 310 million working professionals globally are experiencing PM/M related symptoms.[4]

Myth. Women will always request accommodations when needed.

Reality. 87% of women in the U.S. don't speak to their manager about their menopause symptoms. Yet, PM/M symptoms force 40% of women to adjust how they work on at least a weekly basis.

---

[3] This discrimination overlaps with 'youngism,' when you're expected to get the coffee and be grateful just to be in the room, and 'oldism,' when development opportunities become scarce and your opinions are dismissed. Be sure to check out the study's section on 'lookism' too!

[4] Applying UN Data, Dennis and Hobson found that "47% of the 657 million women globally aged between 45 and 59 contributed to the workforce globally" in 2020.

Myth. It's just a "women's problem."

> **Reality.** Lack of support affects the entire team, reducing both productivity and retention. Global studies report menopause-related attrition rates from 10% to over 25%. That's a lot of experience and expertise walking out the door.[5]

Myth. Accommodations cost too much.

> **Reality.** Menopause-related attrition costs U.S. companies 2.2 billion dollars annually. These are not the interns departing, they're your senior technical lead, your chief engineer, your board member, and your CEO.[6]

> The loss of technical expertise and business acumen is staggering. Pair that with a sudden gap in mentors, champions, and role models for the younger women on your team, and you have an expensive problem. Workplaces must shift their mindset from "Can we afford to?" to "We can't afford not to."

What's Good About Menopause?

Let's take a brief pause to note that perimenopause and menopause are not all doom and gloom. Here are three positive things worth noting about PM/M.

- No more periods (450 down, zero to go).
- No more cramps, menstrual migraines, or PMS.
- And apparently post-menopause comes with a new-found *zest for life!*[7]

---

[5] Check out Hot Resignation, a movement focused on raising awareness of the impact of menopause in the workplace.

[6] The average CEO is 53.46 years old—a prime menopausal symptom age.

[7] "There is no greater power in the world than the zest of a postmenopausal woman," or so the saying goes. This quote is often attributed to Margaret Mead.

SOLUTIONS FOR STEMM WORKPLACES

STEMM workplaces have a powerful opportunity to support women and people AFAB who are experiencing PM/M symptoms, and they face significant costs if they choose not to.

The 2022 Biote *Women in the Workplace Survey* (n = 1,010) found that two-thirds of respondents reported having mostly negative experiences with menopause at work. Allow me to repeat that for dramatic effect: if you have three women or people assigned female at birth over the age of 30 on your team, chances are, unbeknownst to you, two of them are having mostly negative experiences. That can't be good.

Fortunately, workplaces can take meaningful action to provide support. The following actions, drawn from insights shared by our community of contributors, offer practical ways for STEMM workplaces to foster a more inclusive and supportive environment.

ACTION: LISTEN & ACKNOWLEDGE REALITY

The best place to start is by listening to those affected. Television presenter Davina McCall shared similar sentiments on the *ZEO Science & Nutrition* podcast:

> *What happened in the past was that women were expected to suck it up... Women have always been expected to suck up everything.*
>
> – Davina McCall
> *British TV Presenter and Health Advocate*[8]

When someone is brave enough to share their PM/M experience with you, listen and acknowledge them. Avoid the all-too-common tendency to dismiss their concerns or minimize their needs.

Kat Meckle, a mental health therapist and contributing voice, highlighted this 'simple' yet critical action: *validate her experience.*

---

[8] Just one of many great ZOE Science & Nutrition podcasts on menopause. Check out the full episode, *Davina McCall: Make This Choice Every Day to Reduce Menopause Symptoms.*

PM/M is a real medical condition that can be treated. Women do not just 'make up' these symptoms, and it's not for lack of trying. Women need to be validated in these experiences and encouraged to find appropriate care.

– Kat

Did you know that 75% of women in the U.S. who seek medical care for PM/M symptoms are left untreated? While symptoms can be non-specific, your role is to trust her experience and offer support wherever you can.

ACTION: ACTIVELY CHALLENGE BIAS AND GENDERED AGEISM

Bias and discrimination can be addressed, even if you're not ready to say words like "period" or "menstrual" out loud. By focusing workplace training and initiatives on age- and gender-based bias, organizations can drive meaningful change without directly confronting the taboo.

Eliminate gender-diminutive language. Set and maintain expectations to keep women from being labeled with infantilizing and dismissive terms like 'sweetheart' and 'girl' in the workplace.

Ensure equal access to professional opportunities. Seek out patterns. Are women being passed over for development opportunities after they've reached *'a certain age'*? Survey contributor K. Sunshine was left without growth opportunities when her leaders made misguided assumption her ambitions. Are you doing the same?

Check for unconscious bias in decision making. Just as it would be unethical (and in most cases, illegal), to avoid hiring a young woman because she might someday get pregnant, leaders must pause to ensure they are not limiting career progression for mid-career and senior women based on assumptions about their potential for menopause-related symptoms.

ACTION: SUPPORT AN ABUNDANCE OF REASONABLE
ACCOMMODATION REQUESTS

Imagine if one small change could make all the difference for your employee, an accommodation that improves their comfort, productivity, job satisfaction, and likelihood of staying with the company.

Would you support it? Of course you would. Here's how.

Hot flashes. Offer flexible work arrangements, such as hybrid schedules, desk placements away from heaters, and the ability to adjust the office temperature. If uniforms are required, provide material options that accommodate those experiencing skin-related discomfort.

For additional ideas, refer to the UK National Health Service (NHS) Menopause Workplace Pledge, which recommends solutions like ensuring easy access to cold water and bathroom facilities.

Lack of sleep, headaches, and fatigue. Support flexible work hours and locations to help employees manage their energy more effectively. Wendy A. Cocke, founder of Engineering Leadership Solutions, has found that despite experiencing daytime fatigue, she is highly productive during non-traditional work hours.

Having the ability to flex around these times has ensured I'm still able to perform at my best.

– Wendy

Consider your team's energy peaks and valleys. Optimal work hours will likely vary from person to person. Be bold in your approach and focus on outcomes and results, not time spent behind a desk. For more strategies on post-pandemic workplace flexibility, check out Wendy's book *Making Flex Work*.

Stiffness, aches, and pain. These symptoms are not unique to women experiencing reduced estrogen levels, so there's no need to add gender or age when addressing them. Instead, focus on making existing organizational accommodations visible. This might include workstation assessments and ergonomic adjustments, encouraging movement breaks, and offering flexible work options that allow individuals to manage their discomfort in ways that work best for them.

Anxiety, memory lapses, and difficulty concentrating. Cognitive symptoms are often the hardest to discuss openly, but the need for support is real. One contributor shared, "Demanding group settings make my symptoms worse, with flare-ups that last longer both before and after the stress of the meeting." She also recalled that the days she was able to work from home were "the only days I could get any real work accomplished or meet any personal or professional goals."

The level of organizational psychological safety directly affects a leader's ability to support their team. Engineer Vélez-Vega has navigated her extended journey through perimenopause within a highly supportive workplace culture.

> *I've been open about discussing my experiences and haven't felt weak or isolated from my health experiences. Normalizing these life events is part of acceptance and being part of nature.*
>
> *– Vélez-Vega*

In less open environments, leaders should consider whether they are creating safe opportunities for women to ask for what they need or forcing them to burn time and energy justifying their requests to an organization that doesn't fully understand them.

ACTION: UPDATE COMPANY POLICIES

The World Health Organization notes that "those experiencing menopausal symptoms may feel embarrassed or ashamed to draw attention to their experiences and ask for support." As a result, valued employees may remain silent, even when support could make a significant difference.

Inclusive policies can offer that support without placing the burden on individuals to self-advocate. Consider this your call to action: review your organization's policies with these critical details in mind:

> **Employee disclosure policies.** Ensure people can request reasonable accommodations without fear that their specific symptoms, life phase, or age will become widely known.

> **Hiring, promotion, and opportunity policies.** Eliminate bias in decision-making by implementing checks and balances. Evaluate candidates based on their skills and qualifications, not on assumptions.

> **Health insurance policies.** Include menopause support, such as Hormone Replacement Therapy (HT/HRT) in the standard benefits. Ensure coverage for high-quality dedicated menopause practitioners.[9]

And most importantly, ask your team.

They know what they need.

PRACTICAL STEPS FOR PERIMENOPAUSAL STEMM WOMEN

It's time to end the era where women were expected to '*suck it up*' and ignore the impact of PM/M on their work experiences.

> *The inconvenient truth is that perimenopause is a truly challenging time for our brains and bodies and it can make us less 'productive.' How are we to reconcile this?*
>
> – Anonymous

---

[9] Our contributing voices found dedicated menopause practitioners come with a high out of pocket cost and often have long waiting lists. One woman remarked (brilliantly, I might add), "I had to pay very little out of pocket to have a baby, so why should I have to pay more now just because my body doesn't want to make babies anymore?"

While this is not solely a "women's problem" and I assume we all agree the system needs fixing, we also have to take care of ourselves in the moment. Here are a few ideas for supporting yourself and others in your community.

EDUCATE YOURSELF ON THE FACTS

Research is improving, but significant gaps remain. While the volume of data is growing, much of the older research, especially on estrogen risks, is being challenged. Long-held beliefs that even some doctors may still hold, such as "we don't need to talk about menopause until you're 50," can now be countered with updated facts and data. When reviewing any research, be aware of what exactly was tested, oral versus transdermal delivery methods for hormone therapy show significantly different results.

> *I'm doing my best to educate myself as I go along. But having more knowledge at a younger age would really have helped me to prepare myself for what was coming.*

> – Anonymous

As you educate yourself, consider the following.

Recognize the good, the bad, and the ugly of social media. As millennials enter their 40s, conversations about menopause are becoming more popular on social media platforms. But as you know, not everything on Instagram is fact-based. Trustworthy sources I've found include the ZOE Science & Nutrition podcast, the Vajenda blog, and the Balance app.[10]

Talk to your trusted circle. You might discover that someone close to you is going through or has already experienced what you're facing. As one contributor shared, "My best support has

---

[10] The Vajenda, by Dr Jen Gunter, board certified OB/GYN, takes a self-described "fiery" approach to medical facts and feminism. Balance is a menopause support app founded and led by Dr. Louise Newson, a GP and Menopause Specialist.

been through friends. Talking about our experiences and what some of them are doing to find relief."

Review your organization's policies. Uncover how you can reasonably apply current benefits to support your needs.

- Look for specific menopause-related policies in your organization and health insurance.
- Consider how broader benefits, such as sick leave, vacation time, sabbaticals, flexible work arrangements, and ergonomic assessments can help.
- Employee Assistance Programs (EAP) may be able to connect you directly with menopause specialists. This service can also include confidential counseling and assistance interpreting company policies.

STRATEGICALLY SELF-ADVOCATE

Sometimes we need to clearly articulate what we require to the people who can make it happen. With a sensitive subject like PM/M, it's worth taking a few extra moments to reflect on our workplace culture and psychological safety to increase the chances of achieving the results we want.

Consider these questions and actions.

Question 1. Are you comfortable openly discussing your needs with your manager or human resources?

If yes, start an open dialogue to advocate for what you need.

If no, proceed to Question 2.

Question 2. Can you request the support you need without disclosing uncomfortable information with your management team?

If yes, strategically advocate for what you need.

If maybe, call your trusted circle and brainstorm solutions.

If no, proceed to Question 3.

Question 3. Can you access the support you need through EAP or other company resources?

If yes, connect with the available resources.

If no, it's time for some deep reflection. Proceed to Question 4.

Question 4. Is this the right place for you to be working?

Before you answer, invest time reflecting on the value and cost of your current situation. 10% of women experiencing PM/M symptoms at work have chosen to leave their current employer. These women made choices to support themselves when the system around them could not, or would not.

BECOME A TRAILBLAZER

Wherever you are on your journey, you have the opportunity to drive change for those who follow.

First, get loud.

Advocate. Share your story and amplify evidence-based research.

Engineer Vélez-Vega shared her story to ensure hormone-based cancer survivors are included in the conversation.

Kelly is advocating for women who have been mis-diagnosed, dismissed, or have experienced overlapping effects of menopause and other conditions, as she did for 15 years with undiagnosed Hashimoto's thyroiditis.

Sanchari stepped up to raise awareness of how PM/M is experienced in the STEMM workplace in her country.

In India, discussions about menstruation, menopause, and perimenopause are very limited. This silence is reflected in the workforce, where women's labor force participation rate declines at the same time perimenopause becomes a factor.

While I know it is difficult to ask for organization-wide policy changes, we must at least voice our concerns within our groups. In the midst of all this, we must at least try to voice our concerns within our groups. No one will know what we need unless we ask, and therefore no support will be provided, no matter how much others may want to help.

– Sanchari Banerjee
Mother in Science, Leader, and Mentor

Next, leverage your abundance of STEMM skills. How will you advance research, refine tools, and develop better resources to improve the workplace experience for everyone navigating perimenopause?

And finally, stay engaged in the conversation. I'll be navigating PM/M for at least the next decade, I'd love to learn alongside you.

You are invited to join the private LinkedIn Group ELMM PM/M. In this private space, we will share our stories, explore new research, debunk myths, and spotlight insightful podcasts.

Our goal is to build a supportive community for people experiencing perimenopause and menopause, rejecting the notion that these experiences are in any way taboo.

Seventeen

International Experiences

AN ENRICHING MID-CAREER CHANGE OF SCENERY
THAT CAN HELP WOMEN STAY ON THE STEMM PATH

*by Rachael Browning, international engineer, mom, foodie,
and language enthusiast.*

Looking at my colleague, very confused, I asked, "What do you mean we need to make up holidays on the weekend?"

Yep, it happened at least twice a year around the Chinese National Holidays and was locally considered very normal. This was not what I expected to hear after I had already booked my first vacation while on assignment!

For me, gaining international experience like this has helped keep life exciting! I am so happy to be able to share my collective experiences, insights, and expat conversations with you. If you are considering an international role, I hope this inspires you to take the plunge. And if you haven't considered one yet, I hope you find this both informative and entertaining.

– Rachael

There is a story known by many who have lived and worked abroad that truly embodies the experience.

One day, a circle person, living in a circle country with circle friends and family, moves to the land of squares. The squares eat different food, speak a different language, celebrate different holidays, and share their own square values. At first, the circle struggles to fit in, but then they make square friends and eat square foods. While the circle doesn't feel 100% integrated, it also doesn't feel so alone and enjoys its time in the land of squares.

One day, the circle returns home to visit, but it no longer wants to eat and do only circle things. In conversations, the circle suddenly finds itself disagreeing on many points it once believed in and begins to feel like an outsider looking in. The next morning, as the circle gets ready, it looks in the mirror and sees that it is now a triangle, not a circle or a square, but something else entirely. A mix of two cultures and systems of belief, it will never be completely a circle again or fully become a square. It takes some of the good and some of the bad from each and becomes its own unique being.

This is what working internationally can do to us. Many parts of becoming this new person are positive, while others can be plain weird! That said, I believe it is overall a good thing. In all my travels, I have never met anyone who wished they had never gone, seen, or done something as challenging as embracing another culture.

MY JOURNEY

My personal desire to explore and leave my mark on the world is what drove me to engineering. I found an amazing International Engineering Program at the University of Rhode Island, where I was able to pursue both Chemical Engineering and Mandarin Chinese, including multiple study abroad experiences and an internship in Mainland China. Even in my final year at university, while interviewing for jobs, I was clear that I wanted to work on multicultural teams and gain international experience.

Amazingly, all the stars aligned. Right out of school, I joined a Global 500 company where I have grown my career for 14 years. I have worked with colleagues from all over the world, expatriated to both the People's Republic of China and France, supported factories in 11 countries, and traveled to many more.

THE INTERNATIONAL LANDSCAPE

In today's globalized world, we have unprecedented access to people, cultures, information, and plane tickets. Everyone's path will look different, but gaining international experience is easier than ever and can provide an enriching mid-career change of scenery while staying on your STEMM path. However, much like the story about circles, squares, and triangles, there are definitely challenges that depend on the type and level of international work you do, the **culture shock** as you adjust to new environments, and the **reverse culture shock** when you return home.

Your own choices, along with the support you receive from networks inside and outside of work, play a significant role in helping you successfully transition at each stage, especially during mid-career, when many of us must consider not just ourselves, but also our families. Whether you are a mid-career woman in STEMM or an ally, providing support throughout the entire journey, from leaving to coming back home, can help keep life exciting while maintaining a fulfilling career.

PATHWAYS TO AN INTERNATIONAL WORK EXPERIENCE

Many companies that operate internationally value global experience as a career accelerator. You get to experience different ways of thinking, living, and working that can help you grow quickly and enhance your current and future teams through greater understanding. That said, your experience will vary depending on the type, level, and countries of international exposure you have.

Being an experienced mid-career woman in STEMM can strengthen your candidacy for international roles, as you bring significant value and expertise to the table. This is highlighted in Deloitte's research.

To survive and thrive, companies must... use international
assignments to cultivate leaders with global experience to
help run their increasingly broad, geographic operations

– Deloitte

Unfortunately, being mid-career can also be a hurdle to even being offered an international opportunity. Mercer reports that women make up only 20–30% of expatriates in the best-performing industries and countries, with the typical figure closer to 14%. Being vocal about your desires to work abroad and values you bring are critical to being considered.

Challenges to women working abroad can be real - treatment of women, safety, and autonomy can differ country to country.

Women also face challenges based on family status. Gender-biased perceptions about married women or mothers may prevent them from even being considered for international career opportunities, assumptions that she has young kids and won't be able to travel, that her husband has a good job and won't want to relocate, or that she won't want to move until her kids are out of school. For unmarried women, some cultures expect them to have a male guardian or at least permission when traveling. This creates a hurdle even for smaller international exposure opportunities, such as training or conferences.

To minimize the impact of these biases and improve your chances for international work experiences, it is critical to express your desires and pursue them directly. You might start smaller by asking for an international project or trip to demonstrate that you can deliver results in an international environment. Being aware of these challenges and building relationships with sponsors in your organization or network who can advocate for you will also significantly increase your chances.

Business Travel

One of the most accessible forms of exposure is international travel. This might include attending a conference, going on a short mission or research exchange, visiting suppliers, or even touring your own company's factories abroad. Once you build rapport by meeting face-to-face and gain an understanding of the other side, communication becomes easier, faster, and flows more naturally, since trust and shared experiences have been established. You may even find yourself gaining visibility as an information broker. It is also a great way to gain broad exposure to a variety of sites, practices, and people. This exposure can open doors to future opportunities.

EXPATRIATION

Expatriating occurs when your current employer sponsors you, and potentially your family, to relocate to another country to work at one of its international sites. For this type of move, there are usually many supports in place to help you succeed, which can be quite costly for employers. These supports may include cultural training, language training for you and your family, relocation assistance, tax preparation assistance, annual trips back to your home country, and even financial support. As discussed in the pathways section, being mid-career can both help and challenge your chances of securing one of these roles.

Talking to others who have been through the experience is a great first step to understanding what expatriation looks like in your organization and to plan your next moves.

APPLY DIRECTLY

If your employer doesn't offer or support international work, another option is to apply directly to international jobs. This can be challenging both from a work visa and language standpoint, as most "local" jobs require proficiency in the host country's language. That said, many STEMM fields face a high demand for talent. To meet these needs, some countries allow skilled workers to apply for a talent visa directly, enabling them to move and find a job locally. Other countries have employment portals where you can express interest in immigrating and match your skills to high-demand job postings. By connecting talent with employers willing to sponsor work visas, these programs can simplify the process.

If your country of interest doesn't have similar programs, you can also apply directly on employer websites. While this approach can be successful, it may be challenging since many job postings state they do not sponsor visas and actively screen for candidates with legal work authorization.

As with job searching in your home country, leveraging your personal network and securing personal recommendations can help open doors. A personal referral may also fast-track your resume to the hiring manager, bypassing automated screening tools that might otherwise filter you out prematurely.

Higher Education

Like other options, going back to school to pursue further education in a foreign country comes with its own set of challenges.[1] That said, it allows you to target a specific area, country, and language of interest. It also sometimes enables you to apply for a longer-term visa, which may include the right to work in the country after graduation.

The cost of school may be higher or lower than in your home country, but the biggest impact to consider, especially mid-career, is the loss of a full-time paycheck. This can be particularly difficult if you have a family or if a work visa is not possible for your spouse.

Culture Shock

Culture Shock, *noun:*

A sense of confusion and uncertainty, sometimes with feelings of anxiety, that may affect people exposed to a new culture without adequate preparation.

Whether you are living abroad, traveling, or working with international colleagues, culture shock is inevitable. No matter how much you study or research, nothing can truly prepare you for the wide range of challenges you will encounter, especially as a woman in STEMM, except for firsthand experience.

If you are a facts-and-figures person, *Riding the Waves of Culture: Understanding Diversity in Global Business* is a good book to start with. It offers a global perspective on various country-specific cultural norms and topics, including presentation styles, decision-making processes, and even cultural faux pas to avoid, such as buying a nicer vehicle than your manager.

---

[1] See Chapter 12, *Academia*, for Jessica's experience working abroad in academia.

THE NOT SO NICE

Every place has a culture. Regardless of gender, you need to understand how things work, how decisions are made, who the key influencers are, and how things actually get done. Expect it to be different from where you came from, and be prepared to adjust in order to succeed.

As a woman working in STEMM, we are often the only one or one of the few on our teams. This dynamic can make it harder to integrate and may require a different approach compared to others in the workplace. What works for men on the team may be perceived differently when it comes from you.

- A one-on-one lunch outing or invite to the pub after work with a colleague who's a man may be deemed inappropriate.
- The idea of personal space also differs across cultures. Kissing on the cheeks in greeting, resting an arm on a colleague's shoulder, hugging, standing close while talking, or even behaviors such as someone of the opposite gender taking intense interest in your personal life, commenting on your body, or using aggressive speech may become part of your reality.
- These situations can make anyone uncomfortable, so it is important to understand what is considered a cultural norm and what crosses the line into inappropriateness or even harassment.

Globally, women are often perceived as having less technical credibility than men. They may need to prove themselves repeatedly to be taken seriously or to receive the same level of respect as a peer who's a man. In an international workplace, being both an "outsider" and a woman can compound this issue. There are often fewer women with similar experiences who can act as mentors or offer support. Having an ally or advocate in a higher-level position on site who can open doors and speak on your behalf, especially when you are not in the room, can be a valuable way to integrate more quickly and ensure you are able to get your work done effectively.

Challenges like these can occur even in your home country and may be intensified when working for a multinational company, where different corporate cultures collide.

Regardless of your situation, when work plays such a significant role in your livelihood, it can be scary to struggle with these issues, and your mental health may suffer as a result. Please be sure to familiarize yourself with support resources available in a language you are comfortable with. These might include Employee Assistance Programs, local therapists you can communicate with, or even support from the local expat community. Telemedicine apps, some of which allow you to filter by language, and social media platforms can also make it easier to connect with others and offer a safe space for asking questions, making friends, or finding low-cost or free items to help you settle in.

TURNING SURPRISES INTO GROWTH

Change is hard, but also rewarding!

Many things that seem shocking at first often have a bright side, helping you learn more about yourself, your likes, dislikes, and what you want moving forward. For me, one of the most stand-out points of personal growth was becoming more comfortable with setting boundaries.

One day, I was trying to squeeze in a critical meeting. As usual, calendars were full, so I took a chance and proposed an 8:30 a.m. time slot. Coming from the U.S., this felt perfectly normal. But I quickly received a decline from a man who explained that he needed to drop off his kids in the morning and simply couldn't meet before 9 a.m. What surprised me most was how clearly he defended his personal time. There was no "I'll call in from the school parking lot" or effort to bend over backwards, it was a firm, unapologetic no!

I had a similar experience while working in China, where the main mode of transport to and from the site was a company shuttle bus. I blocked off the time on my calendar and made it clear that catching that bus was a non-negotiable stop at the end of the day. It was the only ride home, and I wasn't going to miss it.

When I returned to the U.S., I carried those lessons with me. They gave me the confidence to say "no" when needed or to clearly communicate expectations, like when I had to leave the office on time for school pick-up, for example.

On the personal side, we got an unexpected surprise when I found out I was pregnant a few months into my assignment in France. Resources for life events like this can vary widely between countries. Thankfully, I found a great doctor who spoke English, but I missed out on things like birthing classes due to my limited French.

That said, I had a wonderful experience and benefited from both lower healthcare and childcare costs. Full-time newborn care at a private crèche (daycare) in our neighborhood was around €600 per month, while public crèche cost about €400. In contrast, infant care in the United States was around $1,700 (€1,500) per month, and $1,200 (€1,050) as our child got older.

In France, children transition to *maternelle* (preschool) for free when they turn three years old, whereas in the U.S., free education typically doesn't begin until age five. This meant two additional years of costly childcare back home.

RETURNING HOME, OR NOT

One thing many people and companies don't thoroughly consider or prepare for is repatriation, and this is a missed opportunity. Studies have shown that up to 68% of returning expatriates leave their companies within two years. While there is less research on how to retain returnees than on how to prepare them to go abroad, the issue is thought to be linked to a few key factors.

LACK OF SUPPORT ON RE-ENTRY

Especially for those who have spent significant time abroad, returning home can come with unexpected challenges. Changes in the home country and within the home company often occur, colleagues move on to other roles, professional networks fade and need to be rebuilt, and organizational structures and expectations evolve. Yet, because they are "home," returnees are often expected to navigate everything independently and quickly.

This challenge can be even more pronounced for women, who frequently carry the bulk of household responsibilities and mental load. Children need to adjust to new schools and make new friends. A spouse who was not working during the assignment may now face the need to explain a career gap and reenter the job market.

While there is usually flexibility and understanding when moving abroad, the expectations upon returning are often much less forgiving. Managers and colleagues may act as if nothing has changed. Without the complications of language barriers, cultural adjustments, or visa paperwork, your reintegration timeline is assumed to be the same as that of a local internal transfer or new hire. It's usually shorter, more rigid, and offers little room to ramp back up. Many returning expats are expected to be performing at 100% despite the significant energy reintegration demands both at work and at home. This can make the adjustment difficult and leave you feeling isolated and frustrated. Unlike living abroad, where an expat community or international colleagues might share similar experiences, returning home can feel like you're the only one going through it.

Every situation will require a different approach, but openly acknowledging this transition and offering structured training and reintegration policies for both employees and employers can make a meaningful difference. Even assigning a mentor or integration buddy can help bridge the gap and provide a supportive, judgment-free space for asking what might otherwise feel like basic or obvious questions.

LACK OF RECOGNITION

The expat experience is often life-changing, and the individual usually grows in profound ways. Returning to a previous status quo can feel difficult or even disheartening. Without the heightened visibility and expectations that came with an international role, it's easy to become frustrated by the perceived lack of influence or opportunity to drive change back home.

Even those who frequently travel internationally can experience this shift. When overseas assignments become less frequent, it may feel like the impact they once made is diminished.

Skills developed abroad can also go unrecognized. A new language learned during the assignment may no longer be needed. Professional connections built overseas may no longer serve a purpose in the new role.

As the story of the circle, square, and triangle illustrates, the "circles" back in your home country might not appreciate your new ways of thinking or working. They may even criticize you for it.

REVERSE CULTURE SHOCK & ISOLATION

Like the triangle returning to the land of circles, coming back after spending significant time building close connections abroad can feel deeply isolating. The level of connection and socialization you once had may no longer be there. Even old friends and colleagues might forget to include you in things, either because you've been away for several years or changed your number.

It's important to be prepared for this and not let it discourage you. Know that this is a common experience and that you may need to take the initiative to begin reintegrating.

Reverse Culture Shock, *noun:*

A sense of disorientation or unease, sometimes accompanied
by anxiety, that may affect people returning to their home culture
after significant time in a different cultural environment.

TAKEAWAYS

While there are many challenges, I've never met anyone who didn't at least partially value their time in an international environment. Some friends have even met their spouses and started families abroad, with no plans to return, while others brought their new spouses home.

The experience is different for everyone. What's important is to embrace change, face the challenges, and make the best decisions for yourself and your family. Advocate for yourself and for others, especially those who will come after you. Avoiding isolation and building a strong support network can lead to lifelong friendships. You may even discover that the community, policies, and way of life abroad suit you better than those back home, and choose to stay permanently.

As shown in many chapters of this book, whether we are expats or returning expats, we can't fully control how others treat us, but we can decide what we want to do with our careers. Working internationally, in one or more of its many forms, is a choice we can make. For allies, it's a choice to support and nurture.

For those interested in an international experience, I've provided some time-phased considerations. For allies looking to support others on their adventures, I've added a set of reflection questions just for you.

If you're thinking about taking the leap, know that there will rarely be a perfect time. But you can take a few small steps now to move toward your goal.

Timeframe & actions	Key considerations & reflection questions
Take a week to reflect on your wants and needs. If you have a family, talk with them too.	Are you (and your family) interested in an international experience? Can your partner support extra travel for extended periods?
Take a month to research.	What countries are you interested in? What do job postings, salary, and lifestyles look like there? [2] Are there friends, family, or colleagues who worked abroad who you can talk to? Does your current employer have positions abroad? Is there an expatriation policy at your company? Are there schools, programs, or research institutions you are interested in that accept international students? Is there a language requirement? What will repatriation look like? Are there actions you can take now (e.g., impacts to visas, taxes, healthcare, or future employment).
Make a plan and take action! *This isn't a vacation. Moving internationally typically takes time and planning.*	Express interest at work by sharing that you are internationally mobile. Ask for an international project, training, or site visit. Get started on that graduate or post-doc application. Start a language class!

---

[2] Check out internationally focused resources like SWE's *Gender Balance Overview in STEM* and the Organisation for Economic Co-operation and Development (oecd.org).

Awareness questions	Ally actions
Do you have an employee who has expressed interest in international experiences?	If you're not sure, ask! When someone expresses interest, advocate for them in organizational planning discussions. Assign them to projects with international opportunities (e.g., international clients, business travel, or relocation potential).
Do you regularly travel internationally for work?	Consider inviting a colleague to join you as a learning opportunity.
Do you know someone who's currently abroad or recently returned?	Reach out—check in on how they're doing. Invite them for a coffee and listen to their stories. Even small gestures like these can help them ward off isolation and support their reintegration.

Moving from India to Denmark was one of the best decisions I've ever made.

Being an expat came with many challenges, but facing them head-on allowed me to discover what I'm really capable of. It pushed me beyond my comfort zone and gave me the strength I rely on today as a solo mom.

In addition to research with large-scale infrastructure and time spent with inspiring mentors and peers, living abroad gave me the opportunity to look at the world from a different perspective. I discovered new social expectations and norms, including what work-life balance could actually look like for mothers in STEMM like me.

Although I've now returned to India, the friendships I built and the respect I received as a working mother in science mean that Denmark will always be my second home.

Of course, this journey wasn't always easy. One of the hardest parts of moving across the world was finding a job in my highly competitive field; Structural Biology. As in any new country, I struggled to understand both the local and regional labor markets. The best tool I found to break into new markets was to connect with others. I reached out to communities like STEMPeers, EuroSTEMPeers, and Mothers in Science, joining mentorship programs that helped me understand the local systems, find my place, and feel supported.

I didn't know which networking activity or event would make the difference, but looking back, I believe they all made an impact. My advice: try to actively engage in things you like to do. You never know which skill will come in handy in the future.

If you're thinking about working abroad, I'd say go for it. Yes, it's hard, but it's also deeply rewarding. And you don't have to do it alone, there are support systems out there, ready and willing to cheer you on.

I am grateful for my experience, and for how it transformed how I see myself as a professional. Even when (or perhaps especially when) everything feels unfamiliar, you have the opportunity to learn, grow, and maybe even find a new place to call home.

– Sanchari Banerjee

Section 3

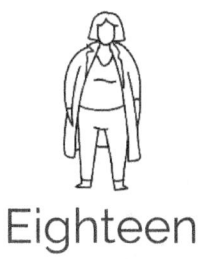

Eighteen

Redefining Success

Beyond the Pipeline Mentality

by Belinda A. Di Bartolo, ex-academic, STEMM coach, and mum proving success looks different for everyone—and that's the point.

When I first entered academia, I had a clear vision of success: publish widely, secure grants, build a reputation, and eventually earn that coveted title of 'Professor'. Like many others, I believed that if I just worked hard enough, stayed focused enough, and proved myself enough, it would all fall into place.

And for a while, it did. I built my research, taught students, mentored early-career academics, and quietly shouldered the invisible labour that institutions rely on but rarely reward.

But as the demands grew heavier, and especially after becoming a mother, I began to see how brittle the system really was. Academia wasn't designed for people balancing family, caregiving, or simply a life outside of work. The system expected relentless output without offering flexibility or meaningful support.

Leaving academia wasn't a decision I made lightly. It felt like stepping away from everything I had built my identity around.

And yet, in leaving, I found something I didn't realise I had lost: freedom.

Freedom to define success on my own terms.

Freedom to use my skills beyond publishing papers or chasing grants.

Freedom to build a career that could grow alongside my life, not consume it.

Through founding BD Stemm Strategies, I now work with others who feel trapped by outdated definitions of success. These are people who are choosing to lead, innovate, and thrive in ways that academia never taught them to see as valuable.

My story isn't rare. It is the norm. And it is why we need to talk about redefining success in STEMM.

– Belinda

THE PROBLEM WITH TRADITIONAL STEMM SUCCESS

THE NARROW PIPELINE MENTALITY

The science world loves a linear path.

Earn a PhD, complete a postdoc, land a tenure-track job, secure grants, publish prolifically, and ascend the ranks to full professor. That's success... at least, that's what we've been told (repeatedly).

But here's the reality: only 12% of STEM PhD graduates in some fields ever secure a tenure-track position, yet academia still trains the majority as if this is the inevitable outcome. What happens to the remaining 88%?[1]

The story isn't so different in industry.

The expected career path often follows the same rigid logic: get the competitive internship, land the entry-level job, move into your first management role, climb to director, and ultimately reach the C-suite.

---

[1] Multiple studies have found that only a small fraction of STEM PhD graduates secure tenure-track positions. At the University of Colorado Anschutz Medical Campus, just 12% of biomedical science PhD graduates obtained tenure-track faculty roles. Broader trends show that tenure-track outcomes vary by field, with approximately 14% of biological science PhDs, 23% of chemistry PhDs, and 21% of physics PhDs entering tenure-track positions within several years of graduation. These figures highlight that across STEM, the majority of PhD graduates do not follow the traditional academic pipeline despite institutional training models that still presume otherwise.

But, much like the academic pipeline, this model ignores reality. Recent research shows that only 3 in 10 professionals actually aspire to a C-suite position, meaning the majority are not seeking a traditional "top seat" but instead want meaningful work, career flexibility, and opportunities for growth and impact.

Many STEMM professionals are left to navigate "alternative" career paths without the institutional support or professional development needed to transition smoothly.

Others stay, grinding away in temporary contracts, low-paid positions, or toxic work environments, convinced not only that their efforts will eventually pay off, but also that stepping outside the traditional model equates to failure.

This is not just an individual problem, it's a systemic failure. The assumption that STEMM careers must follow a rigid pipeline leaves most professionals unprepared for the reality of their career prospects.

At the same time, alternative career paths such as industry research, science policy, entrepreneurship, communication, and consulting are often viewed as second-best options rather than equally valid and rewarding. As a result, STEMM professionals who seek careers outside academia or traditional R&D roles often feel like outcasts, despite contributing just as much (if not more) to science, innovation, and society.

It's time to ask the question that academia, and increasingly industry, refuses to confront: why are we training the majority for a path that only a minority will follow?

THE CONSEQUENCES OF THE TRADITIONAL ACADEMIC SYSTEM

The pipeline model sets unrealistic career expectations, leaving many professionals unprepared for jobs beyond academia. There is little infrastructure (if any) to help STEMM graduates explore careers in industry, policy, science communication, or entrepreneurship.

The model disproportionately excludes women, caregivers, and minorities, making non-traditional career paths feel like "second-best" options. Industries outside academia desperately need STEMM talent, but universities still resist adapting PhD programs to meet these needs.

We do not need minor reforms. We need a radical redefinition of success, one that prepares STEMM professionals for diverse and fulfilling careers.

PROPOSING A NEW DEFINITION OF SUCCESS

A RADICAL SHIFT IN PERSPECTIVE

Academia has positioned itself as the gold standard, the ultimate destination. But in reality, science does not just happen in universities; it happens in industry, in policy, in startups, in non-profits, and in education. Some of the most exciting advancements in biotech, AI, and climate science are coming from outside traditional academic institutions. Scientists founding startups, engineers driving social change, and researchers shaping public policy are the people moving STEMM forward. However, these contributions are rarely celebrated or even acknowledged within the old-school success framework.

If we want a system that actually works for the people in it, we need to rethink what success looks like. We need to value technical expertise and transferable skills equally, because adaptability, leadership, and communication are just as crucial to scientific progress as data analysis and experimental methods. And perhaps most importantly, we need to assess impact differently. We must move away from traditional measures such as publications, funding, and job titles, and instead measure how STEMM professionals are solving real-world problems, advancing sustainability, and making a difference in people's lives.

CORE PRINCIPLES OF A NEW DEFINITION OF SUCCESS

TRANSDISCIPLINARY PREPARATION

Innovation doesn't exist in silos - so why should STEMM careers?

The challenges we face today, such as climate change, AI ethics, and public health crises, do not fit neatly into one discipline. They require collaboration, creative problem-solving, and the ability to work across fields. Yet traditional STEMM education still encourages hyper-specialisation, often at the expense of seeing the bigger picture.

We need to embed interdisciplinary thinking into STEMM education from the start. Imagine a chemistry student learning design to develop sustainable materials, or an AI researcher studying bioethics to navigate the future of machine learning in healthcare. Integrating cross-disciplinary projects, entrepreneurial training, and real-world problem-solving into STEMM curricula will not only make graduates more versatile, it will make them more effective scientists, engineers, and innovators.

CAREER MOBILITY

The ability to pivot should be the norm, not the exception.

Somewhere along the way, we started treating STEMM careers like train tracks: pick one route and stay on it for life. But in reality, career paths are not linear; they are dynamic. The pace of innovation is faster than ever, and the ability to transition between academia, industry, policy, consulting, and entrepreneurship is not a failure, it's an asset.

So why do we still prepare STEMM professionals for one job in one sector? Educational institutions should be actively preparing students to explore. Co-op programs, rotational fellowships, industry internships, and policy placements should be the norm, not the exception. A researcher who spends time working in government policy or corporate R&D will bring richer insights, better problem-solving skills, and a broader perspective back into their field.

What if thriving, not just output, was the benchmark?

And we need to stop acting like leaving our original track is a "plan B." It is time to embrace mobility as a marker of success, not something to be whispered about behind closed doors.

PERSONALIZED VALUATION

Time to throw away the yard stick (or use your own).[2]

Right now, we reward the things that fit neatly onto CVs and grant applications: publications, citations, grant funding, patents, lines of code, and products delivered. But the reality is that some of the most valuable contributions in STEMM do not fit into these traditional metrics at all.

---

[2] See Chapter 11, *Charting Your Own Course.*

Who's mentoring the next generation of scientists?

Who's leading diversity, equity, and inclusion (DEI) initiatives?

Who's translating complex research into accessible science communication?

These contributions are essential to the health of the STEMM ecosystem, yet they're often dismissed as "soft" skills, or what we now refer to as *professional skills* (thank you, Kelly!), something people (especially women) are expected to do on top of their "real" job. [3]

This needs to change.

Success in STEMM should not be measured solely by research output; it should also be about impact. We need evaluation systems that recognise leadership, mentorship, outreach, and interdisciplinary collaboration. The ability to communicate science effectively, contribute to open-source projects, or lead DEI efforts should be seen as just as important as publishing a high-impact journal article.

Because let's be honest, what's the point of pushing scientific progress forward if we're not also making it more accessible, inclusive, and meaningful to society?

WELL-BEING AND SUSTAINABILITY

If you have to burn out to succeed, the system is broken.

It is astonishing that in a field built on logic and evidence, we still normalise exhaustion and treat burnout as a badge of honour. We talk about mental health in STEMM, but then reward the very behaviours that erode it: glorifying 80-hour work weeks, celebrating researchers who "push through" at any cost, and treating holidays or mental health days as luxuries rather than necessities.

That's not success. That is a system failing the people in it.

Let me be clear: if success in STEMM requires sacrificing your health, your relationships, or your identity, then it is not success at all. It's survival. And a system that requires survival mode is not one built for long-term innovation, equity, or sustainability.

---

[3] See Chapter 14, *Pressured Out of Technical*, for more on professional skills.

We can no longer talk about redefining success without putting personal well-being front and centre. A sustainable STEMM career must be one where people can bring their full selves, where rest, flexibility, caregiving, and personal growth are not barriers to success but integral parts of it.

What if thriving—not just output—was the benchmark?

What if we started asking not "How many papers did you publish?" but "How long can you do this work joyfully?"

> **Normalize flexible work arrangements** and career pacing that reflects real lives and diverse needs. Not everyone works best in 9-to-5, office-bound models. Careers are not derailed by parenting, caregiving, or illness. Instead, we need to design systems that flex around the human experience.

> **Embed mental health support into workplace culture**, not just in policies. It is not enough to simply offer support services; we need leadership that models these values, psychologically safe teams, and environments where saying "I'm not okay" doesn't end your career.

> **Reform funding and promotion structures** to remove penalties for career gaps and non-linear trajectories. A year away from publishing should not cancel out a decade of contribution. Success should be measured by long-term impact, not immediate output.

> **Treat life events,** from parenting to burnout recovery, as part of a human career story, not a weakness. Our careers span decades. The system should reflect that by allowing people to pause, pivot, and return without shame or setback.

We should not have to choose between doing the work we love and having a life we love. If STEMM wants to lead the future, it has to build one that people actually want to stay in. And that starts with valuing not just what people produce, but how they feel doing it.

But redefining success is only half the battle. If we want people in STEMM to thrive, not just survive, we cannot stop at theory. We need to redesign the systems around them. From how we train future scientists to how we support career mobility, it is time to get bold.

RADICAL PROPOSALS FOR STEMM EDUCATION AND CAREER MODELS

To truly redefine success in STEMM, we need to do more than change how we talk about careers; we need to change the systems that shape them. That means rethinking not just how we train people, but how we support them across their entire professional journey, in academia, industry, research, policy, and beyond. It is not just universities that need a wake-up call: employers, funding bodies, startups, and government agencies all have a role to play.

Every part of the STEMM ecosystem contributes to shaping how careers are built, sustained, and valued.

A 21ST-CENTURY APPROACH TO STEMM CAREER DEVELOPMENT

Let's start with education and early career training, because yes, the traditional PhD was designed in the 19th century (and yes, for men). It is long overdue for a modern upgrade. But the same goes for how industry trains, retains, and promotes STEMM professionals. Too often, both sectors operate in silos, with rigid expectations and limited mobility.

What we need instead is a flexible, dynamic system that recognises:

- There's more than one way to be successful in STEMM.
- Career paths aren't always linear.
- People's lives, including caring responsibilities, burnout, and values, should be respected, not penalised.

Here's what that could look like across the board:

> **Diverse career pathways and tracks.** We now know that not everyone wants to be a professor or a CEO. So instead, we could offer structured and visible alternatives that reflect the real diversity of STEMM careers:
>
> - In academia, create dual-track PhD or postgrad programs with both academic and applied/industry-aligned options.
> - In industry, create career ladders that reward technical leadership, not just people management.

- Across sectors, build mobility into job design: allow employees to rotate across departments, projects, and even external partners.

Mandatory cross-sector exposure. Whether you are a student, an early-career professional or even a mid-career professional, you should have built-in opportunities to work across sectors, not just rely on luck or personal connections.

- Industry placements for students shouldn't be optional - they should be standard.
- Academics should spend time in policy or community-facing roles. Likewise, industry professionals should be supported to embed themselves in research settings or take on guest lecturing or mentoring roles.
- The more we normalise sector-crossing, the less intimidating those transitions become later in a career.

Career development as core, not optional. It is time to stop treating career development as a nice-to-have. Every STEMM organisation, whether a university, research institute, startup or biotech company, should be actively supporting skill development in areas such as:

- Project and people management
- Leadership and negotiation
- Communication and stakeholder engagement
- Entrepreneurship and innovation. This is not just about preparing people for "non-traditional" careers; it is about recognising that all STEMM careers benefit from these skills.

Career re-entry support for everyone. Breaks happen. Babies happen. Illness happens. Burnout happens. STEMM employers, and yes, that includes universities, need to build career re-entry into the system, not treat it as a special accommodation.

- Create funded re-entry fellowships and upskilling programs for those returning after caregiving, illness, or extended leave.
- Ensure that taking a break doesn't permanently derail someone's trajectory - or force them out altogether.
- Build this into performance reviews, hiring panels, and funding guidelines. This is not just about gender equity. This is about basic workforce sustainability.

Non-linear growth must be normalised. Early-career researchers, engineers or developers should not be expected to lock into one track for life. Allow and actively encourage professionals to explore different roles, sectors, and skill sets.

- Design fellowships that incorporate structured rotations.
- Support people to make sideways or even downward career moves if that helps them grow or realign with their values.
- And yes, this might mean pushing back against the "but we need them to stay focused on [X]" attitude, because that attitude is the problem. STEMM should not require tunnel vision.

Mentorship that matches career diversity. A mentor who only knows one system can only give one type of advice. We should be creating cross-sector mentorship networks that connect early-career professionals with role models who have carved different paths, within and beyond academia, in government, startups, large industry, and community sectors. Navigating STEMM should feel like you have options, not like you're clinging to the one rope someone handed you in grad school.

THIS ISN'T JUST REFORM—IT'S A CULTURE SHIFT

If we want to keep talent in STEMM, we need to make the whole system more humane, flexible, and responsive to the real lives and ambitions of its people. These are not "nice ideas." They're a necessary infrastructure for a sector that claims to be about innovation and progress.

It is not just about the pipeline anymore. It's about building a whole ecosystem that values mobility, inclusion, and sustainability, because that is what modern success actually looks like.

WORKING MODELS TO BRIDGE THE GAP

To successfully implement these types of proposals, we can and need to draw inspiration from existing programmes and propose new initiatives that bridge the gap between academia and the broader professional world. A shift is already underway, as more and more academics redefine what they believe constitutes a successful career path.

Professional Science Master's (PSM) programmes combine advanced STEMM training with skills in business, policy, and communication. Unlike traditional master's degrees, they prepare students for roles in industry, government or policy through real-world internships and applied learning. Programmes such as those at the University of North Carolina (U.S.) or Oregon State (U.S.) equip graduates to enter fields such as regulatory affairs, technical consulting or science policy, redefining STEMM success beyond the academic lab.

Industry-academia collaborations. Work-integrated learning models, such as cooperative (co-op) programmes, allow students to alternate between university coursework and full-time work placements in industry. These collaborations build essential skills and networks while students are still in training. Institutions such as the University of Waterloo (Canada) have led the way in developing strong co-op frameworks that ensure graduates are industry ready.

Interdisciplinary and cross-sector fellowships. Fellowships such as the AAAS Science & Technology Policy Fellowship (U.S.) or Schmidt Science Fellows (UK) encourage scientists to step beyond their fields and apply their STEMM expertise in government, policy or new disciplines. These programmes expand career options and foster innovation by encouraging early-career researchers to engage with the world beyond academia, demonstrating that impactful science takes place across many sectors.

The European Research Council's Synergy Grants. These grants support interdisciplinary research collaborations across countries, sectors and fields (EU). By funding teams of researchers to work on complex, real-world problems, the programme breaks down disciplinary and institutional silos. Projects often link academia with policy, healthcare or industry partners, encouraging a new model of research that embraces diversity of thought and outcome.

Career returner programs. STEMM must make room for professionals returning after career breaks, especially those taken for caregiving, illness or family responsibilities. Programmes like the Daphne Jackson Trust (UK) and the Association of Women in Science (U.S.) provide structured support, including funding, mentorship, and flexible pathways to help returners re-enter the workforce confidently. These initiatives prove that stepping away from STEMM shouldn't mean starting over.

These programs show us what's possible.

Now it's time to build on them, expand access, and embed this kind of innovation across the entire STEMM ecosystem.

DESIGNING STEMM CAREERS FOR THE 21ST CENTURY

To move STEMM away from a rigid, exclusionary definition of success, we need to implement bold, structural changes. It is not enough to critique the system; we must actively reshape it. At the end of the chapter, I've provided a blueprint for institutions, individuals, and policymakers to drive real change.

The following illustration highlights the energy we felt while brainstorming these solutions and many more, far beyond what we could fit within a single chapter or book.

New Programs

- leadership catalyst program
- innovation incubator
- global STEMM
- STEMM career portfolio model
- re-entry fellowships
- 2 year rotation
- research + teaching + consulting + flexibility
- communication
- industry
- policy
- academia

The start of a collective effort to propose programs to support career mobility and ensure STEMM professionals are prepared for the future of work.

You are invited to join the *Beyond the Pipeline: STEMM Women+* LinkedIn group to view our growing list of proposed programmes aimed at bridging academia and the workforce, supporting career mobility, and ensuring STEMM professionals are prepared for the future of work.

THE FUTURE OF STEMM CAREERS

WHY WE'RE DONE PLAYING BY OLD RULES

The question is no longer whether STEMM *should* redefine success; it is whether we are *brave* enough to do it.

If we refuse to challenge outdated norms, we risk losing some of the brightest minds in STEMM to burnout, disillusionment, or professional stagnation. But if we embrace change, we can create a future where STEMM professionals thrive, regardless of whether they work in academia, industry, policy, or beyond.

If there is one thing I've learned through my own journey, it's that rigidity in STEMM careers is a recipe for disaster. We train people in highly specialised fields and then expect them to navigate an unpredictable job market with skills that are not always transferable (or recognised as transferable). And when they struggle to find opportunities outside their niche, we act as though it is their problem, rather than questioning why our system doesn't prepare them for a broader range of careers.

Success in STEMM should mean adaptability, not just endurance. The world needs scientists who can communicate, lead, and problem-solve beyond the lab. Yet traditional academic training often leaves professionals ill-equipped for careers that demand interdisciplinary collaboration, entrepreneurship, or policy expertise. If we truly value innovation, then we need to move away from rigid career pathways that limit growth and start equipping professionals with the skills to thrive wherever their expertise is needed.

WHY THIS REDEFINITION OF SUCCESS IS ESSENTIAL

Currently, it's about survival, about pushing through, sacrificing personal well-being, and proving yourself through a narrow set of outdated metrics. But that's not actually success; that's endurance and self-sacrifice.

Success should mean having choices, being valued for your contributions (not just your citations), and having the ability to build a career that aligns with your skills and passions. It should mean feeling fulfilled in your work without having to constantly justify your worth based on where you work or how many papers you've published.

We don't need to tear down academia to achieve this. We do, however, need to broaden the definition of success in STEMM. Whether you are leading a research team in a biotech startup, shaping public health policy, mentoring the next generation of scientists, or communicating complex science to the world, you are still a scientist.

You are still contributing to STEMM.

And you should be celebrated.

	Actions	Considerations
Institutions	Reform STEMM training and career models.	Create mandatory cross-sector training. Fund applied research projects, not just academic publishing.
	Create hybrid fellowships bridging academia and industry.	Develop 50:50 research-industry fellowship programs. Provide incentives for faculty-industry co-mentorship.
	Expand tenure and promotion metrics.	Stop valuing only grants and publications. Reward mentorship, interdisciplinary work, and public engagement.
	Invest in alumni career networks.	Provide career transition support. Create "boomerang fellowships" to help professionals return to academia after working in industry.
Individuals	Build professional networks beyond your institution or organisation.	Attend industry events, connect with STEMM professionals in alternative careers, and seek mentorship (and more importantly, sponsorship) outside traditional research or corporate paths.
	Develop a personal skill portfolio.	Gain experience in science communication, entrepreneurship, project management, and leadership. Track it and find ways to make your skills visible to others.
	Push for policy discussions.	Organize town halls or initiatives that demand action from leadership.
	Champion personal well-being.	Prioritise rest, set clear boundaries, and model what a sustainable career can look like—because your well-being isn't a luxury, it's proof the system can be better.
Policy Makers	Incentivize industry-academia partnerships.	Offer tax credits for companies that sponsor STEMM fellowships. Develop funding models that integrate corporate and university research goals.
	Support flexible career mobility programs.	Fund career transition grants for mid-career professionals moving between academia and industry.
	Mandate diversity, equity, and inclusion initiatives.	Require institutions receiving federal STEMM funding to report on inclusive hiring and career development policies.

Mental Wellness Moment | Spoon Theory

Have you ever wondered why certain tasks feel easier some days than others or for some people more than others? Christine Miserandino's "spoon theory" offers an explanation. The idea is simple: each person has a finite number of "spoons" (units of energy) to spend each day. Every task costs spoons, and that cost can vary day to day and person to person. Getting out of bed may cost one spoon for an able-bodied, mentally healthy, neurotypical person, but several spoons for someone with chronic pain or depression.

Many other factors can impact spoon availability. Did you get enough sleep last night? Did you have to borrow today's spoons to finish a must-do task yesterday? Are you fighting off any illness? Have you cultivated an environment that is conducive to being efficient with your spoons?

It is important to be aware of your own spoon level and what choices you can make to protect yourself from burnout. Recognize how much taking on an additional task might "cost," and decide whether to budget for it or to say no. Take time for self-care. Ensure you're getting enough sleep. And advocate for accommodations you need to minimize the "cost" of getting through your workday.

To be an ally, learn about spoon theory and how it may apply to others. Show empathy when someone needs more time. Ask what support looks like for them and make proactive adjustments to reduce the cost of their daily tasks.

By prioritizing self-awareness and open communication with a common framework, everyone can perform at their best. The goal isn't to do more, but to cultivate the mindfulness that allows you to thrive.

– Megan Wendell

Nineteen

A Workplace Field Guide

NAVIGATING THE GOOD, BAD, AND UGLY IN STEMM

by Tais S. Kraljević, engineering manager, SHPEtinas director, and advocate for chasing your wildest dreams.

The best role I ever had was one I applied for while ignoring all the advice from the people around me.

Two months after I accepted an internal promotion in Maryland, the COVID-19 pandemic hit, cutting the funding my projects relied on. Feeling both bored and worried, I began browsing job openings on the internal site and came across a role I had been daydreaming about since I started with the company: Mission Systems (MS).

I had worked with MS engineers before and found their work fascinating. However, there were several issues with the job posting. I held a mechanical engineering degree, while the position specifically required a bachelor's in electrical engineering. I had also only been in my current role for a few months, after negotiating a higher salary, accepting a promotion, and using the company's relocation benefits. My mentors and coworkers warned me that applying would be a rash decision and that I probably wouldn't even get the job.

But I knew I wanted that role. I wrote a cover letter explaining why my previous experience with certain mission systems, combined with my strong desire for the position, made me the best candidate they could ever have. I got the job, received another relocation package, and somehow managed not to burn any bridges in Maryland.

The job turned out to be an incredible experience. It exposed me to cybersecurity, a field I never expected to enjoy. I was matched with an incredible and supportive manager, and there was room to take on leadership tasks within the group. I learned, thrived, and had fun doing it. That role introduced me to new technologies, people, and opportunities within the company, and I've been able to use that experience as a springboard to other exciting roles.

I am very passionate about making choices for ourselves, because we are the only ones who truly know what we need. My goal is to encourage every person reading this chapter to develop a system for understanding themselves and their goals.

– Tais

The Women in STEMM movement has been gaining momentum exponentially since the 1970s, and with the most recent statistics, it is clear that the movement is now operating at full throttle.

Between 2016 and 2021, the percentage of women working in STEMM occupations increased at a rate comparable to that of men. During the 2023– 2024 academic year, women enrolled in medical school outnumbered men, accounting for 54.6% of all students. If these trends continue, we will soon see women outnumber men in the medical field and occupy equal space with men across STEMM fields.

These numbers are something all women, women of color (WOC), and LGBTQ+ individuals should be proud of, regardless of how connected you feel to the movement. The numbers do not lie; you are a trailblazer.

However, with the focus on getting women and minorities into STEMM, we have inadvertently created a fairytale-princess type of situation, where the discourse ends as soon as you land the job. There are very few resources or efforts dedicated to supporting women, WOC, and LGBTQ+ individuals as they navigate the rest of their careers. The stories seem to say: "She got the

STEMM job, broke through the glass ceiling, and lived happily ever after. Roll the credits. Next!"

Like the characters in fairytales and fables, we still have plenty to experience, resolve, and overcome after the supposed "ever after." Many changes in your personal life and job will come, and as with any other situation, it can be hard to decide what to do. It is very difficult to see the full forest through the trees.

This chapter aims to fill that gap by providing a guideline for assessing your job and all its context to determine whether it is worth staying, time to make a change, or necessary to leave. Like many things in life, your job and career will include the good (the pros), the bad (the cons), and the ugly (the events that completely uproot your plans).

The first time you make this assessment may take the longest. There is plenty to draw out, plan, and ponder on. The "refresher" assessments will come more easily the more time you've spent on earlier ones.

New Habits

In order to best serve yourself and your interests, you will need to continuously assess any job or position you are in. Before diving into the details of what to consider in your assessment, let's first discuss the habits that will give this knowledge its full power.

- Trust your gut.
- Set clear boundaries.
- Keep expanding your network.
- And check in with yourself.

Trust Your Gut

First, always remember to trust your intuition and gut instinct, and remind yourself that they can help you make the best decisions.

No matter what crossroads you face, it's easy to get caught up in overthinking what you should do or how you should feel. This whirlwind of thoughts can become even more overwhelming when others around you start voicing their own opinions. But you've gotten yourself this far, and you know what you are doing. Do not doubt yourself.

SET CLEAR BOUNDARIES

Second, define your boundaries What are you willing to put up with, for how long, and to what end? This chapter will provide guidelines on the hypotheticals that you should consider when you define your boundaries. Always be aware that you can define your boundaries as non-negotiable and negotiable, but you need to know what you are willing to negotiate those boundaries in exchange of.

It is important to note that career planning is also a key part of defining your boundaries. For example, would you be willing to give up a job you really enjoy in exchange for a higher-paying role that takes you off course from your plan to apply to the engineering rotational program? If so, how high would the salary need to be for the sacrifice to feel worthwhile?

KEEP EXPANDING YOUR NETWORK

Third, never stop building your network. Because women, WOC, and LGBTQ+ individuals are still minorities in STEMM, it can be difficult to find people with similar experiences who can offer the advice and support you need. This challenge can become even greater depending on your specific field or geographic location. A strong support network allows you to tap into a wealth of knowledge. Always remember to nourish your existing network and continue to grow it.

Networking is also essential to shaping your career plan. The more people you meet and learn from, the more informed you will be when deciding the direction you want your career to take. Think back to when you had no idea what a job in STEMM might look like. Now you can recognize the differences between various focus areas and fields of expertise. Give yourself permission to explore roles completely different from your own and consider what aspects of those jobs might appeal to you.

CHECK IN WITH YOURSELF

Lastly, check in with yourself periodically, at least once every six months. It is important to set a quarterly or twice-a-year reminder to assess your job and career. Even if there have not been any major life changes prompting a reassessment, this habit ensures that you remain aligned with your dreams, needs, and personal growth. It also serves as an opportunity to review and adjust your career plan if necessary.

THE ASSESSMENT

"Good" and "bad" are relative terms so everyone will categorize and weigh things differently. Because of this, you must start the assessment by answering these questions:

Assessment | Good and Bad

What matters the most to you right now?

What are you missing from your job today?

What does your ideal job look like?

Compare the results of your assessment to the answers to these questions to give yourself a bigger picture about your own career plan and needs.

Now, let's dive into what you should take into consideration every time you make this assessment.

THE GOOD

Also knows as the pros.

What makes a job worth staying?

YOUR BENEFITS

Your company's benefits directly affect your life and overall well-being. The three that arguably have the greatest impact are health and leave benefits, retirement plans, and education support.

Your health insurance and leave options influence your ability to access preventative, necessary, and emergency care for yourself and, potentially, your family. Preventative care is not covered by many insurance plans, and depending on your family history, this may be especially important. Disability, parental, and medical leave also directly affect your ability to support your family. If you are unsure about the details of your health benefits, reach out to your provider or your company's designated contact.

The company's retirement plan, whether it is a 401(k), a stock-based plan, or another format, is the primary way most people save for retirement. Consider whether your current plan allows you to work toward your desired retirement income. Additionally, does your company offer financial support for continuing education? Ask yourself whether this is important to you or necessary for your intended career path.

You've gotten yourself this far, and you know what you are doing. Do not doubt yourself.

If all three types of benefits align with your needs, count this as a strong reason to stay.

YOUR NEEDS

You should also ask yourself whether your schedule and location still meet your needs and those of your family. Do you have the flexibility in your schedule that you require? Are you planning to relocate in the future? If your current job supports these aspects of your life, count it as another reason to stay.

The details of your day-to-day work are also important and should be thoughtfully assessed. Do you enjoy your job? Think about the difficult or stressful days. Are you able to get through them without feeling overwhelmed? Do you feel motivated and empowered in your role?

If yes, this is another pro.

YOUR FUTURE

Lastly, assess whether your current job fits into your overall career plan. What skills are you building right now? Are you developing a network that will help you reach your dream job? Are you gaining experience in a specific field?

If you see this position as a building block toward a future goal, consider that another reason to stay.

THE BAD

Now, the cons.

What are some of the factors that might indicate it is time to reassess your current job? It is important to understand that realizing it's time for a change does not necessarily mean leaving everything behind. When evaluating whether your job meets your needs, consider it in the context of your team, your broader organization, and the company as a whole.

Start by identifying any gaps you noticed in the earlier section, the good, between what you currently have and what you need. Are your needs being met through your benefits or your schedule? Do you find little or no joy in your day-to-day work? These are valid reasons to reassess your role and consider whether a change is necessary.

If you feel that your current position does not serve a purpose or contribute to your long-term career goals, it may be time to move on. Having no reason to stay is, in itself, a reason to leave. There is no value in remaining in a role that does not actively support your development. In this case, you might start looking for other roles within the same company, especially if the benefits, overall schedule, and daily tasks still align with your needs.

As you think about your career goals and overall direction, you should also assess your ability to grow within the organization. Does the environment support promotions or lateral transfers into different teams and skill areas? Does your leadership genuinely support your career aspirations? If company culture or policy creates barriers to your advancement, it may be time to consider a change. This concern goes beyond just your career path and may reveal deeper issues within the leadership or company's culture that are not be as obvious at first glance. Growth and skill development is imperative to the success of any job in any field.

Over time, you may find that your values no longer align with the company's priorities or culture. Even if you have everything you need in your current role, it is important to ask whether you still agree with what the company stands for. This question might seem minor at first, but disagreement could signal that your priorities have shifted or that deeper cultural issues exist within the company. Ask yourself if you are proud of the work you do. Would you recommend your closest friends to work here? Keep in mind that your answers may change over time. Companies evolve as leadership and industries shift, and your own motivations and values may evolve as well.

One final consideration, though it may seem small, is whether you enjoy working with your direct team. However, this is about more than just liking the people you work with. Do you feel respected by your teammates? Do you respect them in return? Can you speak up when there is an issue without fear of backlash? If you discover significant gaps or concerns when reflecting on these questions, it may be a sign that a team change is needed, even if you remain within the same company.

THE UGLY

While there are many reasons to stay in or leave a job, the conversation is incomplete without addressing your physical and psychological safety. Many harmful things can occur in any work setting that may jeopardize this safety, and you need to know how to protect yourself as these situations arise. It's also important to recognize that this safety should be a non-negotiable requirement for remaining in a job. Although it's impossible to prevent every negative event, you can assess whether to stay or leave based on how your team and company respond to such situations.

These ugly situations can be broken out in three (the "Big Three") main categories:

- Hostile environments
- Discrimination
- Harassment (sexual and non-sexual) and microaggressions

First, you need to know that the United States Equal Employment Opportunity Commission (EEOC) provides definitions for discrimination, harassment, sexual harassment, and a hostile work environment. These "Big Three" directly violate *Title VII of the Civil Rights Act of 1964*, the *Age Discrimination in Employment Act of 1967* (ADEA), and the *Americans with Disabilities Act of 1990* (ADA). This means that if you are in the U.S., you are legally protected.[1]

The Big Three can affect both how you are treated at work and how your performance is assessed. For example, discrimination based on age may lead others to treat you with disrespect or dismissiveness. It can also influence how your work is evaluated. Colleagues or supervisors might assume you lack the ability to handle certain tasks, so they avoid assigning them to you. Even when you objectively perform well, they may withhold full credit for your contributions.

RED FLAGS

Become familiar with these definitions so that you can identify improper behaviors and attitudes early on. As you do this, take time to review and further define your own boundaries. This will help you recognize red flags more quickly and respond appropriately if the situation escalates. Early recognition also allows you to document these instances in case you ever need them for a report.

In most cases, you'll find that email is the easiest and a legally sound way to collect information. Emails provide date and time stamps, which are essential for building a case.

- If there are any verbal or physical actions that make you uncomfortable or break the law, you can document it in your own words and send it as a memo via email to yourself.
- If there is no proprietary, classified, confidential, or controlled information in the email, send it to your personal email as well.
- If there are any witnesses, copy them as well.
- You can copy anyone that you want on the email, as long as you have the copies you need first.

---

[1] It's important to understand the protections available in your country. Even if you're not based in the U.S., reviewing the EEOC's definitions can provide valuable context to guide your research.

This is an essential habit you need to build so that you can have historical information and build a pattern if needed.

Feel free to do this if you are a witness to an event where someone else other than you is affected. A memo inherently does not cause any damage, and you never know when you will need it, so do not hesitate to document.

PERFORMANCE REVIEWS

Regardless of your team culture, documenting your expectations and results is a strong professional habit that is well worth your time. While collecting evidence to support your strong performance requires effort, it can serve as a critical safeguard if bias or inconsistency ever influences how your work is evaluated.

Establish and update expectations regularly, aligned with your project cycles, with yearly documentation as the bare minimum.

Start by meeting with your lead, supervisor, or manager to discuss expectations for the quarter or year. Once you and your leader reach an agreement, type up what you discussed and send it to them in an email, asking for confirmation. Your collected evidence should leave no room for doubt. If, at any point, you cannot agree on expectations or your leader refuses to confirm them, pull in Human Resources (HR). Clearly state that you are simply seeking help, and avoid making any accusations. More details on how to approach this will be provided later in the chapter. The point is, you cannot walk away without having concrete evidence to fall back on.

The expectations you need to document should cover the following:

- Deliverables (*what are you outputting?*)
- Timelines
- Attendance (*e.g., core hours, virtual work permitted*)
- Communication (*e.g., defined cadence, report-outs, 5-15*)
- Issue elevation process (*who to go to when there is an issue*)
- Requirements for promotion or salary increase.
- Definition of not meeting, meeting, and exceeding expectations.

After expectations have been agreed upon and confirmed, regularly collect information on how you are meeting or exceeding each one. The more evidence you gather, the easier it will be to protect yourself in the future. This documentation can also serve as a valuable tool if you apply for a promotion, a new job, an award, or simply need to update your résumé.

HUMAN RESOURCES

Whenever any of the Big Three occurs, it is your right to report the issue to your leadership or Human Resources/Ethics Department. There are different ways to elevate the matter. You can inform your leadership or HR team about the behavior to ensure they are aware in case the situation worsens, or you can submit a full report stating that a serious incident has taken place.

You should consider making a formal complaint to HR if:

- The issue is significant and is impacting your ability to do your job, or
- You suspect the activities are unlawful.

If you're still unsure about approaching HR, know that you are ready and should not wait any longer if you want:

- The bad thing to stop,
- To reduce the risk of retaliation, or
- To lay a legal foundation.

The second and third reasons can double as evidence if you do not have any prior documentation.

After you make a copy and file the complaint, expect to have an in-person interview with HR and prepare for it. Maintain your upper hand by staying calm and doubling down on your position that your concern is aligned with the company's objectives. This is your opportunity to suggest a transfer to another team or division if that is something you would like to pursue. If you are permitted, record the interview. If not, take detailed notes on everything that was said and done, and email it to yourself as a memo. You should never stop documenting.

If you ever report anything, there are two different outcomes to understand:

- Whether your claim is formally substantiated, and
- What steps your leadership or HR team will take to address the situation.

These are separate outcomes. Even if your claim is not legally substantiated (meaning insufficient evidence to prove a law was broken), your leadership and HR group can still take actions to correct the situation.

Unfortunately, any situation of this nature will reveal the true colors of the support systems around you, including your leadership and HR. If you receive no support when escalating any of the Big Three, face retaliation, or notice that people begin treating you differently after you make a claim, it is safe to say that your workplace will not protect your physical or psychological safety. That is a valid reason to leave.

For this reason, if you ever find yourself beginning the process of escalating an issue, it's wise to start job hunting on the side to give yourself a head start.

You may find that your direct team or organization supports you differently than the company as a whole, such as HR or upper leadership. In this case, you might be able to stay with the company but transfer to a different team. If the reverse is true, consider how long you're willing to remain in your role before deciding it's time to leave the company entirely.

At the end of the day, you have to protect yourself.

YOUR PATH

In any situation, whether good, bad, or ugly, knowing yourself and understanding your priorities, boundaries, and needs is key to making the right decisions and changes.

> *I was never emotionally ready to let go, but when the right*
> *opportunity came, I knew I couldn't turn it down. I am glad*
> *I let my gut guide me into my path.*
>
> – Tais

Trust your gut, set clear boundaries, and intentionally build and own your support system. And remember, you always have more power than you realize.

Twenty

Advocacy

COLLECTIVE ADVOCACY TO COMBAT THE GLASS CLIFF

by Jessica G. Borger, Aussie immunologist, equity crusader and mum juggling STEMM, family, and smashing glass ceilings.

In retrospect, I have spent a ridiculous amount of my so-called 'spare time' advocating for gender equity in STEMM. Even more ridiculously, most of my advocacy took place during the COVID-19 pandemic, when I was suddenly juggling full-time work while homeschooling my son and teaching him how to read and write, for an epic 263 days, but who's counting?

Australia was in one of the world's longest lockdowns, and I was in fight-or-flight, adrenaline-pumping, anxiety-driven, highly caffeinated 'on' mode for most of it. As a mid-career academic, I couldn't help but notice, and get angry, about how the pandemic was turning the already uneven playing field for women in STEMM into a full-blown obstacle course.

What started as a few small articles celebrating the brilliance of women in STEMM (because, well, we are) quickly turned into something far bigger. I went from highlighting achievements to calling for real support, such as COVID CVs to account for the career chaos caused by the pandemic. Then, with some colleagues, we dug deeper into the success rate of leadership grant funding in Australia...

and wow. It turns out men were awarded a whopping 23% more grants, raking in an additional $95 million compared to women, to keep their research going and pay their salaries. So, we published our findings, teamed up with advocacy groups, ran an international survey and eventually submitted a position paper to Australia's largest government funding body, the NHMRC. That set off a chain reaction, including public debates, national consultations led by the NHMRC CEO, and even media attention. Safe to say, we got people talking!

I had worked late nights, written on weekends, missed out on time with my son, my husband and friends, and definitely had not made time for myself or my wellbeing. I had dealt with the bigots, the trollers, the deniers, the boys' club, the gaslighters, the tokenisers, and the dismissers.

A year later, I was stuck in crawling freeway traffic, battling a torrential storm, and running late from work meetings to set up the book stall for my son's school market. To make things worse, my cold and flu medication was wearing off, and I was thinking that this whole career-life battle was not working for me. Then my phone rang. It was a media agent asking for my comment on the NHMRC's big announcement: they were introducing a new measure under Australia's Sex Discrimination Act, providing equal grants and funding for men and women in senior fellowship applications.

I burst into tears. Right there in the car. In the rain. In the chaos of being an academic woman in STEMM. I have a tear in my eye as I write these words, because all the hard work and all the emotion created real change.

– Jessica

Advocacy is all about making a difference. It is about speaking up and taking action to change rules, influence decisions and empower people. This can involve anything from shifting the understanding of a single person to increasing support within local communities or working with influential figures in government, academia, and industry.

Advocacy, *noun:*

Proactively taking action and building relationships
within and across groups to drive positive,
structural change on a systemic issue.

Advocacy is an activity designed to influence the policies and actions of others to achieve meaningful change. This can be anything from direct, collective and public actions, such as lobbying or protesting to drive policy change, or more subtle, individual actions like writing an open letter to a key stakeholder or encouraging others to become allies by sharing and discussing their lived experiences.

Advocacy looks different for everyone, and all forms are equally valuable.

Advocacy is also about learning. Be open and willing to listen to others' opinions, even if they differ from your own. Gender, ethnicity, race, disability, religion, and socio-economic status shape each of us in intersectional ways, and everyone has a unique story to share.[1]

Just as others have their own stories, so do you. It is important to be open about your own experience. It is okay to feel uncomfortable, scared or confused at times, especially at the beginning.

Advocacy is about challenging assumptions. For women in STEMM, this means confronting gender norms and stereotypes that perpetuate inequities and disproportionately harm women.

Seeing gender inequities in the workplace often begins with a lightbulb moment. But once that switch is flicked, you realise it doesn't have an off position.

> It's curious how the women in our lab are always asked to take notes in meetings, while the men focus on the scientific discussions. Men are capable of writing publications, so why, exactly, can't they take notes too?

> On social media recently, I saw a world-renowned researcher delivered a groundbreaking keynote, and the comments *were all about her red heels.*

---

[1] See Chapter 8, *A Labyrinth of Identities.*

Interesting. Another team of only men presenting at our weekly seminar. Oh, and it is being chaired by a man too. There are plenty of women in the audience, so clearly they were available to speak or chair. I suppose they were just overlooked... *again.*

At a conference I recently attended, the panel on AI research was made up entirely of men, except for one woman, who was repeatedly asked about "diversity in tech" and never about her actual research. Not a single man on that panel was asked about diversity in AI.

WHY DO WE NEED ADVOCACY?

When you search Google Scholar for "barriers to women in science," you get over four million academic results. The results speak for themselves; there is no denying that barriers do, in fact, exist. These barriers were erected, and continue to be reinforced, by gendered stereotyping, bias, and societal cultural expectations across all STEMM fields. This leads to an unrelenting exodus of women from the pipeline.

I experienced these biases firsthand when my supervisor told me, "You were lucky to get this job. I did consider that you might have another baby." I handed in my notice, and *luckily for him, he didn't even have to wait for me to get pregnant.*

But these biases can also go under the radar, even from those people involved. The **Matthew Effect** in academia often plays out when men take credit for women's ideas. Those already in positions of power gain further recognition, while the original contributions of women are overlooked or dismissed. I have definitely had a man, or several men, speak for me or "clarify" my ideas in meetings, only for the idea to be attributed to them rather than to me.

Gender bias is all around us, but collectively we often fail to notice it. It is important to be attentive and to recognise the ways in which women are judged differently from others.

This can be done in many ways.

Unconscious or implicit bias sneaks into everyday interactions, and **untitling**, a term coined by Amy Diehl, is a perfect example. It occurs when a woman's professional credentials mysteriously vanish, while a man's remain intact. Take, for example, the all-too-common introduction: "We would like to introduce the chairs for the session, Dr. David Davidson and Jessica Borger." Never mind that I am actually an Associate Professor.

Explicit bias is not just about outdated attitudes; it is about deliberate actions that exclude women from opportunities. A colleague on a conference organising committee informed me that I had been considered as a speaker for an international conference. How exciting. Except the committee never actually invited me. Instead, they collectively decided it would be far too much for me. You see, I had just returned from parental leave. Apparently, along with sleep deprivation comes career disqualification. My colleague regretted not saying anything, but it can be hard when you are one of the few women in a room.

When you do see gender bias, as an advocate, interrupt it, and call it out. By speaking up, you also encourage others to do the same. Using "I" statements allows you to express how the behaviour is affecting you without putting the other person on the defensive.

You could say, "I feel really uncomfortable when you talk about women like that. It makes me feel like I can't trust you to treat me with respect."

It's clear that those who benefit most from the status quo are not going to lead the charge for change.

LET'S TAKE A GENDER (IN)EQUITY SELFIE WITH STEMM

If we all took a selfie right now with STEMM, what inequities would we see?

A woman stands in front of her research poster at an international conference, while a senior colleague discusses her work to the crowd that has gathered. Ten minutes into the discussion, he still has not acknowledged her. As he walks away with potential collaborators, he gives out his own contact details.

A woman holds a rejection letter for a major research grant, with reviewer comments questioning her 'leadership potential', while her counterpart, a man four years her junior with fewer publications, has just received funding for a similar project.

A woman at a networking event for early-career researchers stands alone, watching as senior academic men naturally gravitate towards the young men in attendance, mentoring them while she remains on the sidelines, overlooked.

A woman is being interviewed for a senior laboratory head position. The panel is made up entirely of men. They felt she lacked the leadership "presence" needed for the role and hired a man with less experience and less funding. He is brilliant at football, so that will help in the inter-institutional competition. *This was something I actually heard verbatim from a member of an interview panel once.*

It is not enough to simply be aware of the issues we've discussed so far; the next step in becoming an advocate for women in STEMM is to recognise these issues as true barriers to our collective progress. Everyone needs to understand that these situations do not happen in isolation, and their impacts are felt across society.

Have I mentioned there is a current gender pay gap of 16% across STEMM fields?

FIXING STEMM'S LEAKY PIPELINE REQUIRES CULTURAL CHANGE

Historically shaped by a narrow group of the population, including white, cisgender, able-bodied men, STEMM culture reflects antiquated systemic stereotypes, and biases that do not meet the needs of today's diverse graduates. So, how do systemic perceptions shape the realities women face as they enter and navigate the STEMM workforce?

TV and media are excellent at perpetuating stereotypes and **unconscious biases**. We are all familiar with the typical image of a scientist: a white, middle-aged man wearing a lab coat, with dishevelled hair, glasses, and possibly a moustache. This image is reinforced in movies, TV shows, and even some historical portrayals. Indeed, during the COVID-19 pandemic, far more men were being interviewed by major news stations for their expert scientific opinion than women. This stereotype has become so ingrained that it shapes public perception of who "belongs" in science, creating barriers for those who do not fit this narrow image.

Some long-held attitudes in workplaces, broader communities, and even within our homes still associate STEMM careers more with men than women. This results in a lack of encouragement for girls to enter STEMM, and a lack of support for women to remain in STEMM, as they begin to feel devalued and disrespected.

Changing this culture takes intentional effort and support from advocates and allies who actively challenge the status quo.

Our society continues to view women as carers and nurturers, not as the brains behind breakthroughs. There is often an assumption that women will take on the primary caregiving role, regardless of their personal choices or situation. This only increases a woman's mental load as she strives to do it all and more.

Many employers still do not offer flexible work arrangements or critical support in the workplace such as parenting rooms. Nor do they fully recognise the disproportionate burden women often bear when it comes to unpaid care work, further impacting their mental and physical load.

Unsupportive or toxic work cultures emerge due to the absence of equal opportunity policies, ineffective mechanisms to address discrimination and harassment, unclear reporting frameworks, and a lack of accountability. There always seems to be at least one man, often a professor or subject matter expert, who is considered untouchable because he is "too important" or brings in too much funding for the institution. He can be a bully, he can make inappropriate comments, he can put his hand up your skirt.

Why? Because he can. The system lets him.

All of this contributes to a shortage of senior women leaders as role models, because the bias and the barriers become too much for us to continue the fight. This then feeds back into how society sees women in STEMM. They do not see us.

Changing this culture takes intentional effort and support from advocates and allies who actively challenge the status quo, work together to break down biases, and create new opportunities that allow women to be visible.

ADVOCACY RED FLAGS TO AVOID

Before you start advocating for gender equity in STEMM, it is important to be aware of certain problem statements that can hinder meaningful progress. Here are three red flags to watch out for.

RED FLAG: *FIX THE WOMAN*

Let's talk about the idea of "fixing the woman." This approach places all the responsibility for change on the individual woman, suggesting that it is her personal traits or behaviours that are the problem. Women are often told they need to be more confident, back themselves more, stop holding themselves back, negotiate better, speak up, support each other, and balance work and life.[2]

But here is the thing: telling women to fix themselves will not solve the deeper issues in a system that was built by and for men. Instead of focusing on fixing individuals, we should shift the focus from trying to work within a system built for men to changing the system so it works for all of us.

RED FLAG: *IT'S A WOMEN'S ISSUE*

Gender equity often runs the risk of being framed as a "women's issue," inadvertently isolating the problem and making it seem less urgent or relevant to half the community. This framing limits the interest and involvement of allies, particularly men, and overlooks the fact that gender equity benefits everyone.

---

[2] We say this in Australia to mean women in need to trust themselves more (trust in their own abilities).

To engage everyone, especially allies, we need to reframe the issue as essential to operations, processes, and outcomes. Reframing the problem in a more inclusive way helps build broader support for change and emphasises the shared responsibility we all have in addressing inequality. And do not forget, women earn less, which means less money coming into a household and less economic security.

RED FLAG: *ALL WOMEN WANT AND NEED THE SAME THINGS*

Stereotyping or **essentialism** refers to the assumption that all individuals within a particular group share the same inherent characteristics or experiences, often reducing complex identities, such as gender, to simplified generalisations. Intersectionality shapes each woman's unique experience, so it is not as simple as assuming all women will want a parenting room, for example, as not all women are mothers.

BECOMING AN ADVOCATE IN STEMM

STEMMinist, *noun:*

Someone who promotes equality in STEMM.

Being a **STEMMinist** involves raising awareness about gender inequality in STEMM, challenging stereotypes and bias, and supporting initiatives and actions that promote inclusivity. The illustration on page 290 captures some of the many ways we can each be advocates, starting at the bottom with the most accessible actions: learn, listen, and then talk, progressing through to actions that drive systemic change at scale.

The first step to becoming a STEMMinist is to educate yourself on how to create inclusive environments and cultures that benefit everyone, without focusing on "fixing" women. Reading this book is a great way to start!

> **Be a role model.** Promote STEMM education for girls and women by participating in programmes, initiatives, scholarships, and mentorship opportunities.

Help bridge the encouragement gap among parents, educators, and mentors by fostering a growth mindset, exposing children to diverse role models, and challenging stereotypes in media, schools, and daily life. Engaging with high school students at STEMM events, such as speed networking and careers panels, allows me to share my journey while gaining insight into what future women in STEMM are thinking, feeling, and aspiring to.

Amplify women's voices and ideas by championing the women around you and acknowledging their contributions. When a woman you nominated for an award wins, you also win for putting someone forward.

Disrupt bias by "calling in" rather than "calling out" gendered societal assumptions to foster constructive conversations that may lead to reflection.

Celebrating our wins by talking about the hurdles we've overcome is my way of subtly reminding everyone just how tough the journey has been.

Talk to potential allies to amplify your voice, as organisational change often begins with one person's voice gaining momentum, and eventually reaching leadership. Share your stories, and others will share theirs in return. It is that simple.

And don't forget the men!

We need men as allies. They, or you, hold most leadership roles and have the power to drive real change. I was only able to do what I did during the pandemic because the men in leadership at my university backed me completely, without question or moderation. Their trust was rewarded when the NHMRC CEO chose our university for the state consultation, including an executive lunch they attended, where I, as an early-career researcher, found myself nervously sitting at a table of professors! But I held my own, because I knew everyone at that table wanted me there.

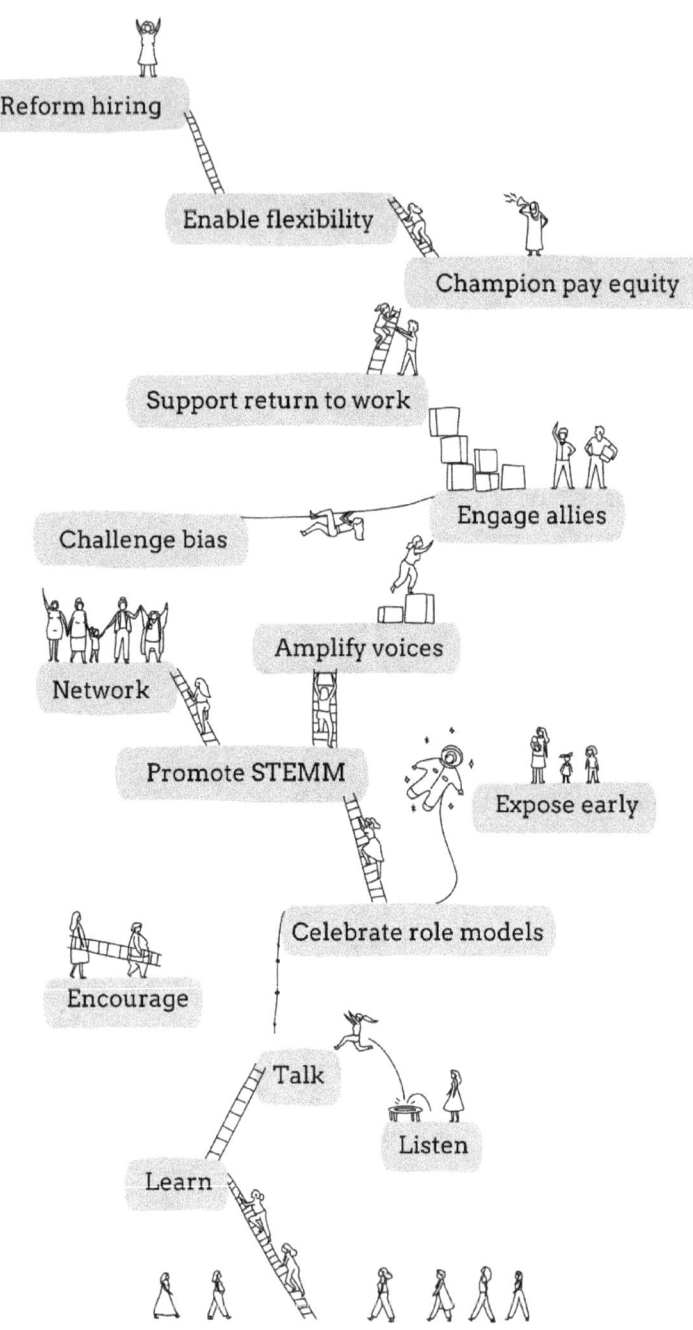

An abundance of ways to advocate, building from individual actions to systemic change.

SOME QUESTIONS YOU MIGHT HAVE

You're probably excited about advocating in STEMM now, and you're not alone. These are some questions I've heard from others who are keen to give it a go.

Question 1. I'm eager to be a better ally to women in STEMM, but I've also heard the term 'advocate.' What do they mean, and can I be both?

> Allyship and advocacy are often used interchangeably in discussions of gender equity in STEMM, but they have distinct meanings, even though they share a common goal of supporting women and marginalised genders in these fields.
>
> Advocacy is about taking action to influence decision-makers and policies that affect gender equity in STEMM. It involves working to change the systemic barriers and inequalities that hinder progress in these fields.
>
> Allyship, on the other hand, involves actively supporting individuals from underrepresented genders, typically those with whom you have relationships or who are within your sphere of influence. It is about doing the hard work to stand alongside them, amplifying their voices, and making space for their contributions.
>
> For example, a woman is talked over in a meeting you are attending.
>
> - **Allyship solution.** Create space for her to be heard in that moment by amplifying her voice or silencing others.
> - **Advocate solution.** Champion new organizational policies and guidelines to drive broad organizational and cultural changes in meeting dynamics, therefore systemically disrupting the biased behavior.

Question 2. I want to be an advocate in my STEMM workplace but how do I avoid **performative advocacy**?

> Performative advocacy refers to actions that are carried out for show or to create the appearance of support, rather than being part of a genuine, sustained effort to address a cause. It often

involves gestures or statements designed to make an organisation or individual appear committed to a particular issue, without taking meaningful action to address systemic problems.

For example, your organization posts on social media about supporting gender equity but continues to have a gender pay gap and is not demonstrating any action to address this disparity.

- **Performative solution.** Respond or 'call out' your organization on social media.
- **Advocate solution.** Advocate for a review of the organization's pay structure and offer to work together to conceptualize solutions such as equal pay audits.

Question 3. What challenges will I face in working to become a better advocate?

As an advocate, the first thing you will face is resistance from individuals or groups who hold biases or stereotypes. Advocating for change often comes with pushback. Whether it's criticism, isolation, or outright opposition, this resistance can be discouraging, but it is important to stay focused on the end goal.

For example, my advocacy approach involved presenting clear, evidence-based data analysis, and strategies to tackle gender inequities, something hard to argue against, but many tried. One response from a reader literally made me laugh out loud, throw my hands in the air, and say, *"THIS is exactly what we (women) mean!"*

> *I don't care about gender equity, I care that every individual gets a fair chance. How would the people at these organisations explain to the parents of a young person that they don't get the job, only because they are the wrong sex? How would they feel were their sons denied opportunities for such stupid reasons?*
>
> – Johnathan A.
> *'Gender Equity When It Suits' Member Discussion Board*

Great punchline, right?

Comments like these can be hard to hear or read, especially given the deeply personal nature of advocating for yourself and people like you. Advocacy can be emotionally taxing, so it is essential to manage burnout and maintain resilience. This means that sometimes you need to take a break. I do, and it is okay. Taking a step back can also create space for other voices to be heard.

Advocating for an issue often requires trust and credibility. This can be challenging, particularly in fields or environments where you are still establishing yourself. Surround yourself with the support of like-minded individuals. Create a network of allies.

Advocating for change often means challenging existing power dynamics. Whether it's within a workplace, organisation or larger system, overcoming institutional resistance can be one of the toughest barriers. This is when your network of allies gives you the power of numbers, the amplification of voices.

Question 4. What if I say or do the wrong thing?

Mistakes are an inevitable part of life. They may feel shitty but they are an important way to learn and unlearn things. If you get it wrong, apologise, learn, and keep moving forward.

It's okay. You've got this!

Question 5. After all this, is becoming an Advocate still worth it?

YES!

I know all too well that advocacy and challenging the status quo, or "how things have always been done," can be easily silenced through unfair power dynamics in STEMM fields. With heightened job insecurity and reliance on those in positions of power who benefit from maintaining the status quo, visible advocacy against gender inequities can feel uncomfortable, intimidating, or even counterproductive. It's important to remember that not all advocacy needs to be public or visible beyond the networks where you feel supported, respected, and trusted.

For example, if you notice a team member struggling to arrive at weekly meetings on time due to school drop-offs, you might work to reschedule the meeting to more family-friendly hours. Such an action could spark further changes, leading to broader organisational shifts, independent of your continued involvement but initiated by your effort. Who knows, but it's fun to find out.

But it is not only about challenging the system for tangible outcomes. Of all the advocacy I have done, the most meaningful moment for me was speaking about my science career in my son's fifth-grade class. Answering questions from vocal, excited, and interested girls was, by far, the most rewarding experience yet.

Advocacy is not about being the loudest or most popular voice, but about being confident in speaking the truth. While the journey towards gender equity in STEMM is far from over, your efforts, along with those of other advocates and allies, will help pave the way for our future STEMMinists.

Twenty-One

Allies

Building Trust, Sharing Power, Creating Change

by Trevor C. George, proud girl dad, HeForSWE co-lead, and engineering leader.

When my company introduced Employee Resource Groups (ERG), I thought they didn't pertain to me. As a straight white man, every group seemed to cater to an identity I didn't share. That isn't to say I wasn't supportive of ERGs, but there was a clear signal to me that I didn't need to pay attention.

Later, the company posted an invitation for people to join the Society of Women Engineers (SWE). I was surprised to see that anyone could join. I reached out to a colleague in HR and asked if there was value in me joining.

She was surprised.

Not that I would ask to join a women's group, but that I wasn't sure I could provide value. She ecstatically encouraged me to join SWE and our women's employee resource group. I was hesitant, of course, because I was concerned about intruding on a safe space for the women in the group.

In my first few meetings with the SWE group, I was pretty quiet, mostly listening to the stories, speakers, and guests. Over time, however, I began to realize I could add value to the conversation as well. I still mostly listened, but I offered support where I could.

Eventually, this involvement led me to formally mentor women through various programs at work and in local colleges. It also led me to become the national Co-Lead for the male affinity group of SWE, HeForSWE. And ultimately, it led me to write a chapter in this book.

Today, I encourage men to attend our women's ERG and SWE conferences to better understand the issues women face in STEMM. I have the pleasure of submitting award nominations for the women I work with, and I tactfully coach others about unconscious biases when they arise. Along the way, I have learned many ways to be supportive of people who are often marginalized in STEMM.

– Trevor

Ally, *noun:*

A person who actively supports
individuals who are marginalized or excluded.

Before we get into how to be a good ally, let's explore what an ally actually is. I often hear people describe **allyship** in narrow terms, such as saying an ally is a man who supports women in STEMM. But that definition isn't quite accurate.

An **ally** is someone who takes action to support anyone who isn't part of the "in-group." In the workplace, this certainly can mean a man supporting women in STEMM. However, it can also mean, for example, women supporting other women, or a senior staff member supporting a new employee who is trying to find their way.

Given the focus of this book, we will concentrate on men supporting women in the workplace. Still, I encourage you to consider how you can support anyone who could benefit from your help, in any aspect of your life, and how the ideas below might apply in those contexts.

So how does an ally provide value to a group or an individual? It turns out, there countless ways to offer support. You might invest time to strengthen your own awareness. You could advocate for someone else. Or you might motivate others to step into allyship.

No matter what action resonates with you most, always keep this in mind: being an ally is about being visible and invisible at the same time. It is not about getting credit. It is about making sure someone else does.

BUILD YOUR AWARENESS

The first step is to learn about and acknowledge the issues at hand. The next step is to spread awareness of the substantial underrepresentation of women and marginalized groups in STEMM programs and corporate leadership.

A good ally is a trusted resource and an active advocate for equal representation. As an ally, my goal is to find opportunities to leverage my network, my position, and my resources to help others and to model the behaviors that promote equality and justice in my field. This book is filled with stories and data that explain what the issues are and why we should care, but there is still so much more to learn. Equality and justice in the workplace are far more nuanced than what can be captured in a single book.

Being an ally is about being visible and invisible at the same time. It is not about getting credit. It is about making sure someone else does.

I encourage you to continue your allyship journey by asking thoughtful questions and staying curious within your community and workplace.

Once you understand the issues, allyship means recognizing them as they happen and seeking opportunities to address them in your daily work.

MODEL YOUR VALUES

So much of allyship comes down to living the values we all say we believe in. When you witness behavior that is not aligned with values like equity and inclusion, speak up and coach those involved. Taking action can have a profound impact.

Several important things happen when you stand up for inclusive behavior.

- You signal to those who might feel excluded or marginalized in the room that you are a safe and supportive presence.[1]
- You model what allyship should look like for others who want to help but don't know what it looks like to do so.
- You open the door for more people to join the effort.

I have been surprised by how many men have reached out to me since I became a visible ally, asking how they could get involved. Modeling good behavior tends to attract other positive actions within your organization.

How you approach this depends heavily on the situation you are in. A good starting point is to assume positive intent. Most people do not set out to say or do something sexist or racist. With this assumption in mind, it's often most effective to pull someone aside for a private, respectful conversation to share your perspective. If public coaching is necessary, you may find that you can redirect or adjust the conversation in the moment without calling anyone out.

> When Cassie's boss mentioned that he had encouraged one of her early-career direct reports to smile more because "she always looks so serious" when he walked past, she immediately told him that telling a woman to smile is not acceptable in the workplace. Her boss, along with the other three men in the meeting, looked at her with confusion.
>
> She recognized in that moment that her colleagues were not trying to be harmful. They genuinely did not know that telling a woman to smile is problematic, least of all because it has become a widely recognized example of a gendered microaggression. They listened and asked questions. She never heard any of them tell a woman to smile again.

This example highlights a way to navigate sensitive topics in a small group without alienating those who have positive intentions.

---

[1] It's important to note: While allies can speak up in support, they should be careful not to speak *for* individuals or assume how someone is affected. When possible, amplify voices rather than replace them, and leave space for those directly impacted to share their own perspectives.

Of course, when actions are more clearly overt and intentionally sexist or racist, different steps must be taken. Most companies have policies in place for addressing abusive, sexist, or racist behavior, and I encourage you to refer to your company's guidelines for how to handle those situations.

SPREAD THE SHARED BURDEN

Low-promotability tasks, as Kelly highlighted in her chapter on women being pressured out of technical roles, are common in any team environment.[2] According to Harvard Business Review, women spend 200 hours per year *more* than men doing non-promotable work. Tasks like preparing a catering order or cleaning up after an on-site event can take time and energy away from more strategic work.

Although these tasks are valuable and necessary, when one person consistently takes them on, it can come at the expense of career growth. While she is handling responsibilities that support the team, other team members may be solving challenges that help them build skillsets and achievements that lead to upward progression. An ally can step in and serve as a visible example of how to share this work. An ally can also intentionally redistribute these responsibilities across the entire team. For example, an ally might suggest assigning a technical task, along with the associated opportunity to stand out, to a deserving but often overlooked team member.

In my office, one of my colleagues volunteered for nearly every cake cutting, event planning, or clean-up task that came up. When I asked her about it, she said she felt bad because no one else would raise their hand, and she didn't think it was fair to leave those tasks for the boss. She felt obligated.

This became a self-fulfilling prophecy. Eventually, it was simply assumed that she would take care of it. I encouraged her to stop taking on these low-promotability tasks by herself. I began assigning the tasks to others, including myself. As a result, we were able to distribute the burden more fairly across the team.

---

[2] See Chapter 14, *Pressured Out of Technical*, for more.

Another colleague shared that, at her company, a series of committees had been formed to tackle different challenges the business faced. Some were tactical, some were strategic, and some were focused on team morale. A woman on the team pointed out that all the women had been assigned to the morale committee, which was responsible for planning events and team-building activities.

This work is certainly valuable. Disengaged or unhappy team members are unlikely to be productive. However, when other team members are involved in cost-cutting measures, strategic initiatives, and productivity improvements, they are building promotable storylines. The team morale committee does not typically offer the same opportunities.

This is where allyship can make a difference. An ally might recommend rotating committee assignments to ensure fairness. An ally can also take steps to ensure that all employees, regardless of identity, have equal access to roles that offer visibility and growth.

JOIN EMPLOYEE RESOURCE GROUPS & SOCIETIES

Employee resource groups have become relatively common in recent years. These are cross-company organizations focused on supporting marginalized individuals within the workplace. They are supported and encouraged by the company and create a safe space for employees to discuss the challenges they face, learn from one another, and explore opportunities for improvement.

Most ERGs have a central mission of supporting and empowering the communities they represent. They provide opportunities to hear personal stories of discrimination and to better understand what is unequal, unfair, or unjust in the world around us. Through these firsthand accounts, we gain insight into what is not working and why.

As an ally, being present for these discussions can offer valuable perspectives on how we can help address these issues. However, a common mistake is for those who are not directly represented by the group to become a little too active in the conversation. Within ERGs, the role of an ally is to listen, to offer support, and to contribute a perspective only when appropriate.

Allies should not be the focus of these meetings. The order of engagement is clear: *listen, learn, and support.*

PROVIDE PLATFORMS

Last year, I recruited several groups of women in my organization to submit proposals to speak at a national conference. Together, we brainstormed ideas for their presentations. I assisted with writing and editing the proposals and made sure all submissions were completed on time. When one of the proposals was selected, I continued to support them by helping with preparation and being in the audience when they took the stage.

Importantly, I was visible to them as a source of support, but I remained in the background when the spotlight was on them. What I found is that when you encourage someone to pursue an opportunity that pushes them just beyond their comfort zone, they often rise to the occasion and expand that comfort zone in the process.

Creating nominations for others to be considered for awards is another powerful way to help people gain recognition for their contributions. This can have a significant impact on their careers, and it requires only a small investment of your time. In the past two years, I have written or edited five award nominations for women in my organization, recognizing both their professional achievements and their work in the community. Some received the awards and some did not, but each one appreciated the gesture and the effort taken to acknowledge their work.

Allyship can also take the form of building structured, repeatable processes that create lasting change. One way to do this is by incorporating award nominations and conference proposal opportunities into regular team meetings. This makes recognition a shared and ongoing practice, rather than a one-time gesture.

BE A MENTOR

Mentorship is a powerful way to make a lasting impact. Whether through internal corporate programs or external partnerships with colleges or primary schools, mentoring creates opportunities for you to support the growth of others. At the same time, the process of synthesizing and articulating your own thoughts in response to questions you may not normally ask yourself can lead to personal growth as well.

Not all mentorship needs to be formal. I have never been a formal mentee in my career, but I can easily point to several people who took the time to support me, shared access to their networks, and coached me when I needed guidance. Similarly, not all mentors need to have followed the exact path the mentee intends to pursue.

Part of being a good mentor is setting aside what may be best for the company and instead focusing on what is best for the mentee. Most of the time, these goals will align. However, as a mentor, your responsibility is to prioritize the development and needs of the individual you are supporting.

Allies should not be the focus. The order of engagement is clear: listen, learn, and support.

All mentors should remain aware of gender biases. It is common for men to receive coaching on business strategy, while women are more often guided on topics such as work-life balance, burnout, and assertiveness. As a mentor, make sure you address not only the areas women are frequently told to improve, but also the skills and experiences that are fundamentally important to any career advancement.

And if you are mentoring a woman who is also in STEMM, I encourage you to draw from what you've learned throughout this book.[3] Help her navigate the systemic barriers, roadblocks, and traps that have been discussed. Support her growth so she can lead and engage with confidence. Actively listen to her. And invite conversations about technical skills and business acumen.

I have formally mentored several people in my career and have often been seen as an informal mentor as well.

---

[3] And consider getting her a copy so your conversations can grow from a shared foundation.

What I have learned through these experiences is:

You often won't have an immediate answer to your mentee's questions. While there will certainly be times when you can offer clear guidance or a well-informed solution, more often you will find yourselves problem-solving together. You might connect your mentee with someone in your network, point them toward a helpful resource, or find another creative way to support their growth and help them move forward.

You can learn together. Recently, I have taken the approach of finding training opportunities that both my mentee and I can complete independently. In our next meeting, we discuss what we learned and explore how to apply it to their specific situation.

You can learn from your mentee. I have always gained something from being a mentor, especially when the mentee asks questions that prompt me to think through different scenarios and reflect on insights from my own experiences.

The best mentors know how to offer an empathetic ear, remain curious, and, when possible, provide thoughtful guidance on navigating challenges and intentionally planning for the future their mentees aspire to.

BE A SPONSOR AND CHAMPION

A sponsor is someone who advocates for you when you aren't in the room. A champion, as Kelly noted in her chapter on the glass cliff, "goes beyond, publicly advocating for you and taking professional risks to advance your career."[4]

Both sponsors and champions ensure their mentees are included in important meetings, provide opportunities that showcase others in the best light, advocate for promotions or raises, and much more. As an ally, you may find yourself advocating for someone deserving of an opportunity simply because you were the only one paying attention to them.

Throughout my career, I have had the opportunity to voice support for colleagues pursuing new roles within the company, as well as for promotions,

---

[4] See Chapter 15, *Glass Ceilings & Cliffs*.

bonuses, and raises. I have also stood up for individuals who were unfairly criticized for the work they had accomplished. An ally can be supportive by serving as a voice for someone who is not present to represent themselves.

In my previous role, I saw 120 interns come through the company doors over just four years. I saw how these tremendously talented team members often struggled to find roles in the workforce. By actively seeking opportunities to connect them with potential job openings, both within my company and externally, I acted as a sponsor by creating opportunities behind the scenes. When I wrote letters of recommendation and personally reached out to hiring managers to improve their chances, I was publicly advocating on their behalf.

Recently, I had the opportunity to identify an emerging leader for a high-profile project. It was an assignment that could have easily been given to someone more seasoned. I remained involved, offering guidance when needed and making sure she received the credit she deserved, even when others attempted to redirect it. She thrived in the role. That's the power of advocacy, and it's so important that we've devoted an entire chapter to it.[5]

BE A VOLUNTEER

As Jane discussed in *Inlet Forces*, we all have an opportunity to thoughtfully support girls with an interest in technical fields.[6] We certainly shouldn't force anyone into any field, but by offering your time, you can create opportunities for girls to explore their technical skills and decide for themselves what interests them.

Here are just a few ideas to get you started:

- Be a coach for a STEMM based team (*e.g., robotics, math team*).
- Be a volunteer at STEMM competitions. Judge at a science fair.
- Host an elementary school field trip to your workplace.

---

[5] See Chapter 20, *Advocacy*, for more.
[6] See Chapter 3, *Inlet Forces*, for a conversation on the distinct differences between pushing and pulling girls into STEMM.

The more you support children as they explore their interests, the more likely they are to discover their passion and pursue it. If that passion happens to be in a STEMM field, all the better.

SUPPORTING FELLOW ALLIES

I almost didn't join our ERGs… or SWE.

I assumed I wasn't welcome.

My colleague assumed I didn't want to join. I assumed the vague wording in the enrollment invitation was meant to be exclusive. It wasn't until I asked what I thought was a silly question that I was encouraged to participate.

Being an ally doesn't come with an instruction manual. But if you're willing to join an ERG and identify as an ally, you're likely also open to feedback on how to offer the best support. Should you be more vocal? Less vocal? Attend certain meetings?

My advice: Ask.[7]

Over the last several years, many men have reached out to me specifically looking for advice on how to make an impact in this arena.

While allyship often involves quietly lifting others, being visibly supportive can open important doors. I have made a point of being seen as an ally through actions rather than self-promotion, which has encouraged numerous colleagues to reach out and ask how they can get involved.

Those discussions echo the themes within this chapter and have led to several colleagues joining ERGs, volunteering, becoming mentors, and proactively seeking out opportunities to champion others.

Clearly, there are many ways to support others as an ally. What makes allyship so impactful is the ripple effect it creates across your team, your environment, and your entire community.

As an ally, you are equipped with the stories of those who have been marginalized in your workplace, and you have the ability to help steer the organization toward greater inclusivity and equity. You can help identify

---

[7] Ask colleagues within the ERG. Ask a peer. Ask AI. Just ask.

biases and inequities, expand networks, support the right people in getting promoted, and redistribute non-promotable tasks. Your actions create space for your entire team to feel supported and welcomed.

This isn't a zero-sum game. As Ashley discusses in the following chapter, the pie can grow.[8] I've witnessed time and time again how businesses and teams are better off for the actions of the thoughtfully applied allyship.

I never expect to get anything in return from being in this role, but it is incredible how often the rising tide has lifted all boats along the way—including mine.

---

[8] See Chapter 22, *The Business Case for DEI*, for more on the top-line and bottom-line benefits of an inclusive work culture.

Mental Wellness Moment | Empathetic Allyship

Over-responsibility is a common experience, especially for women. We often feel responsible not just for ourselves, but for what others think or feel about us, how our kids are doing, and even how our coworkers are performing.

As a new manager, I spent countless thought cycles thinking about my leadership brand, considering past leaders' styles and which ones I wanted to emulate. One leader stands out to me as a true example of empathetic allyship.

Earlier in my career, I was struggling with health issues stemming from my ADHD, combined with (undiagnosed at that time) moderate-to-severe sleep apnea. Even though I was incredibly inspired by the projects at work, I couldn't stay on task. My productivity and quality suffered. When my manager called me in to talk, I knew why.

But she surprised me, in the best way. Instead of criticism, she simply asked, "Are you okay?"

That simple question, asked with genuine care, opened the space for everything I was experiencing to come pouring out, tears included. I felt safe. We worked as a team to figure out how to move forward. I will never forget how she made me feel. I aspire to show that same empathy for my peers and employees, offering understanding instead of judgment and partnering with those who need coaching in tough moments.

This is allyship.

Create space for others to feel safe when sharing without fear of judgment. Show that the person matters, and that asking for help is not just acceptable, it's encouraged. Assume positive intent and meet others where they are. No one is perfect, but if we lead with empathy and listen with curiosity instead of assumption, we can build workplaces where everyone can succeed.

– Megan Wendell

Twenty-Two

The Business Case for DEI

HOW DIVERSITY, EQUITY, AND INCLUSION CREATE BETTER OUTCOMES FOR EVERYONE

by Ashley C. Wynne, engineering leader and mentor, PhD in chemical engineering, and champion for equity and inclusion.

> Diversity doesn't look like anyone.
> It looks like everyone.
>
> – Karen Draper

How many times have you sat in a room at work and been the "only"?

Only woman, only person of color, only veteran, only person over 50? It happens to all of us at some point in our careers, being the only. It can be an intimidating environment, being in a meeting as the only woman, or the only "old guy."

> *32% of women in technical and engineering roles are often the only woman in the room at work.*
>
> – McKinsey and Company

But the room of people that welcomes at least one of every type? That room is a room with diverse thought. Fueled by varied experiences, a blend of ideas, perspectives, and ways to get things done, that room is challenging each other, trying new methods, calling back on past experiences to grow further. That room is thriving. That room is why DEI matters.

DIVERSITY, EQUITY, AND INCLUSION

In recent years, diversity, equity, and inclusion (DEI) has been a trending topic.[1]

While it shouldn't be a divisive topic, everyone seems to have an opinion. A lot of the discourse seems to be between people who have a strong vocal opinion opposing DEI and those who fully understand DEI and comprehend the benefits and advancements diverse communities and groups make to our society.

In recent decades, we have seen significant legislative advancements that are tremendously impactful for equality. For example, in the United States, the Lilly Ledbetter Fair Pay Act of 2009 holds employers accountable for pay discrimination.

More recently, we have seen legislative action in the opposite direction. Administrative directives in the U.S. in early 2025 resulted in an executive order banning DEI practices in federal workplaces. Many private sector companies also rolled back their DEI investments.

The political landscape and popular opinion can influence the perception of DEI and impact how companies invest or divest in related initiatives. But the reality is, businesses that make an inclusive culture a priority are winning in the end, not just in the engagement and workplace satisfaction of their employees.

They are more profitable. The data and numbers speak for themselves.

Before we really dig into the business advantages of investment in diverse workplace cultures, it's critical to understand what DEI is, and what it isn't.

WHAT'S DEI IS NOT

Most importantly, DEI is not the hiring of unqualified individuals to meet a diversity quota.

And DEI is not seeking applicants of specific demographics to achieve metrics and foregoing applicants that don't meet those demographic criteria.

---

[1] Also known as DE&I or Equity, Diversity, and Inclusion (EDI). Sometimes a "B" is added for Belonging, an "A" for Accessibility, or a "J" for Justice.

WHAT DEI IS

Diversity is representation throughout the organization. It's the C-suite and leadership teams that are composed of people of multiple ethnicities, backgrounds, and genders. It's the ongoing recruitment of new hires from multiple universities across the country, not hiring focused on the one university where the CEO was an alum.

Equity is giving people the same resources and opportunities, identifying roadblocks and barriers to success, and acknowledging that not everyone starts from the same place.

Inclusion is workplace cultures where everyone's perspectives, insights, and experiences are equally valued and integrated into the work culture.

Talent, intelligence, valued experience, and expertise are distributed across all populations, but opportunity is not.

DEI is the collective commitment of organizations to recognize inequities among different groups of people and to put forth a dedicated effort to ensure that workplaces and communities are environments where everyone's differences and unique identities are welcomed, respected, and celebrated.

This active investment in culture is beneficial for the entire workplace.

Engaged workforce. A workplace that prioritizes and cultivates a diverse workforce is an environment where all individuals feel safe, embraced, and valued, enabling an experiential and intellectually thriving place of employment.

Improved retention. A diverse workforce supported by an inclusive culture is critical to retention. When employees feel respected, trusted, and have a sense of belonging, they stay.

Stronger recruitment. Expanding the pool of candidates, and subsequently talent, demonstrates clear advocacy for what matters, experiences and expertise from all spaces that will ultimately result in a more innovative and inclusive workplace culture.

DIVERSITY ALONE IS NOT ENOUGH

A workplace needs to be both diverse and inclusive. They are not mutually exclusive but need to be integrated to truly build a culture of belonging.

Today, Gen Z, the up-and-coming generation, expects DEI to be prioritized.[2] Studies of Gen Z employees have indicated that they prioritize companies that share their ethical commitments, including DEI, sustainability, and authenticity.

The future of all workforces will be diverse. Investing today to commit to building an inclusive work culture that welcomes this diverse workforce is critical.

I've found through my experience, as someone who is fortunate enough to work for a diverse technical company, that inclusivity is truly the heartbeat of a diverse and equitable work culture.

DEI in the workplace can take on many different forms and meanings. DEI initiatives can include, but are not limited to, unconscious bias training, supported workplace ERGs, and diverse recruiting practices.

INCLUSIVE WORKPLACE PRACTICES

A dedicated effort to make sure everyone has a seat at the table (figuratively and literally) and purposefully making certain that contributors can share their work is a way to be aware and inclusive.

I have a colleague who is incredibly mindful about this. As the lead presenter, I appreciate how he intentionally invites whoever did the work to speak to their project contributions. By offering that platform to everyone, he demonstrates inclusiveness by ensuring all team members get visibility and appropriate credit for their contributions.

Making accommodations for those who need them is a vital part of creating inclusiveness at work. Take the example of an engineer who uses a wheelchair for mobility. How do we ensure they have equitable opportunities, even if they can't physically reach every space in an outdated, multi-level manufacturing plant?

---

[2] Gen Z is notably the most diverse generation in U.S. history. Similar trends are emerging across many Western European countries, as well as in nations like Nigeria, Singapore, and Malaysia.

Investing in fair pathways for all team members to contribute, regardless of physical ability, is a critical reason why DEI is so important. Laws like the ADA (Americans with Disabilities Act) protect against discrimination and require accessibility and reasonable accommodations. But how can we go beyond compliance to build workplaces that truly offer equitable access and opportunity?

Think about Stephen Hawking, one of the most brilliant physicists in history. Despite living with ALS (Lou Gehrig's disease), which caused significant physical and communicative challenges, Hawking made groundbreaking contributions to science. He continued his work using accommodations such as wheelchair accessible environments and advanced communication technologies. If Hawking had not had the opportunity, and support, to continue his research, the world would have missed out on his extraordinary insights.

This is a prime example of equity and inclusion, and why DEI matters.

EMPLOYEE RESOURCE GROUPS

Workplace ERGs are worthwhile resources and communities for members. Their positive impact on inclusion is amplified when people who aren't a part of that particular community participate in the ERGs as allies and learn from the experiences of others.[3]

For example, you don't need to be a member of the LGBTQ+ community to join an LGBTQ+ ERG. By becoming a member, you access an incredible opportunity to listen to and learn from others' experiences while demonstrating your support.

Celebrating events such as Diwali, International Women's Day, or Black History Month shows members of those communities that you value who they are as people and serves as a learning opportunity for those not part of that community to celebrate the heritage and contributions of people who are.

Bottom-Line Benefits

Numerous publications and studies highlight the importance of a diverse work culture. One of the more notable and prominent studies is a McKinscy and

---

[3] See Chapter 21, *Allies.*

Company 4-part, multiyear study spanning over 9 years of the business impacts of an inclusive workforce and diverse executive-level leadership.

Over the course of McKinsey's reporting, they demonstrated that the financial outperformance of companies with diverse leadership teams continues to grow. Their 2015 *Why Diversity Matters* report found companies in the top quartile for representation of women on executive leadership teams outperformed those in the bottom quartile by 15%. In 2023, that number more than doubled to 39%.

> *Companies in the top quartile for representation of women on executive leadership teams outperformed those in the bottom quartile by 39%.*
>
> – McKinsey and Company

The difference in financial performance doesn't just apply to gender-diverse teams, but also to ethnically diverse teams. McKinsey found that companies with ethnic diversity in the top quartile outperformed other companies financially by 27%.

WORKFORCE WELL-BEING

McKinsey's findings go beyond the financial case for diverse leadership. In its most recent report, McKinsey emphasized the holistic impact of diversity, how representation influences the overall well-being of a company, including finances, capabilities, workforce health, and environmental and social criteria.

The study also found a positive correlation between both gender and ethnic leadership diversity and three dimensions closely tied to employee and community well-being:

- **Community**, including business ethics, corporate citizenship, and philanthropy.
- **Workforce**, measured by talent attraction and retention, and labor practices.
- **Environment**, including operational efficiency and social impact goals like climate strategy.

In a win for champions of DEI, organizations with greater leadership diversity saw a 10% increase across all three dimensions.

The data is clear: diverse leadership drives value. Companies that actively invest in and authentically engage with diversity, equity, and inclusion see better financial returns and meaningful improvements in retention.[4]

Top-Line Benefits

So, we've seen how diverse teams, when supported by inclusive and equitable practices, drive measurable bottom-line results. But what about top-line growth? Can DEI also fuel innovation?

Short answer. Yes

Longer answer. Cognitive diversity drives innovation. The way people think and perceive is so varied that a workplace can only thrive when it is intentionally inclusive of those differences. As Harvard Business Review puts it, "teams solve problems faster when they're more cognitively diverse."

Their study focused solely on cognitive diversity, defined as "differences in perspective or information processing styles." Using the adaptive emergent methodology cube model to measure how individuals process knowledge and approach change, it found that more cognitively diverse teams completed challenges faster. Teams with less diversity struggled or failed altogether.

A *UNC Pembroke* publication reinforced this, noting cognitive diversity as a key factor in avoiding groupthink, sparking creativity, fostering innovation, improving problem-solving, expanding access to talent and skills, and increasing talent retention.

Without cognitive diversity, teams often share similar credentials, technical training, expertise, and even ways of thinking. Over

---

[4] And walk the walk, not just talk the talk. Performative DEI will not yield the same results.

time, this limits innovation, especially when team members prioritize approval or consensus over new ideas.

This is why it's not just about hiring for diversity; it's about retaining and elevating diverse thought. Seek out applicants from different regions, universities, degree programs, years of experience, time in other industries, and life experiences. This is the key to driving a culture of belonging and innovation.

Hiring and, more importantly, *retaining* people with a breadth of experience is about impact, not optics.

- Hire people because you want diverse thoughts and perspectives, not because you want diverse hires.
- Diversity is not about checking a box; it's about exploring how big the box can grow, which directly influences profitability.

The circle of influence of diversity and inclusion is clear. People and businesses all win.

ADVOCATING FOR DEI

In 2025, we are witnessing a major backlash against DEI initiatives. News articles are published daily about companies dropping their DEI programs or shifting away from open support for DEI to avoid backlash.[5]

On the other hand, several prominent companies like Delta Airlines, Costco, and Goldman Sachs have doubled down on their support of DEI programs. These companies have clearly voiced their commitment to promoting and prioritizing diverse workforces.

While the political and popular climate can influence public perception of diversity, equity, and inclusion programs, and companies might choose to invest or divert resources depending on the administration, the research is clear. Investment in inclusive and equitable practices benefits everyone, employees and employers, top and bottom line.

---

[5] At least at the time of publishing...

If your company has decided to shift away from endorsed DEI initiatives, there are many ways to continue fostering that culture without a formalized program.

An inclusive culture is everyone's responsibility.

Here are a few ways to foster an inclusive culture without a formalized DEI initiative:

- Use the correct pronunciation of people's names.
- Use people's pronouns.
- Practice inclusive language.
- Support accommodations for individuals with disabilities or special needs so they can fully participate.[6]
- Review compensation equity and then take action.
- Ensuring coworkers' voices and ideas are heard and acknowledged in meetings, and that their work is appropriately credited.
- Recruit through organizations like SWE, NSBE, SHPE, AWIS, and MedtechWOMEN.

And strategies for building a business case for something more formal:

- Identify why DEI matters specifically for your organization. Consider workforce trends, retention, performance, public goals, and innovation.
- Partner with HR (or available engagement data) to identify current equity and inclusion gaps.
- Correlate your organization's current pain points to the identified DEI gaps to identify value-based actions.
- Quantify impact with simple math, at least to start.[7]
- Connect DEI goals to existing company values.[8]
- Include how success will be measured.
- Keep supporting evidence from this chapter on hand as backup.

---

[6] Accommodations could include physical accessibility, closed captioning for those hard of hearing, or allowing flexible schedules for caregivers.

[7] Often, a rough estimate is enough to pitch a strong idea to leadership.

[8] Or skip the term "DEI" if it's a barrier. In that case, focus on the actions and value they create instead.

Business Case for DEI | In Simple Math

Research show that equitable and inclusive companies see up to a 64% reduction in turnover.

X = investment in DEI initiatives

Y = cost of replacing a mid-career employee (including productivity loss, recruiting, onboarding, and lost mentoring capacity)

If DEI initiatives prevent 64% of potential departures, then: Estimated cost savings = (0.64 x number of potential departures x Y) – X

Even with conservative assumptions, the return on investment can be significant.

FINAL THOUGHTS

As a woman in engineering, my perspective is shaped by my own experience. I have frequently been the only woman in the room. What I find incredibly valuable in my experience is the diversity of individuals, from different parts of the world, different universities, people with hands-on technical experience versus those with formal degrees, and how well everyone works together.

While I can reflect on many great examples of inclusivity, I have also observed numerous instances across several organizations where people were passed over for opportunities because someone's friend in the 'good old boy' network took priority.

The value of diversity is being undermined in popular culture today.

It's up to us to change the narrative and make the future inclusive for everyone.

Conclusion

HOW WE CHOOSE TO MOVE FORWARD

by Cassie Leonard, optimistic realist, excited to see the momentum we can build toward tangible change—together.

When I first imagined building a collaborative book on the complexities and nuances of why women do and don't stay in STEMM careers, the project felt like a pipe dream.[1] Who would want to contribute? And even if they did, would they have the time and energy for it?

This project's authors, just like our brilliant readers, are the very people most likely to be working demanding, high-stakes jobs; most likely to be caught in the ideal worker, ideal parent paradox; and most likely to be facing growing responsibility, increasing stress, and expanding leadership roles, all within a system still shaped by biases and barriers.

But I put the call out into the world anyway, and I'm so thankful I did.

Within minutes, I received my first response (shoutout to Karli!). Within a week, we had a vibrant and dynamic global team of 15, and it just kept growing. I am deeply grateful to each author, collaborator, ally, advocate, and anonymous yet courageous voice.

---

[1] Pun absolutely intended.

It has been a joy and a privilege to be part of this process, from awe-inspiring brainstorming sessions to reading drafts of each chapter as they took shape. I hope you have enjoyed this book's unique perspectives and personalities as much as I have.

– Cassie

THE GOAL OF *BEYOND THE PIPELINE*

We set out with this project to challenge pervasive, often overly simplified or harmful narratives about mid-career attrition for women in STEMM.

We aimed to offer expanded perspectives on many of the seen and unseen drivers that motivate women to "leave" STEMM. Although by now, you might be thinking there is no such thing as leaving STEMM; perhaps we're just reshaping it.

We did our best to provide tools, stories, and resources to illuminate the truth: you are worthy of working in an environment where you are seen, supported, and respected. Through our discussions, we quickly realized there would be no single magic fix. No "wouldn't it be great if every woman in STEMM just..." or "if every ally just..."

Nope, that would be too simple. And it would dismiss the incredible value that more than 9,000,000 STEMM graduates of all genders, colors, races, creeds, sexual orientations, socioeconomic backgrounds, and countless other dimensions of uniqueness bring into our richly diverse professional space each year.

As a team, we agreed to offer a range of perspectives. We accepted that this would inevitably lead to contradictions. And we decided that's okay.

You're smart people.

Hopefully, you've found some benefit as we've shared stories, research, and insights. How would you like to apply what you've learned as we move forward?

Here are a few ideas we've had so far:

Reflect. Consider the major themes that stood out to you within these pages. Was it the breadth or the commonality of the experiences shared? The call to choose your own "yardstick" to measure success? Or maybe the invitation to apply the critical thinking skills you honed during your university studies to navigate your next challenge?

Take time to write down (yes, pen and paper, I believe in you!) the themes that stood out most to you. Consider, free from any judgment, why these resonated with you the most. And if, at any point while reading this book, something felt triggering, offer yourself space, both metaphorically and on the page, to get curious about why.

Share your story. Everyone has a story worth sharing. Imagine if someone heard yours and was affected the way you have been while reading this book. You can start small: open up with a mentee or peer, write a post on social media, or volunteer for a candid panel discussion. Or write a chapter of a book. If you're looking for a bit of encouragement, you are warmly invited to connect with any of the authors of this book on LinkedIn.

Build your village. Your community of support can take absolutely any shape that helps you keep the conversation going. Find people who recognize your strengths, who celebrate your transferable skills, and who cheer for you no matter how you choose to define success. Consider how you are nurturing your authentic community. Are you inviting in diverse perspectives and curious, thoughtful people? Are you making space for allies too?

Be proactive. We're not going to get to where we collectively need to be without systemic change. You can be part of this movement. Engage in (or lead) policy reviews at your workplace, including hiring practices, parental leave, pay equity, succession planning, mentoring programs, and access to business training. Become a champion for someone of merit who has less access than you. Find organizations that are getting it right, and then tell others about them.

Get loud. Truly, the possibilities for advocacy are endless. All we ask is that you get started.

Join our growing community. This may be the end of the book, but it's not the end of the conversation. You are invited to join our growing community of people who don't accept the status quo.

We are working toward a diverse, equitable, and inclusive future that sees and supports women in STEMM for all that they are, never as a drip from some old, leaky pipe that needs to be replaced.

To join the conversation, visit our LinkedIn group: *Beyond the Pipeline – STEMM Women+.*

Whatever path you choose, know that we are grateful for you.

The future of STEMM isn't about fitting into rigid models. It's about redesigning the system so that everyone, each and every one of us, has the freedom to contribute, belong, and succeed on our own terms.

Notes

RECURRING NOTE ABBREVIATIONS

HBR - *Harvard Business Review,* hbr.org   Forbes - *Forbes,* forbes.com
NSF - *National Science Foundation,* nsf.gov   NYT - *The New York Times,* nytimes.com
PEW - *Pew Research Center,* pewresearch.org   WEforum - *World Economic Forum,* weforum.org

INTRODUCTION

"Apollo 13 Infographic: How Did They Make That CO2 Scrubber?" *Houston Space Center,* 10
    Apr. 2019, spacecenter.org.
Employment - Society of Women Engineers. swe.org/research/2024/employment.
Women in Computer Science Dropping since 1980s, developers.hp.com.
"New Tertiary Graduates in Science, Technology, Engineering and Mathematics as a Share of New
    Graduates | Jobs Indicators." *OECD Going Digital Toolkit,* goingdigital.oecd.org.
Oliss, Brendan, et al. "The Global Distribution of STEM Graduates: Which Countries Lead the
    Way?" *Center for Security and Emerging Technology,* 27 Nov. 2023, cset.georgetown.edu.
Anti-Oppression | Canadian Council for Refugees. ccrweb.ca.

MENTAL WELLNESS MOMENT | AN INTRODUCTION

No notes.

1. SHATTERING THE PIPELINE

Hill, Susan. "Science and Engineering Bachelor's Degrees Awarded to Women Increase Overall,
    but Decline in Several Fields." *NSF,* vol. 97–326, Nov. 1997.
Sadler, M.E. "Education during Adolescence." *Nature,* vol. 82, no. 2098, 1910, pp. 325–27.
Climbing the Academic Ladder. National Academies Press, 1979.
Berryman, Sue E. *Who Will Do Science? Trends, and Their Causes in Minority and Female
    Representation among Holders of Advanced Degrees in Science and Mathematics.* Nov. 1983.
Tobias, Sheila. *They're Not Dumb, They're Different.* Science News Books, 1990.
Barinaga, M. "Profile of a Field: Neuroscience." *Science,* vol. 255, no. 5050, Mar. 1992, pp. 1366–67.
Pell, A. N. "Fixing the Leaky Pipeline." *J. of Animal Science,* vol. 74, no. 11, 1996, p. 2843.
Alper, Joe. "The Pipeline Is Leaking Women All the Way Along." *Science,* vol. 260, no. 5106, Apr.
    1993, pp. 409–11.

Hill, Rocky, et al. "Culturally and Linguistically Diverse Teachers in Special Ed." *The J. of the Teacher Education Division of the Council for Exceptional Children*, vol. 16, no. 3, July 1993, pp. 258–69.

Seymour, Elaine, and Nancy M. Hewitt. *Talking about Leaving: Why Undergraduates Leave the Sciences*. Westview Press, 2000.

Watt, Dr Jodi. *Blog – Reconsidering the Leaky Pipeline - Dem Researcher*. 31 Aug. 2023, dementiaresearcher.nihr.ac.uk.

Eliot, Lance. "The Venerable Upstream Parable Helps in These Trying Times, and Applies to the Future of AI Self-Driving Cars." *Forbes*.

Hering, Janet. "Pipelines Are Not Meant for People." *Stukturelle*, 3 July 2023, strukturelle.ch.

Bridging the Gap. "The Leaky Pipeline." *The Duck of Minerva*, 28 Oct. 2020, duckofminerva.com.

"The Pipeline Isn't Leaky." *Ever on & On*, 28 Aug. 2013, biochembelle.com.

2. Values and Choice

Morgan, Kate. "Why We Define Ourselves by Our Jobs." *BBC*, 13 Apr. 2021, bbc.com.

Eccles (Parsons), Jacquelynne. "Expectancies, Values, and Academic Behaviors." *Achievement and Achievement Motives: Psychological and Sociological Approaches*, 1983.

All Women Are Beautiful. "Be A Lady They Said." *And Bloom*, Feb. 2020, andbloom.amsterdam.

3. Inlet Forces

National Association of Colleges and Employers. *Job Outlook, 2022*. naceweb.org.

Honey, Margaret, et al. *STEM Integration in K-12 Education: Status, Prospects, and an Agenda for Research*. National Academies Press, 2014.

Diversity and STEM: Women, Minorities, and Persons with Disabilities 2023 | NSF.

OECD. *Education at a Glance 2023: OECD Indicators*. OECD, 2023.

Government of Canada, Statistics Canada. *Trends in Student Debt of Postsecondary Graduates in Canada: Results from the National Graduates Survey, 2018*. 25 Aug. 2020.

WEforum, *Future of Jobs Report 2023*. May 2023.

Serino, Nicole, and Yucheng Zheng. "Studying the STEM Education Gap Among CEOs Globally." *S&P Global*, 10 Jan. 2023, spglobal.com.

Woolley, Anita Williams, et al. "Evidence for a Collective Intelligence Factor in the Performance of Human Groups." *Science*, vol. 330, no. 6004, Oct. 2010, pp. 686–88.

"Teams Solve Problems Faster When They're More Cognitively Diverse." *HBR*, 30 Mar. 2017.

"The Two Traits of the Best Problem-Solving Teams." *HBR*, 2 Apr. 2018.

Page, Scott E. "Making the Difference: Applying a Logic of Diversity." *Academy of Management Perspectives*, vol. 21, no. 4, Nov. 2007, pp. 6–20.

Larson, Erik. "New Research: Diversity + Inclusion = Better Decision Making At Work." *Forbes*.

"Why Diverse Teams Are Smarter." *HBR*, 4 Nov. 2016.

Carucci, Ron. "One More Time: Why Diversity Leads to Better Team Performance." *Forbes*.

How Diversity, Equity, and Inclusion (DE&I) Matter | McKinsey. mckinsey.com.

Lorenzo, Rocio, et al. *How Diverse Leadership Teams Boost Innovation*. The Boston Consulting Group, Jan 2018, web-assets.bcg.com.

Women in the Workplace 2024 Report | McKinsey. mckinsey.com.

Diversity Wins Interactive | McKinsey. 2020, mckinsey.com.

Why Diversity Matters Even More | McKinsey. 2023, mckinsey.com.

Page, Scott. *The Difference: How the Power of Diversity Creates Better Groups, Firms, Schools, and Societies*. Princeton University Press, 2008.

Glass, Christy, and Alison Cook. "Do Women Leaders Promote Positive Change? Analyzing the Effect of Gender on Business Practices and Diversity Initiatives." *Human Resource Management*, vol. 57, no. 4, July 2018, pp. 823–37.

Eagly, Alice H., and Linda L. Carli. "The Female Leadership Advantage: An Evaluation of the Evidence." *The Leadership Quarterly*, vol. 14, no. 6, Dec. 2003, pp. 807–34.

Olekalns, Mara, and Jessica A. Kennedy. *Research Handbook on Gender and Negotiation*. Edward Elgar Publ, 2020.

Bear, Julia B., and Anita Williams Woolley. "The Role of Gender in Team Collaboration and Performance." *Interdisciplinary Science Reviews*, vol. 36, no. 2, June 2011, pp. 146–53.

Lorde, Audre. *Sister Outsider: Essays and Speeches*. Crossing Press, 1998.

4. IDEAL WORKER VS. IDEAL PARENT

Ware, Bronnie. *The Top Five Regrets of the Dying*. Hay House, 2012.

Brinkley, Douglas. "80 Days That Changed the World." *Time*, 31 Mar. 2003. content.time.com.

CRS Products (Library of Congress). "The Fair Labor Standards Act (FLSA)." *Congress.Gov*.

Kranzberg, Melvin, and Michael T. Hannan. "History of the Organization of Work." *Britannica Money*, britannica.com.

"Diverse Period Practices in Indigenous Cultures." *Help A Girl Out*, 5 Feb. 2025, helpagirlout.org.

"Menstrual Health: A Traditional Chinese Medicine Perspective." *Herbal Reality*, herbalreality.com.

"Permission to Rest | The Benefits of Slowing Down During Menstruation." *Banyan Botanicals*, 26 Apr. 2023, banyanbotanicals.com.

Government of Canada, Statistics Canada. *The Surge of Women in the Workforce*. 17 Dec. 2015. *The Rise of the Dual-Earner Family with Children*. 30 May 2016.

Redmond, Sabrina Wulff Pabilonia and Jill Janocha. "The Rise in Remote Work since the Pandemic and Its Impact on Productivity." *Bureau of Labor Statistics*, bls.gov.

Wells, Rachel. "Office Return: Will 2025 Mark the End of Remote Work?" *Forbes*.

Allen, Terina. "Trump: Federal Workers Will Be Fired Unless They End Remote Work and Return to Office Soon." *Forbes*.

Infra-Annual Labor Statistics: Labor Force Participation Rate Female: From 25 to 54 Years for United States. 15 Apr. 2025, fred.stlouisfed.org.

"Why Gender Equity in the Workplace Is Good for Business." *Professional & Executive Development | Harvard DCE*, 27 Mar. 2020, professional.dce.harvard.edu.

"Worldwide Cost of Living 2023." *Economist Intelligence Unit*, eiu.com.

Braga, Richard Fry and Dana. "1. The Growth of the Older Workforce." *PEW*, 14 Dec. 2023.

"Stress, the 'Health Epidemic of the 21st Century.'" *HCA Healthcare Today*, 1 May 2019, hcahealthcaretoday.com.

Bui, Tina, et al. "Workplace Stress and Productivity." *Kansas J. of Medicine*, vol. 14, Feb. 2021.

"How Stress Affects Your Body and Behavior." *Mayo Clinic*, mayoclinic.org.

Medaris, Anna. "Women Say They're Stressed, Misunderstood, and Alone." *American Psychology Association*, 1 Nov. 2023, apa.org.

McLean, Carmen P., et al. "Gender Differences in Anxiety Disorders." *J. of Psychiatric Research*, vol. 45, no. 8, Aug. 2011, pp. 1027–35.

Artz, Benjamin, et al. "Gender Role Perspectives and Job Burnout." *Review of Economics of the Household*, vol. 20, no. 2, June 2022, pp. 447–70.

"Women Are Nearly Half of U.S. Workforce but Only 27% of STEM Workers." Jan 2021, *Census.Gov*, census.gov.

Ferrante, Mary Beth. "The Pressure Is Real For Working Mothers." 27 Aug 2018, *Forbes*.

Government of Canada, Statistics Canada. *Estimating the Economic Value of Unpaid Household Work in Canada, 2015 to 2019*. 17 Mar. 2022.

Parker, Richard Fry, Carolina Aragão, Kiley Hurst and Kim. "In a Growing Share of U.S. Marriages, Husbands and Wives Earn About the Same." *PEW*, 13 Apr. 2023.

Ramey, Garey, and Valerie Ramey. *The Rug Rat Race*. w15284, National Bureau of Economic Research, Aug. 2009.

The Default Parent Syndrome: More Than Just a TikTok Trend | Psychology Today Canada. Nov 2022, psychologytoday.com.

Anaya, Tessa. *Balancing Work and Family: How Are Parents in the Workplace Supported?* Capterra, 8 Mar. 2023, capterra.ca.

Forbes, Lisa K., et al. "Working Mothers' Experiences in an Intensive Mothering Culture." *J. of Feminist Family Therapy*, vol. 33, no. 3, July 2021, pp. 270–94.

WEforum. *Four-Day Work Week Trial in Spain Leads to Healthier Workers, Less Pollution*. 25 Oct. 2023.

"4 Day Week Research Reports and Pilot Results." *4 Day Week Global*, 4dayweek.com/research.

WEforum. *New Study Shows 4-Day Working Week to Be a Success*. 31 Jan. 2022.

Hurst, Alexander. "Want the Legal Right to Ignore Your Boss Outside Working Hours? Learn from the French." *The Guardian*, 23 Aug. 2024. theguardian.com.

Benchetrit, Jenna. "Australians Now Have the Legal Right to Disconnect from Work. But How Effective Will It Be?" *CBC News*, 28 Aug. 2024. CBC.ca.

Flex Index. *Q4 2024 The Flex Report*. flexindex.com.

Masih, Niha. *Need Time off Work for Period Pain? These Countries Offer 'Menstrual Leave.'* The Washington Post, 17 Feb. 2023, washingtonpost.com.

Levitt, Rachel B., and Jessica L. Barnack-Tavlaris. "Addressing Menstruation in the Workplace." *The Palgrave Handbook of Critical Menstruation Studies*, 2020. ncbi.nlm.nih.gov.

Warren, Rick. *The Purpose Driven Life: What on Earth Am I Here For?* Zondervan, 2012.

MENTAL WELLNESS MOMENT | THE WEIGHT OF OVER-RESPONSIBILITY

Loewentheil, Kara. "359: Over-Responsibility: The Spin." *The School of New Feminist Thought*, 12 Sept. 2024, schoolofnewfeministthought.com.

5. FROM SURVIVING TO THRIVING

Beck, Aaron T. *Cognitive Therapy and the Emotional Disorders*. Int'l Universities Press, 1976

"Reducing Stress through Mindful Practices." *Students*, 25 Oct 2021, students.ouhsc.edu.

Frankl, Viktor E. *Man's Search for Meaning*. Revised and Updated, Pocket Books, 1985.

Fogg, B. J. *Tiny Habits*. Houghton Mifflin Harcourt, 2019.

A New Field of Neuroscience Aims to Map Connections in the Brain | Harvard Medical School. 19 Jan. 2023, hms.harvard.edu.

Seligman, Martin E. P., et al. "Positive Psychology Progress: Empirical Validation of Interventions." *American Psychologist*, vol. 60, no. 5, July 2005, pp. 410–21.

Box Breathing: How to Do It, Benefits, and Tips. 1 June 2018, medicalnewstoday.com.

Vollmer, Becky. *You Are Not Stuck.* St. Martin's Essentials, 2023.

Doyle, Glennon. *Untamed.* The Dial Press, 2020.

Leonard, Cassie. *STEM Moms.* ELMM Press, 2023.

6. BURNOUT

Gregor, Margo A., et al. "'I Need a Break or I Might Quit': STEM Academics' Pandemic Experiences." *The Counseling Psychologist,* vol. 52, no. 1, Jan. 2024, pp. 88–123.

Burn-out an "Occupational Phenomenon": Intl. Classification of Diseases. 28 May 2019, who.int.

Lee, Margaret Y. W., and Kathleen Riach. "Beyond the Brink: STEM Women and Resourceful Sensemaking after Burnout." *J. of Organizational Behavior,* vol. 45, no. 3, Mar. 2024, pp. 477–96.

7. IMPOSTER SYNDROME

"Stop Telling Women They Have Imposter Syndrome." *HBR,* 11 Feb. 2021.

Clance, Pauline Rose, and Suzanne Ament Imes. "The Imposter Phenomenon in High Achieving Women." *Psychotherapy: Theory, Research & Practice,* vol. 15, no. 3, 1978, pp. 241–47.

Ibrahim, Mennatalla. *Women Feel like Imposters in Disciplines That Value 'Brilliance.'* 13 Aug. 2021.

Zenker, Aldana. "An Increasing Number of Female and Non-Binary STEM Students Are Experiencing Imposter Syndrome." *Stem Women,* 18 Apr. 2023, stemwomen.com.

Dabaja, Amar. "Imposter Syndrome." *All Together, SWE,* 3 Mar. 2023, alltogether.swe.org.

"Mentoring Someone with Imposter Syndrome." *HBR,* 22 Feb. 2019.

Psychological Safety and Leadership Development | McKinsey. mckinsey.com.

Moassefi, Mana, et al. "Empowering Women in Imaging Informatics: Confronting Imposter Syndrome, Addressing Microaggressions, and Striving for Work-Life Harmony." *J. of Imaging Informatics in Medicine,* Oct. 2024.

MENTAL WELLNESS MOMENT | PANIC ATTACKS IN THE OFFICE

No notes.

8. A LABYRINTH OF IDENTITIES

Crenshaw, Kimberle. "Demarginalizing the Intersection of Race and Sex: A Black Feminist Critique of Antidiscrimination Doctrine, Feminist Theory and Antiracist Politics." *University of Chicago Legal Forum,* vol. 1989, no. 1, Dec. 2015, chicagounbound.uchicago.edu.

Embassy of France in the United States. "Women Who Made French History – Marie Curie." *Ambassade De France Aux Etats-Unis,* media.franceintheus.org/11939.

Ada Lovelace: Victorian Computing Visionary – Ada Lovelace Day. findingada.com.

Shetterly, Margot Lee. *Hidden Figures.* HarperCollins Publishers, 2016.

"Hidden Voices: Emily Roebling, Engineer of the Brooklyn Bridge." *NYC Public Schools,* 31 Mar. 2022, schools.nyc.gov.

Hedy Lamarr. jewishvirtuallibrary.org.

Hempel, Jessi. "Melinda Gates and Fei-Fei Li Want to Liberate AI from 'Guys with Hoodies.'" *Wired,* May 2017, wired.com.

Jemison, Mae. *Find Where the Wind Goes: Moments from My Life.* Scholastic, 2001.

Astronomy Pioneer Cecilia Payne-Gaposchkin Broke Gender Barriers | Science News. 1 Mar. 2020, sciencenews.org.

Ross, Matthew B., et al. "Women Are Credited Less in Science than Men." *Nature*, vol. 608, no. 7921, Aug. 2022, pp. 135–45.

Andrews-Clark, Taylah. *"Why Intersectionality Is so Important in STEM." The Oxford Scientist,* 8 Apr. 2023, oxsci.org.

Committee on Equal Opportunities in Science and Engineering. *Making Visible the Invisible: Understanding Intersectionality.* 2021-2022 Biennial Report to Congress, NSF, Aug. 2023.

"Responding to Microaggressions and Unconscious Bias." *National Equity Project*, nationalequityproject.org.

Sekaquaptewa, Denise. "Gender-Based Microaggressions in STEM Settings." *NCID Currents*, vol. 1, no. 1, Nov. 2019.

Williams, Joan, et al. *Double Jeopardy? Gender Bias Against Women of Color in Science.* 2014.

Reggiani, Marco, et al. "LGBT + Academics' and PhD Students' Experiences of Visibility in STEM: More than Raising the Rainbow Flag." *Higher Education*, vol. 87, no. 1, Jan. 2024, pp. 69–87.

MENTAL WELLNESS MOMENT | THE IMPORTANCE OF A DIAGNOSIS

"New CDC Data Highlights the Need for Guidelines on Adult ADHD." *Psychiatric Times*, 10 Oct. 2024, psychiatrictimes.com.

9. NAVIGATING MOTHERHOOD ALONGSIDE CAREER

"Women Are Nearly Half of U.S. Workforce but Only 27% of STEM Workers." *Census.Gov*, Jan 2021, census.gov.

Schaeffer, Katherine. "For Women's History Month, a Look at Gender Gains – and Gaps – in the U.S." *PEW*, 27 Feb. 2024.

Quart, Alissa. "The Motherhood Advantage." *Slate*, 26 June 2018. *slate.com*, slate.com.

"Uncovering Culture: A Call to Action for Leaders." *Deloitte United States*, deloitte.com.

WHO. *1 in 6 People Globally Affected by Infertility: WHO. 4* Apr. 2023, who.int.

"Miscarriage - Symptoms and Causes." *Mayo Clinic*, mayoclinic.org.

Ginther, Samuel C., et al. "Metabolic Loads and the Costs of Metazoan Reproduction." *Science*, vol. 384, no. 6697, May 2024, pp. 763–67.

Strandberg, Ann Louise. *The Unspoken Challenge: Breastfeeding While Working Full-Time.* linkedin.com.

"It Takes a Village: Hunter-Gatherer Approach to Childcare Suggests That the Key to Mother and Child Wellbeing May Be Many Caregivers." *EurekAlert!*, eurekalert.org.

"In the Absence of 'the Village,' Mothers Struggle Most." *Motherly*, 9 Nov. 2021, mother.ly.

"How Family Involvement Strengthens Your Community (And Why It Matters)." *Kids Mental Health*, 28 Jan. 2025, kidsmentalhealth.ca.

Reupert, Andrea, et al. "It Takes a Village to Raise a Child: Understanding and Expanding the Concept of the 'Village.'" *Frontiers in Public Health*, vol. 10, Mar. 2022, p. 756066.

Wong, Ruth Grace. *Working Moms Today Spend as Much Time on Childcare as Stay-at-Home Moms 40 Years Ago.* joyfulparentingsf.com.

Semuels, Alana. "'Return to Office' Plans Spell Trouble for Working Moms." *TIME*, 2 Feb. 2023, time.com.

Rodsky, Eve. *Fair Play.* G.P. Putnam's Sons, 2019.

Doucleff, Michaeleen. *Hunt, Gather, Parent: What Ancient Cultures Can Teach Us about the Lost Art of Raising Happy, Helpful Little Humans.* Simon & Schuster, 2021.

The Benefits of Chores for Kids | Bright Horizons. brighthorizons.com.

Matrescence, matrescence.com.

Raphael, Dana. *The Tender Gift: Breastfeeding*. Englewood Cliffs, 1973.

Harrold, Jessie. *Mothershift: Reclaiming Motherhood as a Rite of Passage*. Shambhala, 2024.

Laney, Elizabeth K., et al. "Becoming a Mother: The Influence of Motherhood on Women's Identity Development." *Identity*, vol. 15, no. 2, Apr. 2015, pp. 126–45.

Porges, Stephen W. "Polyvagal Theory." *Frontiers in Integrative Neuroscience*, vol. 16, May 2022.

MOTHER-LEADER INTUITIONSHIP

Ursino, Melinda, and Rivera, Laura Marie, "Exploring Leadership Capabilities Developed as a Mother: Toward a New Theory of Mother-Leader Intuitionship." *Educational and Organizational Learning and Leadership Dissertations | College of Education | Seattle University*, 2025. scholarworks.seattleu.edu/etds-eoll-dissertations.

Intuitionship: To Define and Celebrate the Magic of Motherhood (MOM). intuitionship.com.

The Parent Is the Child's First Teacher | Lifetime Montessori School. lifetimemontessorischool.com.

Denu, Kimberly Battle-Walters, and Janet S. Walters. "Leaning Back: When Purpose Supersedes Position." *Mothers Are Leaders*, Abilene Christian University Press, 2014, pp. 67–86.

Goldin, Claudia Dale. *Career and Family: Women's Century-Long Journey toward Equity*. Princeton University Press, 2021.

Women Have Not yet Reached Gender Equity in Academia, The Fulcrum. 16 Mar. 2022, thefulcrum.us.

Lindahl, Lisa Z. "Is This The Age Of Women in Leadership?" *Forbes*, 5 Feb. 2024.

10. STAY-AT-HOME PARENTS

"How Much Should a Stay-At-Home Mom Make." *Salary.Com*, 5 May 2021, salary.com.

"Paid Parental Leave: Big Differences for Mothers and Fathers." *OECD*, 12 Jan. 2023, oecd.org.

Parks-Stamm, Elizabeth, and Derek Tharp. "Men and Women Use Parental Leave Differently. They're Judged Differently for It, Too." *TIME*, 23 May 2023, time.com.

"More Than a Foundation: Young Children Are Capable STEM Learners." *NAEYC*, Nov 2017, naeyc.org.

Torres, Isabel, et al. "COVID Has Laid Bare the Inequities That Face Mothers in STEM." *Scientific American*, scientificamerican.com.

MENTAL WELLNESS MOMENT | TROUBLESHOOTING COMPLEX SYSTEMS

No notes.

11. CHARTING YOUR OWN COURSE

Hanson, Erin. *Thepoeticunderground: Reverie*. Lulu.com, 2014.

Glass, J. L., et al. "What's So Special about STEM? A Comparison of Women's Retention in STEM and Professional Occupations." *Social Forces*, vol. 92, no. 2, Dec. 2013, pp. 723–56.

Professionals Australia. *Women Staying in the STEM Workforce – an Economic Imperative for Australia: Survey Report. 2021*, members.professionalsaustralia.org.au

Lerchenmueller, Marc J., and Olav Sorenson. "The Gender Gap in Early Career Transitions in the Life Sciences." *Research Policy*, vol. 47, no. 6, July 2018, pp. 1007 17.

Rosenzweig, Emily Q., et al. "Inside the STEM Pipeline: Changes in Students' Biomedical Career Plans across the College Years." *Science Advances*, vol. 7, no. 18, Apr. 2021.

"2021 Highschool Big Data Challenge: Paving the Path to True Equality and Equal Access in Education: Under the Patronage of Canadian Commission for UNESCO." *STEM Fellowship J.*, vol. 7, no. 1, Dec. 2021, pp. 66–82.

Beyond Bias and Barriers: Fulfilling the Potential of Women in Academic Science and Engineering. National Academies Press, 2007.

Dougal, Sonya. *The Challenge of Keeping Women in STEM - NYAS.* 1 Oct. 2019, nyas.org.

"Women in STEM Careers - Where We Are in 2023." *Women in the Workplace*, Randstad, 3 Mar. 2023, randstad.ca.

Walrond, Karen. *The Lightmaker's Manifesto.* Broadleaf Books, 2021.

12. Academia

"Australian Research 'Has a Daversity Problem.'" *ABC News*, 24 Nov. 2017. abc.net.au.

Borger, Jessica. "We Need to Address Gender Bias in Medical Research Peer Review." *Women's Agenda*, 27 Feb. 2022, womensagenda.com.au.

Seneviratne, Prathi. *Are Women Reaching Parity with Men in STEM? | Econofact.* 15 Apr. 2022, econofact.org.

Women in Science. 18 Nov. 2016, uis.unesco.org.

Borger, Jessica G., and Louise E. Purton. "Gender Inequities in Medical Research Funding Is Driving an Exodus of Women from Australian STEMM Academia." *Immunology and Cell Biology*, vol. 100, no. 9, Oct. 2022, pp. 674–78.

Else, Holly. "Outcry as Men Win Outsize Share of Australian Medical-Research Funding." *Nature*, vol. 600, no. 7887, Nov. 2021, pp. 18–18. *nature.com.*

Pohlhaus, Jennifer Reineke, et al. "Sex Differences in Application, Success, and Funding Rates for NIH Extramural Programs." Academic Medicine, vol. 86, no. 6, June 2011, pp. 759–67.

Martinez, Elisabeth D., et al. "Falling off the Academic Bandwagon." *EMBO Reports*, vol. 8, no. 11, Nov. 2007, pp. 977–81.

"Science and Gender." *Nature Immunology*, vol. 11, no. 2, Feb. 2010, pp. 99–99. *nature.com.*

Ross, Matthew B., et al. "Women Are Credited Less in Science than Men." *Nature*, vol. 608, no. 7921, Aug. 2022, pp. 135–45. *nature.com.*

Welle, Elissa. "Women Less Likely than Men to Get Authorship on Scientific Publications, Analysis Finds." *STAT*, 22 June 2022, statnews.com.

Langin, Katie. "Women Scientists Don't Get Authorship They Should, New Study Suggests." *Science*, June 2022, science.org.

Women Fighting Stereotypes and Systemic Discrimination in STEM. education.nationalgeographic.org.

WomensMedia. "Women Leading Women: Supporters or Saboteurs?" *Forbes*, 3 Oct 2012.

13. Rise and Shine

No notes.

14. Pressured Out of Technical

Girls' Superb Verbal Skills May Contribute to the Gender Gap in Math. 15 July 2019, pbs.org.

Hunt, Patricia K., et al. "A Multi-Year Science Research or Engineering Experience in High School Gives Women Confidence to Continue in the STEM Pipeline or Seek Advancement in Other Fields: A 20-Year Longitudinal Study." PLoS ONE, vol. 16, no. 11, Nov. 2021.

New Research Shows Women Are Better at Using Soft Skills Crucial for Effective Leadership and Superior Business Performance, Finds Korn Ferry. kornferry.com.

Goulet, Andrea. *A Short History of the "Soft Skill" vs. "Hard Skill" Divide (and Why It's a Farce).* 27 Apr. 2023, linkedin.com.

Wardell, Amber. "Women's Complicated Relationship With Self-Care Versus Other-Care." *Medium*, 8 Feb. 2024, medium.com.

Babcock, Linda, et al. "Gender Differences in Accepting and Receiving Requests for Tasks with Low Promotability." *American Economic Review*, vol. 107, no. 3, Mar. 2017, pp. 714–47.

Cockett, James, et al. *Career Deflection: Exploring Diversity, Progression, And Retention in Engineering.* Atkins, employment-studies.co.uk.

Fouad, Nadya A., et al. "Women's Reasons for Leaving the Engineering Field." *Frontiers in Psychology*, vol. 8, June 2017, p. 875.

Women Leave Tech Jobs Because They Can't Climb the Ladder - IEEE Spectrum. spectrum.ieee.org.

Hutt, Rosamond. "Why Do So Many Women Leave Engineering? Probably Not for the Reason You're Thinking." *WEforum*, 29 Nov. 2016.

"The Subtle Stressors Making Women Want to Leave Engineering." *HBR*, 23 Nov. 2018.

Cain Miller, Claire. "As Women Take Over a Male-Dominated Field, the Pay Drops." *NYT*, 18 Mar. 2016.

Ramakrishnan, Aditi, et al. "Women's Participation in the Medical Profession." *J. of Women's Health*, vol. 23, no. 11, Nov. 2014, pp. 927–34.

NPR. *When Women Stopped Coding.* Episode 576, 17 Oct. 2014, npr.org.

Newport, Cal. *Deep Work: Rules for Focused Success in a Distracted World.* Grand Central Publ., 2016.

MENTAL WELLNESS MOMENT | REFRAMING

No notes.

15. GLASS CEILINGS & CLIFFS

2024 Women CEOs In America, Changing the Face of Business Leadership. 2024, amazonaws.com.

Get the Data | NORC at the University of Chicago. gss.norc.org.

Linker, Damon. "Hillary Clinton's Authenticity Problem." *The Week*, 17 June 2014, theweek.com.

Cheng, William. "The Long, Sexist History of 'Shrill' Women." *TIME*, 23 Mar. 2016, time.com.

Klein, Philip. *Elizabeth Warren's Candidacy Failed Because Voters Saw through Her - Washington Examiner.* 5 Mar. 2020, washingtonexaminer.com.

"Critics Say Elizabeth Warren Is Too Divisive to Run for President. Are They Right?" *NBC News*, 15 Dec. 2018, nbcnews.com.

CNN.Com - Transcripts. 22 July 2024, show CNAP, seg. 01. transcripts.cnn.com.

Hentschel, Tanja, et al. "The Multiple Dimensions of Gender Stereotypes: A Current Look at Men's and Women's Characterizations of Others and Themselves." *Frontiers in Psychology*, vol. 10, Jan. 2019, p. 11.

Goleman, Daniel. *Emotional Intelligence: Why It Can Matter More Than IQ.* Bloomsbury Publ., 1996.

The Power of Vulnerability | Brené Brown | *TED.*

Greenleaf, Robert K. *The Servant as Leader.* Greenleaf Center for Servant Leadership, 2008.

Wheatley, Margaret Joan. *Leadership and the New Science.* Berrett-Koehler publ, 1992.

"Thanks for the Mentoring but What I Need Is a Champion." *Medium*, medium.com.

Tourjée, Diana. "Women Are Punished More for Being Assholes at Work." *VICE*, June 2016, vice.com.

Cain Miller, Claire. "As Women Take Over a Male-Dominated Field, the Pay Drops." *NYT*, 18 March 2016.

NPR. *When Women Stopped Coding*. Episode 576, 17 Oct. 2014, npr.org.

Ramakrishnan, Aditi, et al. "Women's Participation in the Medical Profession." *J. of Women's Health*, vol. 23, no. 11, Nov. 2014, pp. 927–34.

"If There's Only One Woman in Your Candidate Pool, There's Statistically No Chance She'll Be Hired." *HBR*, 26 Apr. 2016.

"The Most Powerful Woman on Wall Street." *Financial Post*, financialpost.com.

"Krawcheck Seen Bidding Final Adieu to Wall Street." *Reuters*, 9 Sept. 2011. *Reuters,* reuters.com.

Former Hewlett-Packard CEO Carly Fiorina Speaks out - Oct. 24, 2007. money.cnn.com.

"How Brexit Became a 'glass Cliff' for Theresa May." *PBS News*, 1 Apr. 2019, pbs.org.

Associated Press. "Yahoo Boss Marissa Mayer Loses Millions in Bonuses over Security Lapses." *The Guardian*, 2 Mar. 2017. theguardian.com.

English, Duvar. "Turkey's Central Bank Governor Hafize Gaye Erken resigns, cites recent 'defamation campaign' as reason." *DuvaR.english*, 2 Feb. 2024, duvarenglish.com.

Reuters. "Boeing No. 2 Executive's Role Narrowed to Focus on Fixing Commercial Plane Unit." *U.S. News*, 25 Feb. 2025, money.usnews.com.

Gupta, Vishal K., et al. "You're Fired! Gender Disparities in CEO Dismissal." *J. of Management*, vol. 46, no. 4, Apr. 2020, pp. 560–82.

"Women Receive Harsher Punishment at Work Than Men." *Harvard Business School*, 17 Dec. 2018, library.hbs.edu.

Kamaei, Maryam, et al. "Women and White-Collar Crime: A Comparative Study of Iranian and Norwegian Offenders." *Pakistan J. of Criminology*, vol. 14, no. 4, Dec. 2022, pjcriminology.com.

Baum, Ido, et al. *Gender and Corporate Crime: Do Women on the Board of Directors Reduce Corporate Bad Behavior?* no. 2, 2022.

Turner, Sarah. "White-Collar Crime, Sentencing Gender Disparities Post-Booker, and Implications for Criminal Sentencing." *JCLC Online*, Jan. 2023, scholarlycommons.law.northwestern.edu

Baum, Ido, et al. "Elizabeth Holmes Is the Exception: More Women on Boards Lead to Less Corporate Wrongdoing." *ProMarket*, 10 Feb. 2022, promarket.org.

Ogilvie, Sarah. *Not All Women Fall off the Glass Cliff*. prospectmagazine.co.uk.

Elavia, Serena, and Johnathan Tin. "Present Value: Corporate Titan Irene Rosenfeld Reflects on More than 30 Years in the Food Industry." *Cornell SC Johnson*, 1 July 2019, business.cornell.edu.

Wang, Nancy. "Want To Be a Woman CEO? Don't Get Pushed Off a Glass Cliff." *Forbes*, 8 Feb 2020.

Benson, Alan, et al. *"Potential" and the Gender Promotions Gap*. 4747175, 4 Mar. 2024. *Social Science Research Network*.

Exley, Christine L., and Judd B. Kessler. *The Gender Gap in Self-Promotion*. 26345, National Bureau of Economic Research, Oct. 2019.

Bauer, Nichole M. "Gendered Self-Promotion: Differences in How Voters Evaluate Women and Men Who Highlight Their Legislative Accomplishments." *Political Research Quarterly*, vol. 77, no. 1, Mar. 2024, pp. 344–58.

Player, Abigail, et al. "Overlooked Leadership Potential: The Preference for Leadership Potential in Job Candidates Who Are Men vs. Women." *Frontiers in Psychology*, vol. 10, Apr. 2019.

Brandford, Arica, and Angela Brandford-Stevenson. "Going Up!: Exploring the Phenomenon of the Glass Escalator in Nursing." *Nursing Admin. Quarterly*, vol. 45, no. 4, Oct. 2021, pp. 295–301.

Williams, Christine L. "The Glass Escalator: Hidden Advantages for Men in the 'Female' Professions." *Social Problems*, vol. 39, no. 3, Aug. 1992, pp. 253–67.

Reynolds, Jeremy, and He Xian. "Perceptions of Meritocracy in the Land of Opportunity." *Research in Social Stratification and Mobility*, vol. 36, June 2014, pp. 121–37.

A Belief in Meritocracy Is Not Only False: It's Bad for You | Princeton University Press. press.princeton.edu.

"A Point of View: Are You Really an 'Imposter,' or Is It Just Meritocracy at Work? The Problem with 'Imposter Syndrome'." *The Inclusion Solution*, 21 July 2022, theinclusionsolution.me.

Hooks, Bell. *Feminism Is for Everybody: Passionate Politics*. Nachdr., South End Press, 2008.

16. MENOPAUSE & PERIMENOPAUSE

Dennis, Nicola, and Gemma Hobson. "Working Well: Mitigating the Impact of Menopause in the Workplace." *Maturitas*, vol. 177, Nov. 2023, p. 107824. ScienceDirect.

Allmen, Tara. *Menopause Confidential*. HarperOne, 2016.

"Women in Leadership Face Ageism at Every Age." *HBR*, 16 June 2023.

Biote. *Women in the Workplace Survey*. May 2022, biote.com.

The Hot Resignation. www.hotresignation.com.

"It's Time to Start Talking About Menopause at Work." *HBR*, 24 Feb. 2020.

Let's Talk Menopause | Symptoms | Education | Advocacy. letstalkmenopause.org.

NHS England Signs Menopause Workplace Pledge. 15 June 2022, england.nhs.uk.

Cocke, Wendy A. *Making Flex Work*. Engineering Leadership Solutions LLC, 2022.

Menopause. who.int/news-room/fact-sheets/detail/menopause.

ZOE Science & Nutrition Podcast. zoe.com.

How Labour Force Participation Rates in India Vary across Age Groups » CEDA. 8 Apr. 2024

17. INTERNATIONAL EXPERIENCES

Smart Moves – A New Approach to Intl. Assignments and Global Mobility. Deloitte. 2010, deloitte.com.

"Two Minutes to Understand Why Expatriate Gender Diversity Matters (and Do Something about It)." *Mercer Mobility*, mobilityexchange.mercer.com.

Trompenaars, Fons, and Charles Hampden-Turner. *Riding the Waves of Culture: Understanding Diversity in Global Business*. Brealey, 2012.

Mehreen, Hina, et al. "'Homeward Bound': A Systematic Review of the Repatriation Literature." *Intl. Studies of Management & Org.*, vol. 55, no. 2, Aug. 2024, pp. 233–56.

INTERNATIONAL PERSPECTIVES

No notes.

18. REDEFINING SUCCESS

Tregellas, Jason R., et al. "Predicting Academic Career Outcomes by Predoctoral Publication Record." *PeerJ*, vol. 6, Oct. 2018.

Roy, Siddhartha, et al. "Competition for Engineering Tenure-Track Faculty Positions in the United States." *PNAS Nexus*, vol. 3, no. 5, Apr. 2024.

Sauermann, Henry, and Michael Roach. "Science PhD Career Preferences: Levels, Changes, and Advisor Encouragement." *PLoS ONE*, vol. 7, no. 5, May 2012.

Professional Science Masters, professionalsciencemasters.org.

Professional Science Master's Degree in Environmental Science | Office of Graduate Education | Oregon State University. 17 Apr. 2015, graduate.oregonstate.edu.

Welcome Waterloo Co-Op Students! | University of Waterloo. uwaterloo.ca.

"Science & Technology Policy Fellowships." *Programs*, AAAS, aaas.org.

"Schmidt Science Fellows." *Schmidt Science Fellows*, schmidtsciencefellows.org.

"European Research Council." *ERC*, erc.europa.eu.

"Restarting Careers in Research." *Daphne Jackson Trust*, 28 Apr. 2025, daphnejackson.org.

"AWIS Opportunity Scholarships for Career Re-Entry." *AWIS*, awis.org.

MENTAL WELLNESS MOMENT | SPOON THEORY

Miserandino, Christine. "But You Don't Look Sick? Support for Those with Invisible Illness or Chronic Illness." *The Spoon Theory*, butyoudontlooksick.com.

19. A WORKPLACE FIELD GUIDE

NCSES. *The STEM Labor Force: Scientists, Engineers, and Skilled Technical Workers*. NSF, May 2024.

"More Women than Men Are Enrolled in Medical School." *AAMC*, aamc.org.

20. ADVOCACY

Borger, Jessica. "Here's What Is Being Done to Empower, Promote and Retain Australian Women in Science." *Women's Agenda*, 10 Feb. 2019, womensagenda.com.au.

"Should We All Draw up Covid CVs?" *THE*, 21 Mar. 2021, timeshighereducation.com.

Women's Agenda. "Is Australia's Largest Medical Research Funding Body Doing Enough to Retain Women in STEMM?" *Women's Agenda*, 12 Oct. 2021, womensagenda.com.au.

Borger, Jessica G., and Louise E. Purton. "Gender Inequities in Medical Research Funding Is Driving an Exodus of Women from Australian STEMM Academia." *Immunology & Cell Biology*, vol. 100, no. 9, Oct. 2022, pp. 674–78.

"Sign the Petition." *Change.Org*.

"The $400m Reason Female Scientists Are 'Gushing out of the System.'" *Australian Financial Review*, 7 Aug. 2022, afr.com.

"Fund Science on the Basis of Scientists' Work, Not Their Identity." *Quillette*, 17 Dec. 2021, quillette.com.

Britton, Ben. "What We Call Each Other — Professional Titles in Academia." *Medium*, 9 Mar. 2022, bmatb.medium.com.

"Gender pay gaps in STEM and other industries." *The Australian Government Department of Industry, Science and Resources.* 2023, industry.gov.au.

"New Words – 26 March 2018." 26 Mar. 2018, dictionaryblog.cambridge.org.

"Gender Equity When It Suits." *Quillette*, 13 Mar. 2023, quillette.com.

21. ALLIES

"Are You Taking on Too Many Non-Promotable Tasks?" *HBR*, 26 Apr. 2022.

Colantuono, Susan L. "The Key Career Advice No One Bothers to Tell Women." *TIME*, 4 Feb. 2016, time.com.

MENTAL WELLNESS MOMENT | EMPATHETIC ALLYSHIP

No notes.

22. THE BUSINESS CASE FOR DEI

McKinsey & Company and LeanIn.Org. *Women in the Workplace*. 2022, womenintheworkplace.com.

Goldberg, Emma. "How Companies Are Navigating the D.E.I. Backlash." *NYT*, 10 Feb. 2025.

Times. "The U.S. Companies Pulling Back on Initiatives." *Times*, 26 Jan. 2025, time.com.

What Is Diversity, Equity, and Inclusion (DE&I)? | McKinsey. mckinsey.com.

Sahar, Andrade. "How To Bridge Generational Differences at Work." *Forbes*, 17 Oct 2023.

McKinsey & Company. *Diversity Matters Series* (2015–2023). mckinsey.com:

    Hunt, V., et al. "Why diversity matters," 2015.

    Hunt, V., et al. "Delivering through diversity," 2018.

    Dixon-Fyle, S., et al. "Diversity wins: how inclusion matters," 2020.

    Hunt, V., et al. "Diversity matters even more: The case for holistic impact," 2023.

Reynolds, Alison, and David Lewis. "Teams Solve Problems Faster When They're More Cognitively Diverse." *HBR*, 30 Mar. 2017.

Risby, Michelle. "Why Diversity and Inclusion Are Good for Business." *UNC Pembroke*, 27 Oct. 2021, online.uncp.edu.

The Inclusive Workplace: What It Is and Why It Matters | McKinsey. mckinsey.com.

King, Michelle P. "Not Everyone Will Support DEI—Here's How to Keep Moving Forward." *Forbes*, 5 Feb 2025.

Guy, Sandra. "New Approaches to DEI." *Magazine of the Society of Women Engineers*, 2024, swe.org.

CONCLUSION

No notes.

GLOSSARY

Rossiter, Margaret W. "The Matthew Matilda Effect in Science." *Social Studies of Science*, vol. 23, no. 2, May 1993, pp. 325–41.

ACRONYMS

LGBTQ+ Vocabulary Glossary of Terms, thesafezoneproject.com.

Glossary

Advocacy. Taking action to influence decision-makers and policies that impact gender equity in STEMM. Advocacy focuses on addressing systemic barriers and inequalities to drive meaningful change in these fields.

Ally. A person who actively supports individuals who are marginalized or excluded.

Allyship. The practice of actively supporting individuals from underrepresented genders, particularly within your sphere of influence. Allyship involves standing alongside them, amplifying their voices, and creating space for their contributions.

Burnout. A state of physical, emotional, and mental exhaustion caused by prolonged stress.

Capacity for confidence. The ability to build, access, and sustain belief in one's own value and skills, especially in the face of challenge. This ability can be nurtured, supported, and expanded over time.

Covering. Minimizing or hiding socially stigmatized aspects of one's identity to fit in with mainstream culture.

Culture shock. A sense of confusion and uncertainty sometimes with feelings of anxiety that may affect people exposed to a new culture without adequate preparation.

Diversity. The presence of a broad tapestry of identities, perspectives, and experiences woven throughout an organization or setting.

Double bind. A form of gender bias in which conflicting expectations mean a person, typically a woman, is penalized no matter what action she takes.

Equity. Providing everyone with the resources and opportunities they need to succeed. This requires recognizing that people do not all start from the same place, and proactively identifying and removing barriers to access and success.

Essentialism. The assumption that all individuals within a particular group share the same inherent characteristics or experiences, often reducing complex identities (such as gender) to simplified generalizations. Simone de Beauvoir is often credited with popularizing this idea in 1949.

Explicit bias. A form of bias involving conscious, deliberate actions or decisions that exclude, disadvantage, or limit opportunities for others based on aspects of their identity.

Gender-diminutive language. Word choice that subtly devalues or infantilize someone based on gender (e.g., "female doctor" or calling a coworker "girl" or "sweetheart").

Glass ceiling. An invisible barrier that prevents women and marginalized groups from advancing to higher leadership positions, despite their qualifications and achievements.

Glass cliff. A phenomenon where women and underrepresented individuals are more likely to be placed in leadership roles during times of crisis or instability, when scrutiny is high and risk of failure is greater.

Glass escalator. A phenomenon in which men in female-dominated professions experience unearned or disproportionate advantages in promotion and career advancement. The term was coined by sociologist Christine L. Williams in 1992.

Imposter syndrome. A persistent feeling of self-doubt, incompetency, and fears of being exposed as a fraud, despite evidence of competence and success.

Inclusion. In the workplace, inclusion means fostering an environment where everyone's perspectives, insights, and experiences are valued, respected, and meaningfully integrated into the decision-making process.

Intersectionality. The concept that various dimensions of a person's identity intersect to create a unique system of marginalization and privilege. The term was coined by Kimberlé Crenshaw in 1989.

Leaky pipeline. A metaphor used to describe the persistent 'loss' of women and people of color from STEMM career paths. See the illustration in the Introduction for a graphical depiction of the academic and corporate idealizations of the metaphor.

Matilda effect. A form of bias in which women's scientific achievements are misattributed to male colleagues. The term was coined in 1993 by science historian Margaret W. Rossiter, in honor of suffragist Matilda Joslyn Gage.

Matrescence. The process of becoming a mother, similar to how adolescence refers to the transition to adulthood. The term was coined by Dana Raphael in the 1970s.

Matthew effect. The phenomenon where individuals who are already well-known tend to receive disproportionate credit or recognition, often at the expense of other contributors. In STEMM, this can manifest as men receiving credit for women's ideas or efforts. The term was coined by Robert K. Merton in 1968.

Meritocracy (myth of). The belief that success is earned solely through individual talent and hard work, and that systems reward people purely on merit. This view overlooks systemic barriers, biases, and unequal access that disproportionately impact marginalized groups.

Metacognition. Thinking about thinking; awareness of our own learning processes.

Microaggression. Subtle, often unintentional comments or actions that communicate bias or stereotypes toward a marginalized group. Though small in isolation, their cumulative impact can undermine belonging, confidence, and professional growth.

Mother-leader intuitionship. A leadership approach that celebrates both the unique capabilities and traditional leadership capabilities cultivated through maternal experiences. It challenges conventional theories by recognizing and including valuable leadership competencies learned and developed outside of the paid workforce. This novel framework calls on organizations to expand their concept of leadership development by including the strengths that Mothers bring to the paid workforce.

Motherhood advantage. The recognition that motherhood enhances professional capabilities and strategic focus through lived experience.

Performative advocacy. Actions taken more for appearance than as part of a genuine, sustained effort to create change. This often involves gestures or statements that signal support without meaningful action to address systemic issues.

Professional skills. Skills that support effective communication, collaboration, problem-solving, time-management, and emotional regulation. Formerly known as "soft skills," but rebranded in Chapter 14 to reflect their critical value in STEMM careers.

Psychological safety. The belief that you can express yourself without fear of punishment or humiliation for speaking up with ideas, concerns, questions, or mistakes. The term was coined by Amy Edmondson in 1999.

Reverse culture shock. A sense of disorientation or unease, sometimes accompanied by anxiety, that may affect people returning to their home culture after significant time in a different cultural environment.

Scissor effect. A metaphor describing how gendered divergence in career trajectories increases over time, despite equal starting points.

Soft skills. See *professional skills*.

STEMMinist. Also known as STEMinist, someone who promotes equality in STEMM.

Tightrope bias. A form of gender bias in which a person, typically a woman, must carefully navigate being perceived as either too soft or too tough, based on traditionally gendered expectations of behavior.

Unconscious bias. Also known as *implicit bias*, biases that operate below conscious awareness and can influence workplace decisions, relationships, and opportunities.

Untitling. The practice of removing professional credentials from some individuals, but not others, often leading to devaluation of their expertise or status. The term was coined by Joan Acker around 1990.

Value. In this text, *value* in its singular form refers to one's sense of self-worth, including identity, achievements, recognition, self-compassion, and growth.

Values. In this text, *values* in its plural form refer to the principles, beliefs, and standards that guide a person's decisions.

Versatility. The ability to switch between abstract and concrete thinking, quantitative and qualitative reasoning, and micro- and macro-level problem frames. To zoom in and out of a problem keeping both big picture and fine detail in focus.

Acronyms

AAAS	American Association for the Advancement of Science
ADA	Americans with Disabilities Act of 1990 (U.S. law)
ADEA	Age Discrimination in Employment Act of 1967 (U.S. law)
ADHD	Attention-Deficit / Hyperactivity Disorder
AFAB	Assigned Female at Birth
ANDP	Association of Neuroscience Departments and Programs[1]
AWIS	Association for Women in Science
BIT	Built-In Test
CBT	Cognitive Behavioral Theory
COB	Close of Business
DEI	Diversity, Equity, and Inclusion
DSM-IV	Diagnostic and Statistical Manual of Mental Disorders, 4th Edition
EAP	Employee Assistance Program
EDI	Equity, Diversity, and Inclusion
EEOC	Equal Employment Opportunity Commission (U.S. agency)
ELMM	Engineers, Leaders, Moms, and Mentors
EQ	Emotional Intelligence
ERG	Employee Resource Group

---

[1] ANDP merged with the Society for Neuroscience (SfN) in 2005. Today, SfN remains the go-to organization for neuroscience departments in the U.S., advancing graduate education standards and supporting interdisciplinary training initiatives.

EVT	Expectancy-Value Theory
FIRE	Financial Independence, Retire Early
HR	Human Resources
HT/HRT	Hormone Therapy / Hormone Replacement Therapy
ICT	Information and Communication Technology
IDWGS	International Day of Women and Girls in Science
LGBTQ+	Lesbian, Gay, Bisexual, Transgender, Queer, and other identities under the non-normative gender and sexuality umbrella. The plus signifies the inclusion of diverse and evolving identities beyond the acronym.
NCES	National Center for Education Statistics
NCSES	National Center for Science and Engineering Statistics
NHMRC	National Health and Medical Research Council
NSBE	National Society of Black Engineers
OECD	Organisation for Economic Co-operation and Development
PM/M	Perimenopause / Menopause, a combined term developed for this project to acknowledge that midlife experiences often extend beyond the single-day milestone of menopause.
PSM	Professional Science Master's
ROI	Return on Investment
SAHM/SAHP	Stay-at-Home Mom / Stay-at-Home Parent
SHPE	Society of Hispanic Professional Engineers
SME	Subject Matter Expert
STAR/STARL	Situation, Task, Action, Results / Learned
STEAM	Science, Technology, Engineering, Arts, and Mathematics
STEM/STEMM	Science, Technology, Engineering, Mathematics / Medicine
SWE	Society of Women Engineers
TL;DR	Too long; didn't read
WHO	World Health Organization
WOC	Women of Color

About the Authors

Karli M. Auble. Engineer, coach, speaker, author, and mom of three helping you thrive through all things life and labor. Follow along for laughs and connection.

www.lifenlabor.com | LinkedIn: karliauble | Instagram: @LifenLabor

Emily L. Bishop. Emily is an award-winning biomedical engineer turned embodiment coach and mentor, guiding purpose-driven women to create success that honours both their ambition and motherhood. Connect with her on Instagram or LinkedIn.

www.emilylynnbishop.com | LinkedIn: emily-lynn-bishop
Instagram: @emilylynnbishop | Emilylynnbishop@gmail.com

Jessica G. Borger. Advocate, writer, educator, and immunologist, Jess is an equity crusader in STEMM academia. Reach out at LinkedIn.

LinkedIn: jessica-borger | jess.borger@gmail.com

Rachael Browning. An engineer & mom with a passion for pets, people, and our planet. She enjoys experiencing other cultures, especially food and the farming practices that bring it to the table and encourages others to do the same.

LinkedIn: rachael-browning | browningra@gmail.com

Jennifer G. Christensen. Engineer and mom of two boys who thrives on efficiency, problem-solving, humor and giving 110%. Enjoys the outdoors, photography, sports, volunteering, puzzles and non-fiction. Connect with her on LinkedIn.

LinkedIn: jennifergchristensen | jenuwbadger@hotmail.com

Jaymi T. Cormier. Jaymi loves working with research teams to facilitate the design of strategic and impact-focused initiatives. To connect or learn more, please visit her website or connect with her on LinkedIn.

www.cormierinc.ca | LinkedIn: jaymi-cormier-phd-beng-curious-and-daring-explorer

Jane Desrochers. Jane is a #recoveringacademic who approaches the world with an insatiable appetite for learning and a quiet urgency to make things better.

www. innovarastrategicimpact.ca | LinkedIn: janedesrochers
hello@innovarastrategicimpact.ca

Belinda A. Di Bartolo. Belinda is a recovering academic, mum, and founder of BD Stemm Strategies - helping STEMM professionals ditch burnout and design careers that work for real life.

www.bdstemmstrategies.com | LinkedIn: belinda-di-bartolo

Trevor C. George. Mechanical engineer that is constantly reinventing himself through career pivots. Happily married, proud boy-dad / girl dad of 2. HeForSWE Co-lead and supporter of all in the workplace.

LinkedIn: trevor-channing-george | trevorchanninggeorge@gmail.com

Manpreet Kaur. Dr. Manpreet Kaur is an experienced leader with degrees in Engineering and HCI. As part of the sandwich generation, she strives to balance life while leading a global team. She thrives on her love of family, work, travel and volunteering.

LinkedIn: kaurm | kaur.manpreet@gmail.com

Tais S. Kraljević. Writer and engineer passionate about equity, equality, and diversity. Connect on LinkedIn.

LinkedIn: taiskraljevic | tais.kraljevic@gmail.com

Cassie Leonard. Bestselling author of *STEM Moms*, executive coach, and speaker who transforms teams through powerful storytelling, strategic insight, and inclusive leadership. Partner with Cassie to spark meaningful growth and lasting change.

www.ELMMcoaching.com | LinkedIn: cassie-leonard
Cassie@ELMMcoaching.com

Monika McDole-Russell. Executive, servant leader, people developer, advocate for gender equity and animal rights.

LinkedIn: monikamcdolerussell | monika.russell@gmail.com

Laura Marie Rivera. Laura Marie is a seasoned nonprofit leader and proud mother of four. She works in the Arts, Education, and Advocacy, to champion equity, creativity, and community voice. And she enjoys writing for her local newspaper in Seattle.

intuitionship.com | LinkedIn: laura-marie-rivera-intuitionship
drlauramarie@gmail.com

Kelly A. Seiler Vocke. San Diego, CA based electrical engineer with 19 years of experience in aviation, subsea sensor systems, and manufacturing. Ambivalent about career advancement. Happily married with two spirited boys. Enjoys the beach, making stuff, and Viking revelry.

www.kellysv.com | LinkedIn: kellysv
Instagram: @kellyhappening | BlueSky: @kellysv

Mindy Ursino. Mindy is an accomplished leader in the aviation industry, holding a degree in Mathematics and a Doctorate in Educational Leadership. Her greatest lessons in leadership and heart have come from raising her four children.

intuitionship.com | LinkedIn: mindy-ursino | mindyursino@gmail.com

Megan Wendell. Megan is an engineering leader and proud mom of two who champions mental wellness, neurodiversity, and human-centered leadership in STEMM. Her mission is to help build workplaces where all minds are supported, while inspiring the next generation to imagine a future in STEMM where everyone belongs.

LinkedIn: megan-wendell-pmp

Ashley C. Wynne. Chemical engineer, boy mom of two, runner, tailgating enthusiast, and passionate advocate for empowering the next generation of women in STEMM.

LinkedIn: ashleycwynne | Ashleycwynne@gmail.com

Acknowledgements

To my parents, who made "anything you can do, I can do better" feel true—especially for girls. To my husband, who shares the load so we can chase wild dreams. To my kids, my why. And to the women before me—thank you for shattering ceilings. I'm honored to be dancing on your glass.

– Karli M. Auble

To my mom and dad, and my husband, for standing beside me through every season of growth. And to my boys, whose joy and curiosity remind me to live fully—they are my greatest inspiration to follow my dreams and become the fullest and truest version of myself.

– Emily Bishop

Thank you to my parents, especially my mum Ina, for exemplifying hard work and unwavering resilience. My son Abel, whose actions inspire me daily to be an authentic and empathetic leader. My husband Andrew, for supporting my academic rollercoaster ride. To my STEMMinist network for having my back, Monash allies Terry and Steve for allowing my voice to be heard, and Cassie for amplifying my voice.

– Jessica G. Borger

Thank you to my family and friends who have supported me to dream big and travel off the well-worn path.

– Rachael Browning

Thank you to Jason, Lucas and Nolan for supporting my SAHP and working phases—to the boys specifically for making life wild yet joyful. To my parents for their unwavering support, to my middle school science teacher Mrs. Schilling for introducing me to engineering as a path to explore, to Cassie for leading this project, and to the women who have inspired, supported, and challenged me along the way.

– Jennifer G. Christensen

Having the right team around you is a significant enabler of being able to determine your course when you find yourself without a visible path. My journey would have been immensely more difficult were it not for the time, energy, and valuable insight invested by many family members, friends, and colleagues. My sincere thanks especially to John Archibald, Don Bureaux, and Antoine Groulx. I couldn't have done this without you.

– Jaymi Cormier

Thank you to all the collaborators, especially Bridgette, Emily, Jaymi, and Monika. And to Cassie, whose leadership took a "pipe dream" and made it real. Thank you to Lindsey. Your wise words have been a source of safety and strength for almost 40 years. Biggest thanks to Darren - for keeping my belly full of goodies, my imagination full of wacky ideas, and my calendar full of adventure.

– Jane Desrochers

To my husband - thank you for your support, good food and patience through a science career that often made no sense (even to me). And to my children - your chaos, curiosity, and love remind me daily why redefining success matters. You keep me grounded, inspired, and always interrupted - and I wouldn't have it any other way.

– Belinda A. Di Bartolo

Thank you to my wife Jenny and children David and Mel for supporting me to go back to school and co-author this book while working and dadding. Thank you to Cassie for bringing me into such a fun project. And thank you for the women in my life that have taught me so much.

– Trevor C. George

I extend my deepest gratitude to my parents for guiding me toward STEM, especially my father for encouraging me to be "more", my husband for being my equal partner, my siblings for their enduring support, my mentors for believing in me, and Cassie for this wonderful opportunity. To my children, you teach me daily to live and demonstrate the values I wish to instill in you.

– Manpreet Kaur

To every woman.

– Tais S. Kraljević

To the more than one hundred women and allies who have joined this journey, thank you for sharing your inspiring stories. To our authors and collaborators, thank you for your wisdom, your courage, and your precious time. I have learned so much from each of you. And to Patrick and our boys, I love you to the moon and back.

– Cassie Leonard

Special thanks to: Brett Wall, my first and strongest advocate and mentor in medtech; Sandy Kalter, who took me under her wing and taught me to lead with graceful strength; Cris Toner, for believing in me and keeping me accountable; Marnie and Melaina, who cheered me on even when I put career before family, and Sean Russell, for everything.

– Monika McDole-Russell

Thank you to my family, both born and chosen. And to every woman that has opened the door and given me a boost along the way. Together, we can make this world a better and more inclusive place for all.

– Laura Marie Rivera

I'd like to thank my SWEsters and all of the excellent SWE (Society of Women Engineers) programming over the years which has immensely benefited my career and personal life. I have an amazing support system (husband, family, friends, colleagues, SWEsters) and would not have been able to write my piece of this book without it.

– Kelly A. Seiler Vocke

Thank you to my amazing research partner, Laura Marie, my loving family and friends for their unwavering support, and especially to all mothers—our source of daily leadership inspiration.

– Mindy Ursino

I'm deeply grateful to my husband Andrew for his unwavering support, my mom for a lifetime of strength and love, and my late dad for inspiring my ambition. To Sharnece for helping me navigate neurodiversity with self-compassion. To Donna and Christina—thank you for showing me what true leadership looks like. Connor and Scarlett, you are my why and biggest cheerleaders.

– Megan Wendell

To my husband Zach - my MVP, thank you for fueling every wild dream. To my boys, you are my heart and life's greatest joy. To my family and dear friends, your encouragement and support means everything. And to the brilliant women in science I have the privilege of working with and learning from - thank you for leading boldly and rewriting the rules together.

– Ashley C. Wynne

About the Publisher

ELMM Press is committed to expanding representation and equity in STEMM (Science, Technology, Engineering, Mathematics, and Medicine). We publish books and resources that amplify the voices and experiences of underrepresented professionals, including women, mothers, LGBTQ+ individuals, and people of color.

We believe that talent is universal, but opportunity is not. That is why we are working to make STEMM more inclusive, accessible, and representative of the diverse world we live in.

Our work includes:

- Publishing nonfiction business books, workbooks, and children's stories centered on characters and contributors from historically excluded communities.

- Supporting aspiring authors through mentorship and collaboration.

- Partnering with organizations that champion equity and inclusion in STEMM fields.

Representation matters. When we see ourselves reflected in the stories we read, we are more likely to believe that we can achieve our own dreams. At ELMM Press, we are creating a platform where diverse voices are not just welcomed; they shine.

Learn more and join our mission at elmm.press.

ELMMPRESS

What's Next?

STAY CONNECTED, SPARK CHANGE

This book is just the beginning. Keep the momentum going:

Join the conversation. Connect with readers and contributors via our LinkedIn group: *Beyond the Pipeline - STEMM Women+*. Share your story, ask questions, and help us build a more inclusive future in STEMM.

Book impactful speakers. With a dynamic team of 26 authors and collaborators, we bring lived experiences and systemic insights to any conversation. Explore options for keynotes, panels, and book clubs tailored to your workplace, school, or ERG.

> info@elmm.press | www.elmmcoaching.com

Share *Beyond the Pipeline.* Gift a copy to a colleague, mentee, or friend. Bulk discounts are available for teams and organizations.

> info@elmm.press | https://elmm.press

Be an ally. Your voice matters. Leave a review, post on social media, or recommend the book to someone navigating their own STEMM journey. Small actions can spark big change.